Russian Canadians

Their Past and Present

The Chekhov Society of Ottawa

Dedication

This book of collected essays, the first in the English language written by Russian Canadians about themselves, is dedicated to our children. We hope that it will help them understand the occasional emotional duality caused by the historical, religious, ethnic, and political factors stemming from their heritage.

The Chekhov Society of Ottawa

Russian Canadians

Their Past and Present

(Collected Essays)

T.F. Jeletzky

Editor

Co-Editors:

V.I. Grebenschikov	Russian Version
N. Gridgeman	English Version
I. Gryndahl	Coordination of Russian and English Versions

Support for research provided by the Directorate of Multiculturalism of the Department of the Secretary of State.

Borealis Press
Ottawa, Canada
1983

The Publishers gratefully acknowledge the support of the Directorate of Multi-Culturalism of the Department of the Secretary of State, the Ontario Arts Council, and the Canada Council.

Cover design by Peter Shvartsman.

Canadian Cataloguing in Publication Data

Main entry under title:
Russian Canadians

Bibliography: p.
ISBN 0-88887-947-4 (bound). — ISBN 0-88887-949-0 (pbk.)

1. Russians — Canada — Addresses, essays, lectures. I. Jeletzky, T.F. (Tamara F.) II. Grebenschikov, V. I. (Vladimir I.) III. Gridgeman, N. (Norman) IV. Gryndahl, I. (Irene)
FC106.R9R88 1983 971'.0049171 C83-090110-8
F1035.R8R88 1983

Borealis Press Limited
9 Ashburn Drive
Ottawa, Canada K2E 6N4

Printed and bound in Canada

Acknowledgements

The Chekhov Society expresses its gratitude to Professor N.V. Pervushin who acted as consultant and to the following persons who assisted with the preparation of this book: G.K. Belkov*, G.N. Ben-Tchavtchavadze, R. Bogusis, M. Ethier, M. Furimsky*, A.P. Galko, N. Gridgeman, I. Gryndahl*, P.E. Kolibaiev, K.G. de Leuchtenberg*, S.G. Mugué, L. Novikov, N. Smirnov, O. Tanczyk and V. van Veen-Zubok with special mention to T. Galko for providing technical editorial advice.

The Society also wishes to thank Halina Jeletzky and Amy Morin who typed the original manuscript and Linda McCooeye who cheerfully typed and retyped the many versions that followed.

The statistical tables were compiled from information provided by the Program Data Directorate, Immigration and Demographic Policy Branch, Employment and Immigration Commission.

Illustrations courtesy of the National Archives of Canada, the Provincial Archives of Alberta and private collections.

Thanks are also due to Dr. Peter Harker for his encouragement and advice.

* The names of persons who translated portions of the manuscript from Russian into English are followed by an asterisk.

Contributors

Frank H. Epp (Ph.D., University of Minnesota; LL.D., Brandon). Professor of Mennonite History, University of Waterloo and Department of History, Conrad Grebel Mennonite College.

Vladimir I. Grebenschikov (Diploma, Slavic Philology and Eastern-Orthodox Theology, University of Sofia, Bulgaria; Ph.D., Université de Montréal). Professor, Department of Russian, Carleton University; Professor, Russian Language School, Middlebury University, Middlebury, Vermont (1950).

Tamara F. Jeletzky (M.D., University of Kiev). President of the Chekhov Society of Ottawa. (1948).

Andrei D. Klimoff. Former president of the Cultural Aid Society of Toronto. (1950's).

Nataliya G. Kosachova (Ph.D., University of Ottawa). Associate professor, Department of Russian, Scarborough College, University of Toronto. (1950).

Edward P. Laine (Ph.D., McGill). Archivist, Public Archives of Canada, Ottawa.

Mstislav I. Mogiljansky (Institute of Aeronautial Enginering, Leningrad). Former chairman of the International Service of the CBC/Radio-Canada, Montreal. Author of "Concise History of Canada" (Toronto, Sovremennik, 1976). (1949).

Nikolai V. Pervushin (Doctor of Humanities, Honoris causa, Norwich University). Professor emeritus, Department of Russian, McGill University. One of the founders and member of the International Symposium for the Study of Dostoevsky. Honorary director, Russian Language School, Norwich University, Northfield, Vermont.

Richard F. Piotrovsky (M.D., Harbin University, China). Member of Russian Canadian Cultural Aid Society, Toronto. (1966).

Constantin V. Ponomareff (Ph.D., University of Toronto). Associate professor, Department of Russian, Scarborough College, University of Toronto. (1949).

Feliks J. Yaroshevsky (M.D., Psychiatry, First Medical Institute, Leningrad). (1973).

Tova Yedlin. Associate professor, Department of East European Studies, (History), University of Alberta.

* * * *

The authors listed above represent all waves of immigration, being members of the first and subsequent generations who settled in Canada. The date in brackets at the end of each entry indicates the date of immigration to Canada.

Contents

Part One

Main "Streams" of Russian Immigration to Canada

Part Two

The Life of Russian Canadians in Canada

List of Illustrations

Introduction

The title of this book alone, as well as its central theme, already draws attention to the meaning of the words "Russian" and "Canadians of Russian descent". It is not as easy to give a precise definition of the term "Russian" as it may first appear.

To be Russian can be said to mean "to belong to the Russian nationality". However, if one examines the definition of nationality as stated in the Encyclopedia Britannica[1], it becomes evident that there is no universally accepted interpretation in this case. In some countries, for example, nationality is defined either in terms of "belonging to a nation or to a sovereign state" or in terms of birth on a specific territory, namely:

> . . . by one rule of international law, a person who is born within the territory of a given state and is subject to its laws, acquires that state's nationality by the mere fact of his having been born on that state's territory.

According to another law, however, "nationality is inherited according to the nationality of one or both parents". Further, we find that "differences in the national legislature and the absence of universal laws or practices complicate the search for a solution to the many problems dealing with the definition of nationality".[2]

The foregoing considerations present various possibilities for defining the term "Russian" and can help explain some of the discrepancies found in census data on Russian immigration.

The definition based on the "territorial principle" as stated in the Encyclopedia Britannica appears acceptable only where the majority of the population belongs to one ethnic group or race. In such countries, the erroneous mixing of the concepts of "nationality" meaning ethnicity or citizenship acquired by birth on a specific territory is not very significant.[3] In a multinational state, however, such as Russia before the Revolution or the U.S.S.R. of today, these concepts do not coincide as citizenship is shared by people whose language, religion and cultural backgrounds are entirely different.

Despite its inaccuracy, the "territorial principle" is the one most widely used in determining nationality. Consequently, people born in Imperial Russia before the Revolution or within the boundaries of the Soviet Union after 1917, are often labelled as "Russian" even if, ethnically, they are not.

The names "Russia" and "U.S.S.R." are not interchangeable, reflecting totally different entities, so that any reference made to one or the other is very specific. The latter was formed on the territory of old Imperial Russia after the Revolution of 1917 and the years of civil war. The Russian Soviet Federated Socialist Republic, the largest of fifteen republics of the Union, and formerly known as Great Russia, was proclaimed in October 1917. The official declaration establishing the U.S.S.R. was proclaimed in December 1922.

The practice of labelling as Russian all persons born on the territory of both Imperial Russia and the U.S.S.R. is misleading and causes discrepancies in statistical data. Many new Canadians who were automatically registered as Russian when landing in Canada choose to correct this error. When receiving their Canadian citizenship or during census-taking, they identify their nationality according to the ethnicity of their parents and not the "territorial principle". This has resulted in a statistical increase in the number of Ukrainians, Byelorussians, Jews and others who came from Russia.

Let us take the census data for 1961 and 1971 as examples. In 1961, data on ethnic groups included 119,168 Russians. In 1971, this figure dropped to 64,475. As there had been no considerable emigration of Russians during this period, why the discrepancy in these figures? Research in citizenship undertaken by the Department of the Secretary of State concluded that:

> . . . the figure of 119,168 is most likely an exaggeration. It includes Mennonites who came to Canada from Russia, and representatives of the other groups such as Poles, Ukrainians and Finns who belonged to the former Russian Empire.

This article also stated:

> . . . we shall only examine "true" Russians, or as they were sometimes called, the "Great Russians".[4]

It stands to reason, therefore, that the present book will also limit itself, as much as possible, to the "narrow" ethnic meaning of the word "Russian".

It would be incorrect, however, to equate "Russian" with "Great Russian" at all times. Great Russians, who are natives of the central and northern parts of Russia, live side by side with other nationalities that are not Russian in the ethnic sense of the word. The problem as to who can be considered a "true" Russian is further complicated by population migrations, mixed marriages and sociopolitical influences, both within and outside the Soviet Union.

Soviet passports distinguish between "citizenship" (i.e., all people are Soviet citizens) and "nationality", the so-called "Fifth Item" in the document. When the first passports were issued in the 1930's, entries under this "item" were made rather arbitrarily. At the present time, however, when a person becomes of legal age and receives his first passport, he has the right to choose his nationality according to that of one of his parents.

In other countries also there are similarly no universal rules to define nationality for Russian emigrants born outside the Soviet Union's borders. Some are registered according to the territorial principle (i.e., by place of birth or permanent residence), others according to the nationality of their parents who, in some cases, either took the citizenship of the country in which they lived or retained their "stateless" status, holding the so-called Nansen Passport.*[5]

In the general chaos that followed World War II, people who lost all their documents simply declared their nationality without any supporting evidence. When filling out questionnaires or going through the screening process conducted by immigration officials, it was not uncommon for Soviet citizens to furnish incorrect information in an effort to escape forced repatriation. Consequently, former Soviet citizens of Russian and other origin registered themselves as Poles, Ukrainians, etc., pretending that they were not subjects of the USSR at the beginning of World War II.

The foregoing facts create difficulties in analyzing the statistics regarding the Russian ethnic group. As it is not within the scope of this book to verify either the accuracy of census data on Russian ethnic groups or of immigration statistics, we can only suggest possible reasons for the discrepancies existing within the statistical data available.

The Canadian Bureau of Statistics classifies immigrants and the population as a whole according to various categories, some of which can indirectly point to persons of Russian origin. These categories are:

a) former citizenship;
b) last place of residence;
c) place of birth;
d) language (mother tongue);
e) ethnic origin;
f) religion.

Information on the number of Russians is more readily obtained in the larger cities where there exist cultural groups and religious communities. The very fact that an individual would join such a group is evidence that he considers himself Russian. It is more difficult, however, to compile data on those people who, for some rea-

---

* Fridtjof Nansen, 1861-1930, Norwegian polar explorer and statesman, who, in 1921, became the first High Commissioner for Refugees at the League of Nations. He was responsible for the protection and settlement of political refugees over one million of whom came from Russia. His work resulted in the establishment of the International Identity Certificate known as the Nansen Passport for stateless persons. This document gave the bearer the right of residence, employment and social security.

son, stay outside the community or who even try to conceal their Russian origin by changing their name.[6]

In the long run, the most realistic criterion for defining the nationality of an immigrant is his own declaration, that is, what he considers himself to be and how he registers himself during census-taking. In general, such "self-definition" is often a reflection of the individual's desire to continue family traditions, to maintain ties with the religious community and to preserve the Russian language, which he considers his native tongue. Such behaviour is also typical of some people of non-Russian origin who became "russified" and adopted Russian culture as their own.

The different factors that unite Russians, as well as the contradictions existing among different Russian groups, are easier to understand when one examines their roots and the reasons that led to their eventual emigration.

To know the past is to understand the present. With this in mind, we have presented the material in two parts: a historical review, including the background to various waves of immigration, and different aspects of contemporary life in Canada.

Part 1 — Historical Review

The historical review includes a description of the different "waves" of immigration and is divided chronologically into four main periods: immigration before World War I, between the two World Wars, post-World War II and the 1970's. Separate chapters are devoted to immigration from China and the Germans and Mennonites who came from Russia.

Before World War I

The first "wave" saw intellectuals of the end of the 19th and beginning of the 20th centuries who rebelled against the tsarist régime and were attracted to America and the intellectual freedom it offered. Here also we find Doukhobors searching for full religious and social independence who rejected subordination to any established order, as well as immigrants from south-western Russia and Eastern Austro-Hungary whose desire it was to escape extreme poverty and to acquire a piece of land.

Between World War I and World War II

During the period between the two World Wars, Russian immigrants were few in number, yet more diverse in their make-up than their predecessors. Among those who came to Canada at this time were representatives of the "white" immigration — adversaries and opponents of the Soviet régime — who left Russia after the 1917 revolution.

At the same time, however, this "wave" also included immigrants from Poland and Eastern Austro-Hungary whose views were diametrically opposed to those of the above group and who sympathized with the USSR.

Post World War II

The immigrants who came to Canada after the Second World War comprised former Soviet citizens and members of the "old" immigration who lived outside of Russia between the period of the two wars. On the whole, this "wave" was anti-communist in nature.

Recent Immigration — the 1970s

The recent "wave" of immigrants from the Soviet Union, sometimes called the "third wave", is predominantly Jewish in ethnic origin. With respect to cultural background, it is Russian in the majority of cases.

Part 2 — Different Aspects of the Life of Russian Canadians

The second part includes chapters describing the religious, socio-political and social activities of Canadians of Russian descent. The frequently distorted image of Russian ethnic communities, based either on ignorance of the group in general or on prejudicial descriptions of it, prompted us to mention some of the contributions made by Russians in the areas of science, arts and community life. Initially, we intended to devote a special chapter to this topic but the information collected was too voluminous to be included in a book of this size. It is more appropriate that a separate publication be based on these findings.

Concluding Remarks

In an effort to present as comprehensive a view as possible, we selected authors who represent all waves of immigration. It follows, therefore, that one cannot expect them to share common views. Therein lies the concept behind this book of collected essays: to present a "profile" of various points of view.

The role of the Chekhov Society has been to coordinate this project. The views of the Society do not necessarily coincide with those expressed by individual authors who bear the final responsibility for their material.

The views presented in this book do not necessarily reflect the thinking of the entire Russian ethnic community.

Ottawa
1982

T. Jeletzky

Notes

1. *Encyclopedia Britannica*, 1956, Vol. XVI, p. 151.
2. Morison, J.L., 'Nationality and Common Sense'', *Bulletin of the Departments of History and Political and Economic Science, Queens University*, Kingston, Ontario, Canada, N37, Oct. 1920, the Jackson Press, Kingston.
3. Kurganov, E.A., *The Nationalities of the USSR and the Russian Question* (in Russian), Frankfurt/Main, West Germany, 1961, 263 p., Part 1, Ch. 1, pp. 5-20.
4. *The Canadian Family Tree*, Citizenship Branch, Dept. of the Secretary of State, Centennial Edition, Ottawa, Canada, 1967, p. 273.
5. Nansen International Office for Refugees, *Report on Liquidation of the Office*, Geneva, June 14, 1937.
6. *Ethnic Change of Name, Ontario*: A Pilot Study, Toronto, 1965, p. 45.

E.W. Laine

ON DOCUMENTING THE RUSSIAN PRESENCE IN CANADA*

The Russian presence in North America dates back to the eighteenth century when Russian explorers and adventurers began to colonize Alaska and the Pacific coast. Although this early settlement of Russians did not extend to the territories that were later to become part of Canada, it was not without importance in the ultimate shaping of the Canadian nation. For example, the *modus vivendi* reached between the Russian-American and Hudson Bay Companies undoubtedly had a significant effect in preventing the entire Pacific Northwest coast south of Alaska from becoming American.[1]

About the time of Canada's confederation in 1867, people from the Russian Empire began to immigrate to this country, injecting a new and more direct kind of Russian presence into the lifestream of Canadian society. Evidence of this can be found in the 1871 census of Canada, which reported 607 persons of Russian origin. By the 1881 census, this trickle had grown to 1,227.

However, it should be noted that the statistics compiled by the Census Office then not only included those of Russian ethnic origin in its count of "Russians" but Finns and Poles as well, for Finland and Poland were both under the Russian tsar's hegemony. Canadian census-takers eventually excluded Finnish and Polish immigrants from their head-counts of Russians in the census of 1901, by which

* This article has been prepared with the support of the Public Archives of Canada. I also with to acknowledge the assistance of two of my colleagues at the Archives, Dr. George Bolotenko and M. Stephen Salmon, whose critiques of earlier drafts of this article have proved most useful and beneficial. (Author)

time the Russian population in Canada had risen to 19,825.

Even so, it should not be assumed that all these people were necessarily of Russian ethnic origin for some were German-speaking Mennonites or Ukrainian-speaking "Little Russians" who were reported as, or perhaps had simply reported themselves as, "Russian" on the basis of their former citizenship.

Even this apparently simple question of citizenship was to become blurred as a result of the territorial rearrangements made in Eastern Europe after World War I. For example, the immigrants who had already left or were streaming out of those territories which had been ceded by Russia to her neighbours, or had declared themselves independent states, often did not know whether to report themselves to the Canadian authorities as Russians or as new citizens of those countries to which their homelands now belonged. Thus, the fact of citizenship as well as ethnic identity had become a problematical and confusing issue for many of the 100,064 Russians and other East Europeans included in the Canadian census of 1921.[2] In fact, this difficulty has continued to plague Canada's statistical reporting to the present. Therefore, apart from the valuable evidence of the LI-RA-MA Collection (discussed later in this article), there is little source material available for determining the true extent of the ethnic Russian element in this country.

If these census reports have obscured the issue of the ethnically Russian component in Canada, other government sources have provided another important avenue for defining the nature of this presence more precisely. Indeed, until recently, the records of the federal government and its agencies constituted the chief source for documenting the Russian past in this country.[3] For example, the records of the Privy Council contain Orders-in-Council granting free land to Russian congregations for the building of churches to encourage the settlement of these newcomers.[4] Such documentation attests to the positive measures which were taken by the federal authorities to assist Russian settlement here.

However, the files of other government departments might suggest a more ambivalent view concerning Russian immigration in-as much as certain records deal with the illegal entry of Russian aliens, while others document the importation of Russian labourers by the Canadian Pacific Railway under armed guard or report the deportation of Russian undesirables.[5] Information about these and other matters is scattered throughout the holdings of the Federal Archives Division of the Public Archives of Canada.

The Ethnic Archives Section of the Public Archives has recently acquired a major collection that received much attention in the media under the rubric of "Russian consular records".[6] This collection, which is now referred to as the LI-RA-MA Collection, consists of the papers of Sergei Likhachev, Konstantin Ragozin and

Harry Mathers, all of whom were at one time members of Imperial Russia's consular corps in Canada. Moreover, Likhachev and Ragozin were later employed as agents of the Canadian government to deal with matters affecting the Russian immigrant community. Thus, their papers also came to reflect the concerns of the Government of Canada regarding the integration of "Russian" immigrants into Canadian Life.

These three men assembled a mass of records dating from about 1900 to 1922, which related to all aspects of immigration, settlement, social adjustment, military service, cultural and religious affairs of Armenians, Doukhobors, Estonians, Finns, Jews, Lithuanians, Mennonites, Poles, Russians, Ukrainians and other people originating from the Russian Empire and settling in Canada. Nor did they neglect to document the nature of Russo-Canadian relations in such matters as fisheries, trade and commerce, wartime co-operation and Canada's involvement in Russia's Civil War.[7] In that respect, this collection can also provide scholars with new evidence relating to Canada's international role and its purposeful emergence into independent nationhood between the turn of the twentieth century and the 1920s

As the collection is still being processed, it should be understood that the following remarks concerning its potential value as a historical source are tentative.[8] By all appearances, the richest material seems to centre on the immigration of Slavs and, in particular, Ukrainians from the former Russian Empire. (Of course, the mainstream of Ukrainian immigration to Canada during that period came from Galicia and Bukovina and was, therefore, largely outside the purview of the Russian consular officials.) These immigrants came mainly from the two western Russian provinces of Volynia and Podolia, which were largely populated by Ukrainians, with sizeable numbers also coming from the vicinities of Kiev and Ekaterinoslav. Instead of heading out to Western Canada *en bloc*, many appear to have gravitated first toward urban centres such as Toronto, Montreal and Halifax or, perhaps, the work camps and mining towns of northern Ontario, and then moved from these industrialized areas into the hinterlands. From this preliminary evidence, the experience of these people does not bear out Sifton's* stereotype of the immigrant Slav "in the sheepskin coat" who was ready to take up farming immediately upon entry into Canada. Nevertheless, the proof or disproof of this impression must await a more detailed statistical analysis of these records.

As already mentioned, Jews, Finns and peoples of the Caucasus region also appear to be well represented in the records of the LI-RA-MA Collection. It seems that much of the so-called "Russian"

---

* Clifford Sifton, Minister of the Interior, 1896-1905.

immigration to Canada in the period documented by this collection came from the borderlands of the Empire or from those non-Russian minority groups which were relegated to the periphery of Russian society for having maintained their own ethno-cultural identities. In other words, comparatively few immigrants seem to have been attracted from the ethnically Russian provinces and, of those who came from there, even fewer were identifiably Russian in ethnic origin. Hence, in the context of this collection, the term "Russian immigration" serves as little more than a label of convenience for an ethno-culturally heterogenous peoples, many of whom were "Russian" only in the sense that they were subjects of the "Tsar and Autocrat of all the Russia".[9] Nonetheless, we do discover undeniably Russian names with some frequency in this collection and learn of Russian immigrants to Canada from Viatka, the region known as as New Russia (Black Sea littoral), and from other areas as well. In this regard — that is, in establishing the ethnic Russian component of immigration to Canada from the Empire — the collection should do much to clarify the problem concerning the reporting of "Russians" in the Canadian census statistics before the mid-1920s.

Most of these observations were drawn from the "nominal case files", the larger of the two series in the collection. This series consists of approximately 12,000 case files, each relating to a particular individual. Typically, such a file contains a completed questionnaire or application form which includes the respondent's personal history — for example, age, nationality (meaning ethnic origin), religion, marital status, place of birth or Russian residence, date of departure from Russia or of arrival in Canada, port of entry, place of residence after emigration, military service, relatives and dependents, etc. In most cases, a photograph of the individual is also included. The purpose for which these case files were created varies, although most involve passport applications or registration with Russian authorities in compliance with their civil and military regulations. In any event, it is clear that these files were created only with the co-operation of the individual respondents and, therefore, do not include information concerning those former Russian subjects who had no desire or need to reveal their existence to the consular officials.[10] Nevertheless, this sample of case files in the LI-RA-MA Collection concerning pre-World War I "Russian" immigrants is certainly large enough, and detailed enough, to awaken the curiosity of a host of historians, sociologists, genealogists and other researchers.

Although the case file series just described may be of use to the quantifiers, the other major series in the collection, the "subject policy file" series, will undoubtedly appeal to the scholarly researcher of the more traditionalist persuasion. There are some 5,000 files in this series which deal with such topics as: charities; deportations and extraditions; education; trade and commerce; recruitment; enlistment and conscription into the Canadian (CEF) and Russian armed forces as well as other military or war-related matters; churches; family breakdowns; work injuries; non-payment of wages; crimes and trials; personal assistance of various kinds, including aid in settling minor family problems; ethnic groups, including the anti-tsarist movement amongst "Russian" immigrant groups in Canada; estates and inheritances; shipping; internment of Russians; etc. Because of its size and richness, this part of the collection gives a strong sense of bridging the historical and geographical gulfs between the donor and host societies as well as providing an overview of the whole migration experience. Undoubtedly, it will prove to be one of the chief sources of information for a better understanding, quantitatively and qualitatively, of the Russian presence and experience in Canada.

Even a random selection of files from this series indicates the richness and variety of evidence contained within the collection. For example, there is an unsolicited report by one Mowbrey S. Berkeley to the Russian Consul-General in Montreal detailing the general socio-economic condition of Russian subjects settled on the western prairies. In addition to outlining their numbers and areas of concentration, Berkeley discusses their pronounced ability to adapt to their new homeland and the hardships they faced in adjusting to it. Another file documents the experience of a Reverend Harris who, in about 1914, founded a "Russian Mission" in Halifax to feed, clothe and house the local Russian destitute. The work of Berkeley and Harris shows that many members of the host society did not always regard immigrants with callous indifference or worse, but sometimes with interest and sympathy offering assistance to help them succeed in Canada. Even the Canadian government would occasionally show compassion for the immigrant as, for example, in the lukewarm co-operation that it extended Russian authorities intent on extraditing such alleged criminals and escaped felons as J.A. Mustonen. Canadian officials were apparently reluctant to hand anyone over the Russian judicial system, deeming it inferior to the Canadian judiciary and its sense of British "justice" and "fair play".

On the other hand, there were many instances of utter disregard for the humanity of the individual immigrant by Canadian society and its institutions. For example, immigrants who came to the new land were at times exploited and abused by unscrupulous contractors. Some fought back in small ways, trying to organize workers from Russia into concerted action by forming the Russian Workingmen's Union which, it seems, was very strong in Vancouver. Among the organizing activists were men of Russian stock who, for their pains, were rewarded with rapid and unceremonious deportation.

Nor were the Russians alone in being discriminated against as an alien "race", for other former subjects of Russia also encountered similar treatment. For example, the files of Hjalmar Lahtinen and Edward Aho document how these two immigrant Finns were unjustly imprisoned as examples to other "brawling" foreigners because they were without friends or influence in an alien society. Unable to speak other than their native language, they could not properly defend themselves and so were easily convicted of crimes they did not commit. Evidently, the "new world" was not quite the paradise which many of these immigrants had been initially led to believe it was.

The forces of Canadian xenophobic nativism notwithstanding, this series still attests to Canada's basic need for more "foreigners" to augment its agricultural and industrial labour force. Hence, we find such grandiose projects as that proposed by the Grand Trunk Railway to import 10,000 Russian labourers to help build its railway lines. Indeed, it was out of this need for more human labour than the original "founding" peoples could supply that Canada's multi-cultural society was developed and realized.

However, as this collection also documents, the interests of "Mother Russia" did not always agree with those of Canada. The Russian Consul-General in Montreal frequently made fierce protests to the Canadian government regarding the latter's designs to entice the "flower of the Empire" to foresake their homeland. Even in Russia it was understood that the emigrants often proved to be among the most industrious and vigorous people of that country. Thus, the mother country knew the value of those it was losing to the tides of the emigration movement. Now it is time for Canada to learn more about those whom she had gained - and one principal means is by documenting the valued Russian presence in this land of ours.[11]

References

1. In Canada, the principal manuscript sources relating to this area are found in the records of the Hudson's Bay Company at the Public Archives of Manitoba, Winnipeg. Microfilm copies are available at the Public Archives of Canada, Ottawa, in MG 20 *passim*. (Including certain records of the Russian American Company - MG 20 F 29, 2 reels, HBC 5M49 and HBC 5M50, vols. 1-2) Note, however, there are restrictions governing the use of these microfilm copies; interested researchers are urged to contact the British Archives Section, Manuscript Division, Public Archives of Canada first.

2. The Canadian census data noted throughout the article are from the Dominion Bureau of Statistics, *Census of Canada*, decennial censuses, 1871-1921 (Queen's/King's Printer, Ottawa), as prepared by the Census Office (under the Department of Agriculture to 1912; thereafter, to 1918, the Department of Trade and Commerce) and, after 1918, the Dominion Bureau of Statistics.

3. A general listing of the records of the Government and its agencies at the Public Archives is published in Terry Cook and and Glenn Wright, *Historical Records of the Government of Canada.* (Ottawa: Public Archives of Canada, 1981.) Specific references to Russian immigration are obtainable from the Manpower and Social Development Records Section, Federal Archives Division, Public Archives of Canada.

4. For example, see Canada, Privy Council, in the Public Archives of Canada (PAC), RG 2, Orders-in-Council, P.C. 1104, 27 June 1929, concerning a grant of land to a "Russian Greek-Orthodox Church" at Samborg, Saskatchewan.

5. For records concerning the above, see *ibid*, no. 402, 12 February 1917, and Canada, Department of Justice, in PAC, RG 13 A2, Vol. 179, File 730, respectively.

6. For example, see "Soviet Documents Boon for Canadians,"*The Citizen*, Ottawa, 20 August 1980, p. 86. Essentially the same story was sent across Canada by wire by the Canadian Press. The background history of these papers has been told in John H. Brown, "The Case of the Disappearing Russian Embassy Archives, Washington, D.C. (1922-1949)", (unpublished conference paper, 1980).

7. See "An Odyssey of Canadian Archival Heirlooms End," *The Archivist* 7,6 (November - December 1980), pp. 4-5.

8. Unfortunately, volume and file numbers cannot be cited for the following materials from the LI-RA-MA Collection because the collection is still being processed and, thus, its arrangement has not been finalized.

9. Note that it was the custom of the Russian consular officials, no less than that of the Canadian census-takers and other government agents, to "Russify" the reports pertaining to these immigrants. For example, Ukrainian, Finnish and Swedish names were often spelled or transliterated into Russian and, particularly in the case of the Finns and Baltic peoples, patronyms were supplied. On the other hand, it is clear that many of the immigrants themselves, perhaps in cases of mixed marriages or for political or other reasons, also chose to report themselves as ethnic Russians. Evidence of this occurs when individual immigrants have chosen to describe themselves as "Russian" both in terms of their citizenship and nationality in spite of other documentation relating to them which is strongly indicative of their non-Russian origins.

10. Apart from the fact that the collection conveyed this impression, the author has been informed by more than one person of the reluctance of immigrants from Russia to have any contact with the authorities of their old homeland.

11. Bearing this purpose in mind, the Russian Archives Programme was created by the Ethnic Archives of Canada to collect and preserve the archival material related to the Russian presence in Canada. Organizations and individuals interested in supporting this programme by donating their inactive records and papers should contact the Co-ordinator, Russian Archives Programme, Ethnic Archives, Public Archives of Canada, Ottawa, Ontario, K1A 0N3.

M.I. Mogiljansky

One

THE FIRST RUSSIAN SETTLERS IN CANADA

Late last century, there was what amounted to a mass migration of Russians into Canada. They were Doukhobors, nearly 8,000 in number, and in a way they can be regarded as the first Russian immigrants. Their settlements and their checkered history over the following 80 years are well documented and described in some detail in the next chapter. But the Russians who were the first to step on American soil were those who helped discover Alaska.

Geographically and prehistorically, North America is much more closely linked to Siberia than to Western Europe. Anthropologists agree that the initial peopling of this continent was done by Mongolian man via the Bering Strait a mere 15 or so millenia ago.[1] At that time, there was a land bridge of tundra (today the shortest distance between the Siberian Chukchi peninsula and the American Seward peninsula is only about 50 km).

When and how the first wanderers reached the American shores from Siberia has sunk into oblivion. However, according to the historian Fedorova, the Canadian explorer MacKenzie, who discovered the river bearing his name and who was the first to reach the Pacific coast by land, knew of stories among the aborigines about a lost settlement of white people. These people "came from beyond the sea, were bearded, tall, wore long coats and worshipped the cross and icons."[2]

Fedorova refers to A.V. Efimov, Richard A. Pierce, D.J. Ray, S. Farelly and A.L. Birkenhof on the subject and quotes from letters of Herman, the Russian missionary in Alaska who is now revered as St. Herman of Alaska. In his letters, written to the Father Superior of the Valaam Monastery at the beginning of the 19th century, the missionary related his talks with the local Indians that led him to believe that the first Russian settlers came in 1571 and that the people working for the Russian-American Company presumably met the descendants of these settlers called "Russian Indians." Some historians speculated that these settlers were a "group of Novgorodians fleeing from the terror of Ivan the Terrible (and who) took ship and eventually reached Alaska via the Arctic Ocean".[3]

However, Pierce, Efimov and Fedorova consider that the first Russian settlers in North America were not Novgorodians but survivors of the crew of the fleet of Semen Dezhnev,[4] the Russian seafarer who, in 1648, investigated the existence of a strait between the Chukchi Peninsula and the land beyond. Dezhnev's fleet of seven craft was scattered during a severe storm and four ships were never seen again. There is speculation that they could have reached the Alaskan shore and stayed there, eventually mixing with the local tribes.

Dezhnev was under the impression that the "Big Land", or Alaska, was an island, as did some of the later explorers (Fig. 1). His report on the discovery of the strait between Asia and this "Big Land", which was later called the Bering Strait, was sent to the *voyevoda** of Yakutsk. It apparently never reached Russia which explains why, as of the 1720s, Peter the Great ordered the exploration of eastern Siberia and the adjacent parts of North America without making mention of Dezhnev's discoveries.

The first expedition sent by the Tsar included the geodesists Evreinov and Luzhin who were ordered to "go to Kamchatka and further, as you were told, and describe the places there, finding out if there is a continuation of land between Asia and America."[5]

As the results of this expedition were not satisfactory, Peter the Great sent another in 1725 under the command of Vitus Bering,[6] a Danish explorer who was in the Russian Imperial Naval service. However, it was only Bering's second expedition in 1741 which finally confirmed the suspicion that Alaska was part of a continental landmass and not an island.** In his report, Bering also described the strait, that was later called the Bering Strait.

The crew of Bering's ship, the *St. Peter,* which landed near the mouth of the Copper River in the summer of 1741, became the first Russian visitors in recorded history to reach North America from Asia.

The immediate consequence of Bering's discoveries was the spreading of the news of an apparently unlimited source of a high-

---

* Voyevoda — equivalent to a governor of a province.

** Indications that a strait did indeed exist can be found as early as 1709 as shown in the map by Lvov (see Fig. 1).

quality fur, that of the sea otter. This news drew Siberian hunters and traders like a magnet.[7] Eventually, the chaotic activity of small bands of *promyshlenniki* (traders-hunters) was replaced by some sort of order. Trading companies were created and later consolidated into the famous Russian-American Company.[8] Permanent settlements were founded, the initiative being taken by G.I. Shelekhov who, in 1783, explored the coast of Alaska to Cape St. Elias.[9]

However, the main work of establishing settlements and opening up the new land was carried out by Alexandr Baranov who began his many years of activity in the New World in 1790.[10]

During the first years of the 19th century, the Russians sent expeditions from Alaska to the shores of British Columbia and California, where they built Fort Ross in 1812, just north of the 38th parallel.[11]

It is not known if Russian manufacturers, trading with the Indians of Western Canada built forts or factories, but they explored such possibilities.

One attempt that ended in disaster was made in 1808 and is described by V. M. Golovnin in his *Famous Shipwrecks*.[12] Golovnin relates that the Russian sailing ship *Sviatoy Nikolai* headed from Novoarkhangelsk (the capital of Russian America) along the shores of Vancouver Island in order to purchase furs from the Indians and to find a place suitable for the construction of a fort.

This ship was wrecked on the rocks of the Strait of Juan de Fuca, which separates Vancouver Island from the mainland. Its captain, Bulygin, his young wife Anna and the entire crew were captured by the Indians. The American historian, Hector Chevigny,[13] asserts that Anna Bulygina was the first white woman to set foot on the shore of New Albion which, at that time, was the name of the land between Russian Alaska and California.

The years 1867-1871 were crucial. In 1867 Russia sold Alaska to the United States. That year also saw the birth of the Canadian Confederation. In 1871, British Columbia became a province of the Dominion of Canada.[14]

At that time, the boundaries between Alaska and what was to become British Columbia and Yukon were not settled. There are no data regarding how many Russian settlers and traders returned to Russia and how many moved south to California where fertile land and a gentle climate were readily available. One may assume that some hardy souls took a liking to the new land and, rejecting California and Russia, preferred to stay in Canada. These people could be considered the earliest European pioneers in Western Canada before Confederation. Even today, many of the shops in the old parts of Whitehorse have faded Russian names in English characters displayed on store fronts.[15] This may suggest that some people from Russia, who worked for the Russian-American Company at the time

Alaska was sold, did not return to Russia or go to California but stayed to become the first Russian Canadians. There is a considerable amount of data on relations between the Russian-American Company and the Hudson's Bay Company. This aspect of history is documented in the articles of Canadian historian R. A. Pierce, in particular, in *Russia and British Columbia to 1967.*

The ties between the Russian-American and Hudson's Bay Companies were strong. After Sir George Simpson became the manager of the Canadian company, even more frequent agreements were made on various questions, such as the prohibition of the sale of alcoholic beverages to Indians. Simpson often visited Russians in Novoarkhangelsk and, 1841-42, travelled by sled and carriage across Siberia from Alaska to St. Petersburg as part of his celebrated "overland journey around the world."[17]

Some old residents of Vancouver [18] say that the city was built on the site of an early Russian settlement by people who came from Alaska and other immigrants during the gold rush in British Columbia in the last century, and after the Canadian Pacific Railroad was built.

Indirect indication of a close relationship between Russians and Indians in the last century can be found in the works of the well-known Canadian anthropologist Marius Barbeau,[19] who noted the influence of Russian culture on the crafts of Indians of the west coast. This is illustrated in the photographs of Indian totem poles whose carvings depicted figures copied from the interior of a Russian Church (Figs. 2 and 3). One possible explanation for the paucity of information about early Russian immigrants is that, even after the railroad was built, and in spite of all endeavours, the government was not successful in attracting a large number of immigrants and was content with each settler who came irrespective of his national origin, political views or education. The few Russians who emigrated, mainly from the western provinces (Ukrainians and Poles) preferred to go to the United States where industry and agriculture were developing rapidly and where there was still an abun-

---

* The "Old Believers" (Strarovery or Raskolniki)—adherents of the old faith as it was practised before Patriarch Nikon introduced Church reforms in the middle of the seventeenth century. The reforms included revisions of the religious ritual and Russian prayer books and were met with hostility by conservative members of the clergy and Boyars. The split that followed divided not only the Church but Society as a whole. The harsh policy of repression against the Old Believers by Church and lay authorities led to more resistance, sometimes self-immolation of groups and entire families. It is estimated that by 1700 at least 20,000 perished by suicide alone, not to mention many more who were sentenced to death. (Ed.)

dance of fertile soil offering better opportunities to engage in various forms of agriculture. If a large group of settlers from the same area or belonging to the same religious denomination came to Canada at the same time, then it attracted attention as, for instance, in the case of the Russian-Germans and Doukhobors.

In addition to the Doukhobors, small groups of other sects such as the Baptists and Adventists, began to arrive in Canada from Russia in the first years of the twentieth century. They settled predominantly in Saskatchewan. At the same time, some Russian Old Believers settled in northwestern Alberta.*

Immigrants from Russia and other European countries who were members of sects whose religious beliefs did not allow them to bear arms, were attracted to Canada where they were not required to do military service. In Russia, however, where there had been general conscription and where, neither before nor after the revolution, consideration was not given to religious convictions and exceptions not made for sectarians, each war resulted in a great number of people fleeing abroad either to avoid conscription or as deserters. Some of these "refugees" emigrated to Canada during the Russo-Japanese War of 1904-05.

In 1905, some participants in the famous revolt on the battleship *Potemkin* arrived in Canada from Romania.* One of the soldiers, a certain Mikhail Zerniuk, worked at a meat processing plant where he agitated for the founding of a trade union, as a result of which he was dismissed.

The unsuccessful Russian revolution of 1905 and the subsequent government reprisals forced some of the leaders to escape abroad. Others were arrested and exiled to Siberia from where they fled, some turning up in Vancouver.

In contrast to the people who came to Canada to get land of their own, "political" immigrants settled in large cities. For example, a Russian Progressive Library was organized in Toronto in 1911; it had a large collection of political literature and was the place of frequent meetings of Russian revolutionaries of various stripes: Bolsheviks, Social Democrats, Social Revolutionaries, Anarchists, Syndicalists and others.

The Russian Progressive Club was founded two years later. With approximately 400 members, the club was the site of continuous meetings until 1917. After the revolution, many returned to their homeland.

---

* The revolt, which started on June 13, 1905, was not supported by the crews of other Russian ships. The mutineers killed their officers and escaped to Romania where all those who had been unable to hide were arrested and handed over to the Russian government.

In 1917, a similar club existed in Montreal, known as the Circle of Russian Revolutionaries of Montreal; Russians not involved in politics but who wished to preserve ties with the Russian-Orthodox religion founded a Russian church in 1914.

At the same time, there were attempts to organize labour. In 1913, a man known by the name of Kukhar, a fugitive revolutionary from exile in Siberia, founded the first trade union of carpenters in Toronto. There was a large group of labourers in Windsor which attracted people by its proximity to Detroit with its better chances of employment. One of the eldest members of the large Russian colony in Windsor was Alexei Maslov who arrived in Canada in 1909 from the province of Minsk, Byelorussia. In fact, the majority of "Russians" in Canada at that time came from poor Byelorussian *gubernias** of the old Russian Empire and had Byelorussian rather than Russian names.[20] In Windsor, at that time, there was a Russian Social Revolutionary Organization which had almost 650 members in 1917. It was dissolved in 1919-21. The Russian-Orthodox Church in Windsor was built in 1916.

It would be a mistake to assume that the Russian immigrants were interested only in work provided in the cities and industrial centres (Fig. 4). Most of them arrived in Canada in search of jobs, planning to save enough money to return home and acquire land, cattle, and so forth. Others who decided to adopt Canada as their new homeland went mainly to the West (Figs. 5, 6 and 7) to develop virgin land which was in abundance in the almost uninhabited prairies or in British Columbia. There, it was possible to obtain a large homestead free of charge which, after several years became the personal property of the farmer. Because such possibilities no longer existed in the United States towards the end of the nineteenth century, a flood of immigrants poured into Canada after 1886 when the last spike was driven in the Canadian Pacific Railroad that traversed the country from sea to sea. By 1914, the number had reached two and a half million; of these, more than half a million were from Germany, Poland, Russia, Scandinavia and Italy. As stated in the Introduction, however, it is impossible to determine how many of these people were "genuine" Russians.

---

* Gubernia — administrative distict.

Notes

1. Barbeau, Marius, *Migrations sibériennes en Amérique*, Mexico, 1958, p. 48.

   Efimov, A. V., *Iz istorii velikikh russkikh* geograficheskikh otkrytiy (From the history of great Russian geographic discoveries), Moscow, 1950, pp. 52, 53, 182, 258-264.

   Efimov, A V., "Otkrytie Ameriki so storony Asii" (The Discovery of America from Asia), *Voprosy Istorii* (Problems of History), Academy of Sciences of the USSR, Institute of History, Moscow, 1964, vol. 12.

   Boas, Franz, *Race, Language and Culture*, Collier, MacMillan, London, 1966, pp.234-330, 334-355, 525-529.

   Magilovich, I.P., *Istoria otkrytiy i issledovaniy severnoy Ameriki* (History of the discovery and exploration of North America),Moscow, 1962.

2. Fedorova, S.G., *Russkoye naselenie Alaski i Kalifornii* (The Russian Population in Alaska and California), Moscow, 1971, pp. 14-16, 51-53, 64-79.

3. Farelly, T.S. "A Lost Colony of Novgorod in Alaska", *The Slavonic and East-European Studies Review*, Vol XXII, Menasha, Wis., October, 1944, pp. 33-38.

4. Pierce, R.A., *The Russian Period of Alaskan History*, Anchorage, 1968.

   Efimov, A.V., *op.cit.*, 1964.

   Fedorova, S.G., *op.cit.*

   Coxe, William, *Account of Russian Discoveries Between Asia and America* (with supplement: A comparative view of the Russian Discoveries with those made by Capts. Cook and Clarke)(The Third edition, T. Cadell, In the Strand, London, MDCCLXXXVII),Published for University Microfilms Inc., Ann Arbor by Argonaut Press Ltd., New York, 1966, 387 pages.

5. Solovyev, S.M., *Istoriya Rossii s drevneishykh vremen* (History of Russia from Oldest Times), Moscow, 1962, Book IX, Vol. 18 p. 532.

6. Golder, F.A., *Bering's Voyages* (An account of the efforts of the Russians to determine the relations of Asia and America) in 2 volumes, Octagon Books, New York, 1968.

   Polevoy, B.P., "Iz istorii velikikh geographicheskikh otkrytiy" (From the history of great geographic discoveries). Part of the book, *Ot Alaski do Ognennoy zemli* (From Alaska to Tierra del Fuego), Academy of Sciences of the USSR, Institute of Ethnography, Moscow, 1967, pp. 111-120.

7. Fainberg, L.A. *Ocherki etnicheskoy istorii zarubezhnogo severa* (Review of the ethnic history of the North outside of Russian territory) Moscow, 1971.

Orekov, V.I. *Ocherki iz istorii russkikh geograficheskikh issledovaniy* 1725-1765 (Review of history of the great Russian geographic explorations, 1725-1765), Moscow 1960,pp. 20, 52.

8. Okun, S.B., *The Russian-American Company* (Translated from Russian edition of 1939 by Carl Binsburg), Cambridge, Mass., 1951.

Okunzov, Ivan K., *Russkaya emigratsia v severnoy i yuzhnoy Amerike* (Russian Emigration in North and South America), Editado por la Revista Sembrados, Buenos Aires, 1967, pp. 18-34.

Bancroft, Hubert Howe, *History of Alaska*, Volume XXXIII, San Francisco, A. L. Bancroft & Co., 1886, Chapters XVII, pp. 375-383, XXVI, pp. 530-568, XXVII, pp. 568-590.

Golovnin, V.M., *Obzor russkikh koloniy v severnoy Amerike* (Review of Russian colonies in North America), St. Petersburg, 1862, (written in 1812).

Wrangell, Rear Admiral Ferdinand Petrovich, with additional material by Karl-Ernst Baer, *Russian America*, Statistical and ethnographic information, translated from the German edition of 1839 by Mary Sadonski, edited by Richard A. Pierce, The Limestone Press, Kingston, Ontario, 1980

9. Khlebnikov, Kirill Timofeevich, *Materialy k istorii russkikh zaseleniy po beregam vostochnogo okeana* (Materials on the history of settlement on the Pacific Coast), St Petersburg, 1861.

Fainberg, L.A., *op.cit.*

Fedorova, S.G.,*op.cit.*

10. Khlebnikov, K.T., *Baranov, Chief Manager of the Russian Colonies in America*, The Limestone Press, Kingston, Ontario, 1973.

Bancroft, H.H., *op.cit.*, pp. 315, 333, 514-520.

Baranov, A.A., "Russian Heritage Studies in USA", *Russian American*, Nov, 1975, No. 5, New York, 1976, Nos. 6-7.

Chevigny, Hector, *Lord of Alaska, Baranov and the Russian Adventure*, New York, 1942.

11. Efimov, A.V., *op.cit.*, 1950.

Okunzov, I., *op.cit.*

12. Golovnin, V.M., *Primechatelniye Korablekrushenia* (Remarkable Shipwrecks) St. Petersburg, 1853. (Note: The original book of the same name in three volumes by A.D. Duncan was translated by Golovnin, who added a fourth volume in 1822 on shipwrecks of the Russian fleet.)

13. Chevigny, Hector, *Russian America, The Great Alaskan Adventure*, Viking Press, New York, 1965, pp. 135-147.

14. Careless, J.M.C., *Canada, A Story of Challenge*, Cambridge, 1953.

15. Belkov, G,K., Personal observations, 1970.

16. Pierce, R.A., *Russia and British Columbia to 1967*, Glenbow Museum, Provincial Archives, Calgary, Alberta, 1973.

17. Simpson, Sir George, *An Overland Journey Around the World*, Lea and Blanchard, Philadelphia, 1847.

18. Author's interview with Vancouver old-timers; Capt: V. G. Balzaud and E.E. Andreyev, in 1965.

19. Barbeau, Marius, *op.cit.*, pp. 44-47.

    __________, *Totem Poles*, National Museum of Canada, 2 vols., Bulletin No. 119, Vol. 1, pp. 405-407, Vol. 2, pp. 831-833.

20. Sokolowski, J., *The Russians and Byelorussians in Alberta* (Papers and proceedings of the conferences and meetings on Central and East European studies, ed. by Tova Yedlin), The Division of East European and Soviet Studies, University of Alberta, Edmonton, February-April, 1976, p. 32.

21. *Ibid.*, p. 1.

N.G. Kosachova

Two

THE DOUKHOBORS

Because of the specific religious and social practices of the Doukhobor group in Canada, it is necessary to treat them as a separate and distinct entity within a Russian community. Indeed, some Doukhobors disclaim any connection with Russians rejecting entirely the principle of nationality. . .

The Canadian Family Tree, 1979, p. 190.

Historical Sketch

From a numerical and economic point of view, the Doukhobors of Canada are not very significant and would not, from this standpoint, merit a long chapter. However, they are of extraordinary interest from the human, religious, and political point of view. Not only do they have a fascinating historical background but their coming to this country and their experiences and treatment as a non-conforming group, furnish an object lesson on how a nation-state can attempt to accommodate such a group.

Doukhobors, the religious sectarians-pacifists who left Russia in 1899 and settled in Saskatchewan and British Columbia, occupy a special place among the Russian population of Canada.

As the earlier Doukhobors refused to recognize written language, there is no archival information available on the origin of their sect. The Doukhobor movement is believed to have started as a result of the split caused by the reforms of Patriarch Nikon (1605-1681). The term "Doukhobors" was first mentioned in 1785 in the report on "icon rejectors" by Bishop Amvrosii of Ekaterinoslav who wrote that they "rebel against all sacraments of the church and reject the presence of the spirit, i.e., they are Doukhobortsy (spirit wrestlers)."* Doukhobors later changed the interpretation of this term insisting that they were "spiritual wrestlers" i.e., that they fought for Christian faith together with the Holy Spirit.[1]

While recognizing Christ, the Doukhobors reject the church, dogmas, rites, icons, priesthood and the Bible but, at the same time, have their spiritual leaders whose will they obey implicity. They assert that God lives in the hearts of people who hear God's guiding voice when need be. The symbols of Doukhobors' belief — bread, salt and water which are laid out on a table during prayer meetings — embody the principal elements of earthly existence.

Their only ceremony, a waist-deep bow on entering a prayer house or on meeting another Doukhobor, is a bow to the divine spirit present in a human being. During their prayer meetings, Doukhobors sing hymns and psalms, which are passed on from generation to generation with constant changes and additions — the so-called *Book of Life*.

God's guiding voice, they believe, is present in every human being. They, therefore, reject the right of autocrats, of the state or of any institution to guide their actions. Hence, their refusal to swear allegiance to either a Russian tsar or an English king. Herein lies a major contradiction between the theory and practice of the Doukhobor movement: while denying the authority of a tsar, they have, since the last third of the 18th century, obeyed their sole spiritual leader whose power is absolute and which has become hereditary. They ascribe to him the endowment of prophecy and intuition. Since God is present in every human being, they reasoned, killing another person constitutes the vilest sin no matter what the circumstances, be it war, robbery, or anything else. Hence the unshakeable pacifism of the Doukhobors and the initially negative attitude towards education which, as they allege, implants not only knowledge but militaristic ideas.[2]

Doukhobors believe in the superiority of the spirit over the flesh and reject attachment to material wealth because this leads to spiritual impoverishment.

Until the middle of the 18th century, the Doukhobor movement concentrated in the Ukraine, later shifting to Central Russia, the Don and the Trans-Caucasus.

The first communities were set up in the village of Goreloye, Tambov Province, where the leader, I. Pobirokhin, proclaimed himself the living Christ.

Initially, the Doukhobors influenced only the orthodox peasants in their vicinity. It was not until the Cossacks, who protected the southern state border, began to assimilate the ideas of pacifism that the government of Catherine II paid serious attention to them.

---

* In the sense of wrestling *against the holy spirit.* (Ed.)

It was decided to suppress the sect and exile its leaders and active members. However the Doukhobors kept expanding their ranks. Stricter measures ensued, in particular against soldiers who refused to go to war. Under Tsar Paul I, the Doukhobors were condemned to corporal punishment, hard labour, and subject to seizure of property.[3] But this did not stop them either: in 1806 the newly-recruited Doukhobors laid down their arms in the battlefield.[4]

The situation changed when Alexander I ascended the throne in 1801. He looked upon the sectarians with benevolence[5] and allotted them a place in Kherson Province, a land with a good climate, fertile soil and excellent conditions for settlement. A large village sprang up on the Molochnaya River to which Doukhobors began to move from other places.

By 1828 the Molochnaya River had become a major population centre comprising nine villages with 3,985 inhabitants. Doukhobors settlements were also established in Siberia and some 3,000 lived in Saratov, Tambov and Orenburg.[6]

In the beginning, the Doukhobors lived in communes* on the Molochnaya River where they thrived on communal agriculture and cattle breeding. Trade for the commune was carried on by the elders. The leader paid the taxes for everyone. Leader Savelii Kapustin introduced an unwritten constitution: hereditary leadership, a 24-member Council of Elders who conducted communal affairs, and prohibition from using the services of government jurisdictional bodies. Along with this there was an assembly, attended by all men and women. Its functions consisted of praying and discussing everyday matters. This enabled the leader to size up the mood of the commune and to act accordingly.

By 1816, however, the commune had begun to fall apart as a result of leadership being hereditary: Kapustin's son and grandson were unintelligent and weak-willed. Disregarding established traditions, they indulged in hard drinking and debauchery. Power was shared by two families, the Kapustins and the Kalmykovs.[7]

When Nicholas I, a convinced enemy of pacifists, came to the throne in 1825, he regarded Doukhobors as a threat to his absolute

---

* The author draws a distinction between commune and community. A *commune* designates a number of Doukhobor families living under one roof and eating in a common dining hall; such communes existed in British Columbia until the fall of 1938. A *community* means former communal Doukhobor families living in separate, self-contained homes, but still united by common beliefs and having one leader. In this article, Doukhobors living as a group in a commune will be referred to as Community Doukhobors and not Communal Doukhobors as the author believes they should be called. The reason being that this is how this group is called in most English-language publications and by the Doukhobors themselves when speaking English.

power and introduced numerous restrictions such as forbidding Doukhobors from hiring substitute recruits to replace them in military service.

In 1832, Kapustin's sixteen-year old grandson, Illarion V. Kalmykov, became the leader. He was a weak-willed degenerate who was a pawn in the hands of the Elders' Council. Debauchery and shady business continued. The Doukhobors were well aware of this but kept silent. Rumors spread of torture and killing of the discontented. Nicholas I ordered an investigation: it resulted in the discovery of several mutilated bodies. The Tsar decided to punish all the Doukhobors and exiled them from their prosperous and cultivated homeland on the Molochnaya River, where they had lived for 40 years, to the Mokrye Mountains (in the Trans-Caucasus), a wilderness with soil conditions suitable only for cattle-breeding.[8] There, nine villages were set up, with another four in the vicinity of Elizavetpol where the land and climate were better. The next to move here were the Cossacks-Doukhobors who had already settled in the Caucasus.[9] Twenty-seven families who had re-converted to orthodoxy remained on the Molochnaya River. Later, about 1,000 Doukhobors returned to this place.[10]

In all, about 4,000 Doukhobors went to the Caucasus, but by 1890 their number had reached 20,000 presumably as a result of emigration from Russia proper. They raised cattle, sheep and horses for, at that time, they were still not vegetarians. Trade prospered, providing them with grain, vegetables, and fruit. The land was in common prossession, but stock was individually owned. Hard work, unpretentiousness and the ability to adapt to a harsh environment led to prosperity.[11]

Tranquil times returned after Alexander II came to the throne in 1855. The government and the church left the Doukhobors alone because the Caucasian villages being regarded as penal colonies, were exempt from military service. The hospitable and physically strong Doukhobors were liked and respected by the local population.[12] Prosperity, however, put an end to equality. A wealthy upper class came into existence, bringing with it the exploitation of "brother by brother." The commandment "thou shalt not kill," was forgotten: the Doukhobors began using rifles to protect their cattle. They also started drinking and smoking.

Illarion's son, Peter, turned out to be an able and strong leader, but he took little interest in the spiritual aspects of Doukhobor life. His favourite pastime was hunting.[13] He married Lukeria Gubanova, an intelligent, strong-willed young lady, whom he appointed his successor.

"Lushechka" ruled wisely for 22 years, an era now considered to have been the best in Doukhobor history. Having managed to establish excellent relations with government officials and the local population, Lukeria secured numerous privileges. Contrary to Doukhobor conviction, she compromised with the government and detailed several hundred men to assist in the transportation of ammunition during the Russo-Turkish war. In return she was granted 1,500,000 roubles and new fertile lands in the vicinity of the town of Kars (which was won back from Turkey), near Tiflis.[14]

Childless herself, Lukeria chose as her successor Peter V. Verigin, a great grandson of Savelii Kapustin. Verigin was literate, highly-principled and a strict follower of tradition. At Lukeria's insistence, he left his wife, pregnant with a son who was to become a Doukhobor leader in Canada under the name or Piotr Chistiakov.[15]

Lukeria's death in 1886 caused a split in the Doukhobor ranks. A struggle for power ensued between P.V. Verigin and Lukeria's brother M. V. Gubanov, whose supporters informed the gendarmerie that Verigin called himself Christ and tsar. The assembly, however, recognized Verigin as their leader. Immediately after the elections, he was arrested and exiled to the north for 16 years.[16] The split lasted until the departure of Verigin's supporters for Canada.

The opposition led by Gubanov found themselves in the minority; the only laws recognized by the majority were Verigin's directives from exile. In the Caucasus, for example, where military service had already been introduced, young men would join the army but, obeying Verigin's orders, would not fire in combat.

While in exile, Verigin suffered no privations because Doukhobors visited him regularly, providing him with money. Personal contact with other political exiles contributed a good deal to Verigin's intellectual growth. In particular, he was influenced by Tolstoy's teachings.[17] As a consequence, in 1893-94 Verigin ordered his followers to return to the traditional way of communal life: to cease all lawsuits among the members, to remit debts, to make all property common and to stop paying taxes to the state. Moreover, following Tolstoy's dictates he introduced vegetarianism, prohibited the use of alcohol and tobacco, and suggested abstinence from sexual intercourse because "Doukhobors must enter into a struggle against the Prince of Darkness and children may be an obstacle to God's cause."[18] The requirements of vegetarianism and sexual abstinence alienated many of the Doukhobors, but the staunch followers formed a strong, blindly obedient group.

Accompanied by two other Doukhobors, Verigin's brother met Tolstoy in 1894. The famous writer was delighted when he learned of their life-style. He had, in fact, been misled, however, for the Doukhobors had been insincere when they said they lived as a commune without a leader.[19]

Nicholas II, who ascended the throne in 1894, demanded that the Doukhobors take the oath of allegiance or be subject to punishment. Verigin would not take the oath and ordered the Doukhobors to do the same and to refuse military service. Those who had already joined the army were to return their uniforms and arms. The arms required for the protection of their property, for hunting and sport were to be publicly burned on St. Peter and Paul's Day, June 29, 1895 to symbolize the Doukhobors' rejection of compromise.[20]

The Doukhobor-soldiers carried out the order and were severely punished and sent into exile. The peasants, nonetheless, also complied with their leader's decision and burned a large quantity of weapons and firearms in a huge bonfire on the night of the Peter and Paul holiday.[21]

Gubanov's group had warned government officials that something important would happen. Troops were sent to the Doukhobor settlements. In the village of Orlovka the Cossack cavalrymen drove their horses into the crowd and beat the people with whips. Repressions began. Cossack troops were billeted in Doukhobor villages where they went on the rampage. About 300 people were put into prison and the rest (4,300) were resettled on malarial lands in the vicinity of Batum. What property could not be loaded onto carts had been sold to Gubanov's people for next to nothing.

Those who arrived in Georgia were settled in groups of four or five families in mountain villages; they had no right to own land, to leave the village in search of work or to communicate with other Doukhobors. Despite the clandestine help the Doukhobors received from their brethren in Kars and Elizavetpol, more than 350 died during the first year. Nonetheless, the Doukhobors continued their passive resistance.

Tolstoy raised his voice in their defence. He wrote letters and appeals to both Russian and British newspapers.[22] The Doukhobors themselves sent petitions to higher authorities, requesting either exemption from military service or permission to emigrate. At last they were allowed to emigrate at their own expense on condition that they never return to Russia.[23] The money towards their emigration was raised by Tolstoy in Russia, by Chertkov in Britain and by the Doukhobors themselves who gave up all their possessions. In addition, Tolstoy donated his royalties from the novel *Resurrection* (30,000 roubles) and the English Quakers set up a relief fund.[24]

Among several possible destinations, Cyprus was chosen as the most hopeful, and in August 1898 an advance contingent of 1,126 moved there. Things turned out badly, however; there was no proper leadership, and the hot climate and lack of customary foods (especially milk) contributed to unhappiness, ill health and high mortality.[25] This situation led to increased attempts to move to a better homeland. In the end, Canada was chosen. Among those who supported such a move was Aylmer Maude, the English friend, translator and biographer of Tolstoy and the exiled anarchist, Prince Piotr Kropotkin.

So it came about that a small reconnaissance party, including two Doukhobors and their families, moved across the Atlantic accompanied by Maude himself aboard the *S.S. Vancouver*. It docked at Quebec City on September 10, 1898.

On December 6 of that year, the Government, through Privy Council, granted permission for resettlement in Canada, promising the Doukhobors exemption from military service, freedom of religion, and land grants.

P.V. Verigin insisted that the Doukhobors in Canada live in communes but that each family be separately housed and own two horses and a cow. The rest of the stock was to be common property and field work was to be done collectively. The first 7,400 Doukhobors came to Canada from Russia in 1899[29] (Fig. 8). Although as far back as 1895 Verigin proposed that the sect be called the "Christian Community of Universal Brotherhood" to make it clear that the Doukhobors regarded all people as brothers. Communal life began only after the departure of the Doukhobors from Russia.[27]

In Canada, the Government granted Doukhobors three large territories in Saskatchewan: north-east of Yorkton (South colony), north of Yorkton (North colony) and near Prince Albert. In all, this amounted to 400,000 acres.[28]

Under severe winter conditions, the first temporary homes were built and Canada's first Doukhobor village, Mikhailovka, was founded. Because young men of military age had to stay in Russia, the able-bodied amounted to only about 20 per cent of the newcomers. These men soon left in search of work at railroad construction sites, saw mills and farms, while the women, the old men and the children stayed behind to till the land. There was hardly any money with which to buy stock and implements. Ploughing was carried out by harnessing 10 to 12 women to a plough and it was the women who felled trees, skidded logs, pulled carts and even built cabins and houses. The Doukhobors might have never succeeded in Canada had it not been for their heroic women who bore the burden the first two years. Nevertheless, many people had to make do, living in dugouts or tents.

During the first year of immigration, a good deal of help came from Quakers who provided the Doukhobors with large amounts of food, seeds, medicine and even with 69 head of cattle.[29]

The Canadian Government made plots of land available on the basis of 160 acres per family (homestead). If, within three years, the family had cultivated a certain amount of land and erected household building, the plot became their property.[30]

The Doukhobors built no fewer than 55 villages in the vicinity of Yorkton and the land was cultivated jointly by all members of the community.[31] The land near Prince Albert was divided by the Government into mile-square individual lots with even numbers for

Doukhobors and odd numbers for non-Doukhobors. As a result, only 10 villages were set up here; most Doukhobors had to settle as single families and cultivate the land individually. Villages would be given typical Doukhobor names — Terpenie, Osvobozhdenie, Tikhomirnaya, etc.*

In 1905, Doukhobors who had been exiled to Yakutiya arrived in Canada. This was, essentially, the end of mass immigration of Doukhobors to this country. Only a handful, mainly members of the Verigin family, would arrive later.

The lack of leadership (P.V. Verigin was still in exile), freedom from persecution and contacts with Canadians greatly influenced those Doukhobors who lived on individual plots among other settlers. They began to change, becoming wedded more to individualism than communal life. Soon they became known as Independents.

At about this time, a group of several dozen strong-willed resolute and deeply committed men stood out among the Doukhobors.[32] Looking upon poultry and cattle as their junior brothers in God, they insisted that these should not be made to work for man and accordingly "set free" several hundred cows, horses and sheep.[33] Articles manufactured from animal bones and skins, such as sheepskin coats, boots, buttons, harnesses, etc., were burned. The members of this group subsequently became leaders of the "Sons of Freedom" movement. They renounced material possessions to preach Christ's teachings to the people. [34]

In October 1902, over a thousand "Sons of Freedom" started on their march through Doukhobor villages calling on sympathizers to join them; they were heading south in search of better lands and "to meet Christ."[35] Near Yorkton, the police separated the women and the children from the marchers and sent them back home. The men continued the march until they reached Minnedosa, Manitoba where, hungry, cold and exhausted, they were forced into railroad coaches and sent back to their villages.

In 1902, P.V. Verigin's term of exile came to an end and he left for Canada to join his mother and brother. He founded a new village, Verigino, which later became an administrative centre. Being regarded by many Doukhobors as God, he acquired the nickname "Gospodni" (Peter the Lordly). Since 1901, the Canadian Government has insisted that Doukhobors should register their homesteads individually, take the oath of allegiance to the Crown and be naturalized. The Doukhobors, however, insisted that their land be registered on the community's behalf only. P.V. Verigin was able to settle the issue temporarily by getting permission to have 2,000 plots of land registered on behalf of three Doukhobors elected by the

* Translates to Patience, Deliverance, Quietly Peaceful.

community.[36]* In the beginning, Verigin encouraged his people to look for work outside the community with the intention of accumulating money to buy agricultural machinery. However, contacts with Canadians still further enhanced the division of the one-time homogeneous Doukhobor community into three distinct groups: (1) the conservative majority, who obeyed Verigin's orders and stood for communal life; (2) the more prosperous Doukhobors from near Prince Albert, who preferred individual homesteads (Independents); and (3) the most radical, the Freedomites. The last group stood for complete freedom of man and beast and for plain living. They were particularly zealous in guarding the Doukhobor traditions and when Doukhobors "went astray" would lauch a protest, often in most peculiar ways. Governments, they would reason, were created by people; therefore, it is absurd that people should be subordinate to their own creation. People should live as close to nature as possible. Civilization, education and private property make life unnatural and, therefore, should be done away with. It is not without reason that the Doukhobor historian Maloff calls the Freedomites "the counterweight" on the scale of Doukhobor society.[37]

Indignant over the discrepancies between Verigin's teachings and his political compromises, the Freedomites insisted that his directives should be interpreted in the opposite sense. In May 1903, they stripped to the skin and began their march through Doukhobor villages to protest against the accumulation of material wealth and to propagate the idea of identity with nature. They were promptly arrested and imprisoned. On their release, a few fanatics trampled the wheat sown with the aid of machines and set fire to several mowing and threshing machines.[38]

According to the Doukhobor historian Sukhorev, "the nudes" acted under the influence of the nudists of Oregon who tried to persuade the Freedomites "to restore the lost primeval paradise of Adam and Eve" who had never worn clothes.[39]

At this juncture the Independents were in the minority (850), the Community Doukhobors numbering 7,852.

By 1907 the Canadian Doukhobors had made astonishing progress. The illiterate peasants who started from scratch had built 61 villages and their population increased to 8,700.[40]

With the arrival of Verigin, who had rallied around him the majority of the Doukhobors, "the Christian Community of Universal Brotherhood" came into its own. Each village had become a separate commune whose members worked together in the fields and jointly handled their money reserve, stock and implements. Only

---

* Woodcock and Avakumovic give 2,770 as the number of registered homesteads; *op. cit.*, p. 187.

clothes and some personal belongings were considered private property.

Gradually, communal enterprises such as flour mills, silos, a brick factory and wholesale stores would be organized. The communal office served as a link with the outer world. The Doukhobors led a simple life, excess and luxury being banned by the leader. Domestic crafts and sensible improvement of lifestyle were encouraged. The village shops produced furniture and footwear. The women spun, wove, embroidered and knitted. The food was plain but nourishing and wholesome. Religious activities consisted of praying during gatherings. The children were not allowed to attend Canadian schools; there were, however, several Russian schools where the teachers were either Doukhobors themselves or, occasionally, Russian intellectuals. As the adults could hardly speak any English, the commune members were, in effect, cut off from Canadian society. As a result, the old Russian mode of life remained unchanged: steam baths with birch twigs, Russian stoves, national costumes, traditional meals with kvass* and pies, etc. All members of the family would eat their meal with wooden spoons from a common bowl. Diseases were treated by old women using homemade medicine.[41]

At the same time, by developing the virgin lands of the west, the Doukhobors made an important contribution to Canada's history.

In 1905, Peter Vasilyevich Verigin's son, Peter Petrovich Verigin (later known as Chistiakov, "the Purger") joined his father in Canada, bringing with him his mother, wife and children. (One of the children, Peter Petrovich Iastrebov, later died in a Soviet concentration camp during Stalin's rule). Peter. P. Verigin turned against his father upon arrival in Canada, publicly denouncing his extravagant way of life and his being on too friendly terms with his relative, Anastasia Golubeva. Six months later P.V. Verigin sent his family back to Russia.

By 1907, the issue of land registration had come to a head. The new Minister of Internal Affairs, Frank Oliver, insisted on literal observance of the law that provided for land registration on an individual basis. At the time, Verigin was in Russia sounding out the political climate after the 1905 revolution and exploring the possibility of moving back to Russia. While he was away, the Independent Doukhobors had their plots registered and obtained their ownership. This was a major decision and its consequences were far-reaching. The unregistered Doukhobors lost 258,880 acres of land, including the buildings, which were given to those who had submitted claims for these partially developed plots. Each family

* Traditional Russian non-alcoholic beverage.

could keep 15 acres for its use but without right of ownership. In one stroke, the Community Doukhobors had lost all their property and had to look elsewhere to build new settlements.

In the summer of 1907, the Freedomites stirred again. About 70 of them began another march to the south where, they said, Christ was waiting for them. The march lasted a whole year. On New Year's Day the participants stripped naked and walked in the snow-covered streets of Fort William. In the spring they burnt all their clothes. The police arrested 19 people and sent them home.

Soon after, an opportunity presented itself for the community to move to another place. As there was no need to become naturalized and take the oath of allegiance in order to buy land second-hand in Canada, Verigin acquired several thousand acres in a mountainous area of British Columbia near Waterloo Station (later Brilliant), Grand Forks, Pass Creek, and Slokan Junction. Several fruit plantations were bought as well. The plots were heavily timbered, the soil fertile. The climate was favourable for fruit-growing and bee-keeping. Everything seemed to agree with the Doukhobors' aspiration for living close to nature.[42] By 1924, the communes had bought 21,648 acres[43] in Verigin's name; he, in turn, bequeathed it to the community. The Doukhobors migrated in groups and by the end of 1912 about 5,000 of them had settled in British Columbia.

As migration continued, Doukhobor state-granted plots were vacated and given to those who wanted them — often the Independent Doukhobors. But, in 1918 the law concerning these plots changed and the rest of the land was purchased by individual Community Doukhobors, who had stayed in Saskatchewan, and who later passed this property on to the community. A sum of $71,445 had been borrowed for this purpose. To pay the debts, Verigin introduced strict austerity and a policy of hard work.

Only the Independents and about a thousand Community Doukhobors had stayed behind in the Prairies. Cattle breeding was on the decrease. In British Columbia, the Doukhobors engaged in logging, gardening and bee-keeping. Being very practical, Verigin coupled unpaid communal labour with seasonal work. Those working elsewhere paid a tax to the commune. Gradually, the migrators acquired saw-mills, a brick factory, two fruit canneries, flour-mills and silos. By 1924, their property was estimated at $6,410,822 with a debt of $1,113,300.[44]

Thus, while claiming to be against acquisition of material wealth, Verigin encouraged agriculture and trade. In the words of Woodcock and Avakumovic, he "transfigured from living Christ to company president."[45] His slogan was "toil and peaceful life".

In Saskatchewan, each Doukhobor family had a separate house and prepared its own meals. In British Columbia, the Doukhobors began living communally (35 to 50 people to a house with common meals and property, each family having a separate room). Two such houses made up a "village", i.e., a commune owning a plot of land. Strict austerity was observed. Maloff recalls two restrictions in particular, when at one time the Doukhobors were not allowed to buy salt and kerosene to be used for lighting. Surplus products were turned over to store-houses.

Adornments and luxury articles were also prohibited. The Community Doukhobors found themselves almost completely isolated because private trade, trips to town and visits with neighbouring farmers were forbidden. Mothers taught their children to sing psalms and instilled into them the necessity for modest behaviour and respect for parents and old people.[46] The clothes were very plain, children and many adults going barefoot in the summer. Entertainment consisted basically of choir singing and various games. Punishment within the community was inflicted by depriving the culprit of a flour ration from three to thirty days and, in extreme cases, by banishment from the community. Thus, an individual, without money or knowledge of English, was placed in a very difficult position.[47] This communal way of life, however, gradually eroded, coming to an end in the 1930s.

After the migration of Verigin's followers to British Columbia, over a thousand Independent Doukhobors were left on the Prairies. They preserved their beliefs, retaining their pacifism. But, living among Canadians, they lost their belief in the divinity of their leaders and grew so antagonistic to communal life that, by 1910, they left their villages and settled on privately-owned plots. They were joined by many Community Doukhobors who had not yet left for British Columbia and who had easily acquired some land. When the town of Blaine Lake was built on their territory, the Independents made it their centre. Here, in 1916, the "Society of Independent Doukhobors" was set up, led by its secretary, Peter Makaroff, a young lawyer, who was the first Doukhobor to receive a higher education. He also headed the opposition to Verigin who had prohibited social intercourse with the Independents.[48] British Columbians disliked the Doukhobors because they were exempt from military service and would not support trade, manufacturing most of their own goods. During World War I, the Doukhobors, being in a priviledged position, were trying to help Canada by contributing money to the Patriotic Fund and jam to the Red Cross.[49] Even so, demobilized soldiers demanded, unsuccessfully, that the Doukhobors' lands be given to them.

The restrictions and austerity imposed by Verigin during the first years in British Columbia were short-lived. In 1916, the Doukhobors' way of life underwent some changes: commune members began accumulating money of their own and morals began to deteriorate. Doukhobors took to visiting neighbouring towns, learned about the movies and acquired a taste for liquor, tobacco and meat. With these changes came social inequality: the "Elders" and the "Officials" together with Verigin's relatives and retinue, became a privileged class.[50]

The post-war years, especially 1921-22, were difficult for the commune. To repay the loan, Verigin stressed the need to apply even more stringent measures than before. He established a daily living expenses quota of 10 cents per Doukhobor which led to discontent.[51]

Under the pressure of the Government of British Columbia, the children from the communes started attending school in 1911. The following year, the Doukhobors complained that the teaching was conducted in a militaristic spirit, did not meet the needs of the peasants' children and led to assimilation with the Canadian population. This resulted in a drop in attendance.

In 1915, Verigin and the Government reached a compromise: Divine Law would be taken off the curriculum and militaristic ideas suppressed. Although not all school-aged children were attending school, this was the first step towards literacy.

For unknown reasons, the children stopped going to school in 1922, which got the Doukhobors into trouble with the Government. The following year, some school buildings were set on fire in retaliation for the fines imposed on Doukhobor property by the Government. Verigin asserted that Community Doukhobors had nothing to do with it as his own house and sawmill had also been burnt down.[52]

In the meantime, the Doukhobors had been profoundly shaken by the news of the Bolshevik Revolution of 1917 and the abdication of the Tsar. Many of them began to think of returning to their homeland. They believed that they shared the same ideas with the Soviet Government: both the Doukhobors and the new Government were against the Tsar, both wanted peace, and the "soviets" (councils) themselves looked very much like Doukhobor assemblies. In reality, the Doukhobors were ignorant of the Bolshevik Party's political platform. In 1922, Verigin wrote a letter in which he expressed his wish to return to Soviet Russia and stated the conditions therefor: exemption from military service, registration and compulsory education. He received no reply.

Verigin continued to be the Doukhobor's spiritual leader until his death in 1924, when a bomb, set by unknown malefactors under the train coach in which he was travelling, exploded. As Verigin had failed to appoint a successor, the Doukhobors were left without a leader. On learning of his death, the creditors brought a lawsuit against the community. The Doukhobors had to contract a loan for $350,000 secured on nearly all of their multi-million dollar property instead of on a part of it.

The majority of Doukhobors decided to choose as their new leader Verigin's son Peter Petrovich Verigin (or Chistiakov, the "Purger", as he preferred to call himself), who, at that time, was the leader of those Doukhobors who had moved from the Caucasus to the Sal'skie Steppes near the city of Rostov-on-the-Don. Chistiakov was considered a supporter of the Soviet régime. Woodcock and Avakumovic see him as a mixture of spiritual leader and Bolshevik commissar.[53] Compared to other Doukhobors, Chistiakov was well-educated, having completed grammar and technical school in Tiflis. However, he was said to be lacking in his father's common sense; instead, he was impulsive and given to drink and fits of rage.[54]

Having accepted the offer to be leader, Chistiakov dispatched an order from the USSR to Canada stipulating that the children start attending school again. This improved the Doukhobors' relations with the Government of British Columbia. In 1927, he arrived in Canada, leaving his wife and children behind.[55]

On arrival, he immediately took a keen interest in the financial position of the community. In 1928, the debt totalled roughly $1,200,000.[56] To get out of debt, Chistiakov called on the Doukhobors to unite. He made their life easier by permitting them to sell surplus grain and fruit to communal silos and canneries. If they found work elsewhere, they were permitted to keep what money was left after paying taxes. In a letter addressed to the Doukhobors, he called on them to donate money towards an internal loan that would enable the community to discharge its debt. The Community Doukhobors and even the Independents responded willingly, raising about $350,000.[57]

In between the leadership of the two Verigins, the young generation had begun to assimilate and forget Doukhobor traditions and the Russian language. In 1928, Chistiakov called a meeting in Saskatchewan at the farm of an Independent Doukhobor, V.I. Popoff, which led to the founding of a new Doukhobor organization, the "Society of Named Doukhobors". The resolution adopted at this meeting stated that "the Doukhobors shall not resort to violence to resist evil; all disputes shall be settled by an ad hoc committee; marriage shall be based on love; divorce shall be by mutual agreement; he who has committed a crime shall be banished from the community; education shall be encouraged on condition that teaching is free from imperialistic ideas or hatred".[58] In particular, Chistiakov called for an expansion of the Russian school network. Soon afterwards, new Russian schools and libraries were opened. "The Society of Named Doukhobors" was Chistiakov's idea of uniting Community Doukhobors and Independents who compromised with the Government and of keeping in check the Freedomites who could now be banished from the commune. But the

Freedomites chose to interpret the resolution "the other way around" and started vigorous demonstrations against education, saying that the leader was testing them. To the call for an expansion of communal economy, they replied that one should not be concerned with worldly and material things. They resumed burning schools and public buildings and demonstrations in the nude.[59] Gradually, the new organization got down to the business of raising money to repay the debt.

Although Verigin-Chistiakov had come to Canada without means, he very soon started living in "style", drinking, gambling, brawling, and generally displaying a somewhat violent, unholy nature. Yet most Community Doukhobors took it for granted.

In 1929, he suggested that the Doukhobors raise money for the "White Horse" on which to set out on a long journey. The Doukhobors once again responded to the call, raising $525,329. Chistiakov loaned this money at interest to the same Doukhobors who had contributed it. The migration plans did not materialize.[60]

In 1931, a delegation from the "Society of Named Doukhobors" left for Germany where it was to establish contact with the Politburo and obtain permission to immigrate to the USSR. The political naiveté of the Doukhobors and their total ignorance of life in the USSR is evident from their petition to Stalin, in which they called themselves "the first champions of communism" and asked why they had received no reply from him. "For several months", they wrote, "we have been knocking on your door. We are forced to keep spending money here, in a foreign land, money that belongs to our comrades in Canada who sent us to contact you. Is this all in vain?" The petition ended with "Dear comrades! The thousands of workers and peasants who chose us as delegates are expecting news of our trip to Soviet Russia where, as we have already said, lie all our aspirations and hopes."[61] The reply was negative.

Speculating on the reasons for the refusal, the Doukhobor historian Sukhorev came to the following conclusion in 1944: ". . .there are reasons to believe that the Soviet Union was going through a critical period of espionage and counter-revolution activity of the reactionaries, as became clear after the Zinov'yev-Kamenev trial. . . It is possible that the noble aspirations of the Doukhobors. . .were interpreted as being to the detriment of the USSR and that was the reason for denying entry."[62]

Sukhorev was unable, of course, to foresee Khushchev's denunciation at the 20th Party Congress of Stalin's political course; nor could he have known of the fabrication of the Zinov'yev-Kamenev trial, in particular.

According to Woodcock and Avakumovic, Chistiakov's behaviour from 1930 onwards was scandalous. While the country was suffering from economic depression and the Freedomite movement had become widespread, Chistiakov was irresponsibly abusing his absolute power over the Community Doukhobors. Woodcock and Avakumovic regard him as a nihilist to whom nothing was sacred. The Canadian authorities were indignant with him. The last years of his life were a series of court trials (for drinking, assault, perjury, etc.) and prison terms.

Chistiakov's behaviour and the Freedomites' escapades earned a bad reputation for Doukhobors in general. The Canadian public knew of the Doukhobors only from hearsay and from newspaper reporting of Freedomites' scandalous activities. Few people knew that the Freedomites were a small group of fanatics denounced by the majority of Doukhobors.

In the meantime, more and more Doukhobors had begun leaving the commune. By 1936, over 2,300 members had left, with 3,083 remaining in British Columbia and 386 in the Prairies.[63] The village of Krestovaya had become a Freedomite centre.[64]

During the 1930s a strong influence on the Doukhobors was exercised by a leftist Russian workers' organization which united prerevolutionary Russian emigrants and whose centres were the "Russian Workers' Clubs," situated in different cities. These clubs later became part of the "Federation of Russian Canadians."

The most cultured among the Doukhobors were the Independents who had been educated at Canadian schools, some graduating from university. They frowned upon Chistiakov's scandalous behaviour. A small group of them had established contact with Russian Workers' Clubs and, in June 1934, a congress was convened in the village of Verigino at which the "Progressive Society of Doukhobors" was formed. Items discussed at the Congress were published by "Kanadskii Gudok," a Toronto-based pro-communist newspaper. The majority of Doukhobors, however, were against the new group. "In the last days before the Congress, all the Doukhobors began to stir, meetings were called, large delegations were elected at nearby places in order to ensure a majority over the 'progressive part' of the Congress", remembers G. Okulevich.[65] The Society prepared a declaration using marxist rather than Doukhobor terminology and announced as its principal goal "the undertaking of cultural and educational activities among the Doukhobors" (organizing schools, self-education and amateur performance groups, lectures, libraries and wall newspapers "for the purpose of fighting bad behaviour"). The second important goal was the struggle against militarism and fascism, against "exploitation of the working class by capitalists and against the Government's terror and violence upon the working people."[66] To carry out these activities, a central Executive Committee was elected. At the request of the Society, the "Kanadskii Gudok" editorial staff made available one page to the Executive

Committee and named it "The page of the Progressive Society of Doukhobors."

In 1936, the Third Congress of the Progressive Society of Doukhobors suggested that the page be renamed "Doukhobors' Life", so that, according to G. Okulevich, "the very name would not prevent other Doukhobors from regarding this page as their own".[67] Chistiakov called the members of the Progressive Society "Bolsheviks and non-Doukhobors". The Society ceased to exist in the early 1940s.

In June of 1934, Chistiakov convened the Second Congress of the Society of Named Doukhobors at which he stressed that the Doukhobors should stay away from politics. At that time, the Independents were showing interest in the new Canadian political party, the Cooperative Commonwealth Federation (CCF) and began to break away from Chistiakov. In 1937 they severed all ties with him, rejected the leader's cult and dissociated themselves from the Verigin dynasty.[68]

The main event of the 1930s was the collapse of the Christian Community of Universal Brotherhood.

The year 1938 was the time to pay off the mortgage, with debts amounting to $360,580. The creditors — two insurance companies — started a lawsuit and, as Chistiakov claimed to have no money, the court awarded them nearly all of the Community Doukhobors' lands which, together with the buildings, were estimated to be worth three or four million dollars and which had fed several thousand Doukhobors. It never became clear where the money raised for the "White Horse" and the tax money from those doing outside jobs had disappeared to. Okulevich writes that Chistiakov used the money "uncontrolledly". Some $360,000 went for the communes' needs and about $250,000 remained in the form of various properties which, subsequently, were inherited by Chistiakov's grandson, I.I. Verigin. The rest of the money, according to Okulevich, "had been squandered, spent in drink and gambled away".[69]

There is, however, a different point of view. Woodcock and Avakumovic believe that Chistiakov had achieved a great deal and should not be blamed for all the troubles. He had paid off a lot of debts and taxes, purchased new lands, erected buildings and cleared forests. All of this was done at the time of an economic depression when the demand and prices for goods and labour had dropped to a disastrously low level.[70]

The creditor insurance companies suggested that the Doukhobors buy back the land taken away from them. Many Community Doukhobors in Saskatchewan and Alberta did so and, in the process, became Independent Doukhobors. In British Columbia, the Provincial Government bought the Doukhobors' land from the creditors and offered it for rent to the previous Doukhobor owners.

However, having lost its stock and money, the commune found itself ruined: the irrigation system, immovable property and fruit plantations deteriorated gradually. Having lost their land, the Doukhobors also lost interest in its upkeep.

Soon after, Chistiakov set about reorganizing the Christian Community of Universal Brotherhood into the "Union of Doukhobor Communities of Christ" (UDCC), which was supposed to unite not only Doukhobors, but also Molokans, Baptists, Quakers and Mennonites. In the fall of 1938 he convened a congress at which the UDCC was formed comprising 37 communities of British Columbia and the Prairies. Chistiakov defined the fundamentals of the new economic policy as follows:

> We will no longer live . . . in a commune. We shall live in villages just as we did in Russia. . . Each family shall have a house and a plot on which to grow the necessary vegetables. The field behind the villages shall be cultivated jointly. . . The profits from the communal enterprises shall be distributed among community members. . . The community shall be taking care of the weak, sick, the orphans, the widows and the old. . .[71]

But by now Chistiakov had fallen seriously ill, dying in February 1939. His followers elected as leader his son Peter Iastrebov (the "Hawk") who lived in the USSR. As nobody knew of his whereabouts, the leadership passed temporarily to the eighteen-year-old Ivan I. Voikin, Chistiakov's grandson on the female side, who came to Canada in 1928 and assumed the name of Verigin after Chistiakov's death. The Independents, however, refused to recognize him as hereditary leader.

During World War II, the Canadian Government exempted the Doukhobors from military service and the demand for labour during the war saved them from complete ruin after the disintegration of the communes. The Doukhobors sought employment at railways, saw-mills and in construction. By the middle of the 1940s the Doukhobors in British Columbia were no longer "sons of the soil", but rather a "semi-rural proletariat".[72]

The hardships of war brought the UDCC and the Independents closer together. Even the Freedomites calmed down a little, although not for long. In 1943 they burned down the jam factory and I.I. Verigin's house in the town of Brilliant.

In 1945, an all-Doukhobor Congress was held at Brilliant, as a result of which a new all-embracing soriety, the "Union of Doukhobors of Canada" (UDC) was formed, numbering 8,000 members. The Congress resolved that the Doukhobors consider Christ their only leader, which meant the abolishment of "leadership". It also condemned the Freedomites' demonstrations in the nude, terrorism, and came out against the military use of atomic energy. Shortly after, the UDCC left the Union of Doukhobors of Canada and the Freedomites were expelled from it. In 1950 the UDCC took part in a pro-communist peace congress despite the protests of the majority of the Doukhobors who believed that the Congress pursued political rather than religious goals. Soon after, the UDCC ceased to exist.[73]

In the post-war years, the former Community Doukhobors and Independents emerged as prosperous people. The Freedomites, however, continued to regard material welfare and collaboration with the government during the war as a betrayal of Doukhobor ideals and began setting fire to the Community Doukhobors' property. From 1944 to 1962, the Freedomites' terrorist activities increased and spread to their neighbours, the Community Doukhobors. Arson and bomb explosions alternated with government investigations that led nowhere because of the tangled testimony and absence of witnesses. The Freedomites' leaders were Ivan Lebedoff and Mikhail Orekoff, nicknamed "The Archangel".

By 1950 communal life had come to an end and with it many years of social isolation. Gradually, the former Community Doukhobors, like the Independents started to built modern houses for themselves, buying furniture and cars, and going to movies. Naturally, the Freedomites, who numbered about 2,500 by 1950, disapproved of this trend towards assimilation.

In the opinion of Woodcock and Avakumovic, the Freedomites' terrorist activities were, in the beginning, a protest against material well-being and later, became a reaction to the unsuccessful attemps of the police and lawyers to find a rational solution to an irrational situation.

In 1949, a certain Stefan Sorokin* arrived in Canada as a displaced person and soon became the Freedomites' unquestioned leader, uniting them into the "Christian Community and the Brotherhood of Reformed Doukhobors" in 1950. In 1952 he pointed out the necessity of moving to new lands. He, himself, made two trips to Uruguay where, failing to buy land for the Freedomites, he acquired a plot for himself and settled down. The Freedomites sent him money from time to time, still thinking of him as their leader.

By 1950, the British Columbia Doukhobor Research Committee was formed and, two years later, made available its findings to the public. Manifesting a friendly and impartial attitude towards the Doukhobors, the committee had investigated the main causes of trouble between the Government and the Doukhobors. The commit-

---

* According to Woodcock and Avakumovic, he had fled from the USSR in 1929, wandering for 20 years in Asia Minor and Europe, shifting allegiance from one religion to another. He was not a Doukhobor. *Op. cit.*, p. 328.

tee resolved that a compromise solution to most of the problems be found, that only the dangerous criminals be subjected to punishment and that Doukhobor terrorists, who disobeyed the sect commandment of not using violence to resist evil, be deprived of the privilege of exemption from military service.

Following the report of the Research Committee, the Government of British Columbia made some concessions such as mitigating punishment for going nude in public, recognizing Doukhobor marriages, etc.

In 1953, the Freedomites realized that Sorokin (who held them in check somewhat) would not be coming back to Canada* and terrorism broke out again. Almost the entire village of Krestovaya was burned down during the summer and the Freedomites set out towards Slokan Valley. But the police stopped them, took the children of school age and sent them to boarding schools. Thereafter, round-ups of children aged seven and over were organized every year for the same purpose. Over a six-year period, 170 children in all were separated from their parents and sent to school. Finally, in 1959 the majority of Freedomites promised to bring their children to school; they kept their word. Many older children, however, were hostile towards the authorities and later joined the ranks of terrorists; most younger children stuck to their studies. In 1957, news arrived from the Soviet Union via the Red Cross that Peter Iastrebov, the would-be successor to the Doukhobor leadership, had died in Stalin's prison camps from pellagra (a disease of malnutrition) in August 1942. Ivan Ivanovich Verigin then became the official leader of the Doukhobors.

Following their unsuccessful attempt to move to Uruguay, the Freedomites decided to try their luck in the USSR. In 1958, a Freedomite delegation went to the Soviet Union where they were allowed to inspect lands in the Altai region. Back in Canada, the delegation registered 2,440 Freedomites who wished to return to their motherland. The Canadians authorities promptly agreed to assist with transportation and resettlement costs provided the Doukhobors signed away their claim to Canadian citizenship and the Soviet Government agreed to accept them. However, the final formal agreement never came.

The summer of 1958 saw more incidents of arson and explosions. For the first time, terror was directed not only against the Doukhobors but also against Canadians: railways and power lines were blown up and bombs were placed in hotels and even in a bus station.

At that time, the Government of British Columbia renewed its

---

* Sorokin finally returned to Canada in the 1970s and has since been living in British Columbia.

proposal that the Doukhobors buy back the land that had earlier been taken away from them. The one-time Community Doukhobors accepted but the Freedomites, who regarded such an act a compromise with the government, blew up P. Verigin's grave (doing so for a second time in 1961) as well as the entire village of Utesheniye. There was a total number of 106 cases of arson and bomb explosions in 1961.

1962 was the most difficult year, with 274 acts of terrorism. After 1962, mass terrorism began to subside.[74]

By the end of 1963 nearly all of the land had been bought back by former Community Doukhobors. Plans were made to return to communal life, but to no avail.

Then came a period of calm. Having become individual proprietors, the Community Doukhobors began to meld with the Canadian way of life. All that remained of communal life was a small number of jointly-owned agricultural machines for land cultivation, consumer co-operatives through which they bought wholesale goods, and a flour mill.

* * *

A few words about those Doukhobors who remained in the USSR. According to Woodcock and Avakumovic they were concentrated mainly in the Caucasus where they numbered 20,000 during the 1960s. Before Stalin's death, little news reached Canada about the Soviet Doukhobors. After 1953, correspondence between relatives was resumed and since that time a number of individual Doukhobors and Doukhobor groups visited the USSR to participate in various congresses and festivals. Among frequent visitors were such leading Doukhobors as I.I. Verigin, E.A. Popoff, K. Tarasoff and others. As far as emigration was concerned, only Anna P. Markova, I.I. Verigin's mother, who had lived in exile in the USSR since 1935, succeeded in emigrating to Canada (her second husband, P. Markov, had died in prison). She was allowed to leave in 1960 as a result of the Doukhobors' having interceded on her behalf with N. Khrushchev during his visit to the United States.

In the USSR, the Doukhobors had assimilated to a large extent as a result of compulsory education and military service. For example, I.I. Verigin's stepbrother, Peter P. Markov, was sent to the war where he died in the Battle of Berlin.

During the 1930s the Doukhobors, as everyone else, underwent collectivization, which caused them no difficulties since they had long been leading a communal life. The more prosperous among them, however, were sent into exile or to prison camps as kulaks. Those who survived in the camps had been exonerated and allowed to return to their native lands after Stalin's death.

According to Woodcock and Avakumovic, the Doukhobors were better off, on the whole, in the post-Stalin era. Today, their economic status is good compared to other collective farmers, although not as good as that of their Canadian counterparts.[75]

The Doukhobors in the 1980s

Ethnographic Sketch

Today, there are between 20 and 30 thousand Doukhobors living in Canada.[76] They fall into three well-defined groups: the Independents (who account for about 65%); the Community Doukhobors (about 25%); and the Freedomites (about 10%).

Large groups of Doukhobors live in Saskatchewan, Alberta and British Columbia, with several hundred scattered in various cities and towns of Canada. Assimilation has greatly changed their way of life, leaving intact only their pacifism and rejection of the church and its sacraments. Many of their convictions and customs are changing further as a result of general education and contact with non-Doukhobors. Mixed marriges are common and more and more children are given English names. Marriages, births and deaths are registered. In the past, marriage was arranged by agreement between the parents of the bride and groom and contracted in the presence of close relatives, without intermediaries. Today, the marriage ceremony is often performed in Canadian style: the marriage takes place in a City Hall, sometimes in a church, and the wedding reception in a rented hall amidst a crowd of guests, often with dancing and drinking.[77] The interment ceremony has also changed. In the past, the family and close relatives would dig the grave and wash the dead body. Relatives would bring the traditional borshch and noodles for a noonday meal to the house of the deceased. Now, the services are provided by an undertaker. Prayers for the deceased have been shortened from ten to one or two hours and the funeral banquet is often held before carrying the body to the cemetery.[78] Vegetarians are becoming fewer in number. More and more people are beginning to eat meat on the grounds that vegetarianism was not part of the Doukhobor movement at the beginning and that it was introduced as a temporary measure. However, on Doukhobor holidays, as if by an unwritten law, only vegetarian food is served. In the past, several people would eat from the same bowl, which was placed in the middle of the table.[79] Today, this custom no longer exists. Canadian food and drinks are liked as much as Russian ones. The young (fourth generation) have taken to dancing and would rather speak English, some of them unable to speak Russian at all.

Respect for the elderly and implicit obedience to their will — some of the main precepts of the Doukhobors — are on the wane. The children feel equal to their parents and teachers. Juvenile delinquency appeared.[80] In the past, all generations of a family lived under the same roof. Today, many old people live separately on their old-age pension. Russian games, such as "gorelki", "platochek" and "lapta"* are no longer popular and have been replaced by football, hockey and other Canadian sports. The women no longer weave fabric for clothes, buying material or ready-to-wear clothes in shops instead. Outwardly, the life of most Doukhobors today resembles that of ordinary Canadians.

The Independent Doukhobors

Settlements of Independent Doukhobors are concentrated in Saskatchewan (8,000) and Alberta (1,000). Their religious centre is the town of Blaine Lake. In addition, some 3,500 live in British Columbia and several hundred in Ontario and other Canadian provinces. Independents are organized into the "Society of Independent Doukhobors".

There are more farmers among them than among the Community Doukhobors in British Columbia. Others have taken up various professions. In outward appearance, the Independents live like Canadians (same clothes, homes, furniture, television sets, radio, cars, etc.). Many young people study at universities and, after graduation, find their way into Canadian business and academic circles.

A Vancouver lawyer, Peter S. Faminov, recalls that when, as a nine-year-old boy, he was sent to school by his father in 1925 (the first doukhobor child to go to school in Alberta), his grandfather called it a shame. "At that time, Verigin damned all schools, but my father stood his ground," Faminov explains.

A good many Independents are members of various Canadian public and municipal organizations. A few of examples recorded by the author in 1969 are N.A. Popoff, former president of the Chamber of Commerce and mayor of Blaine Lake; V.P. Sherstobitov, secretary of the International Machinist Association; N.N. Kalmakov, Vice-president of the Canora Credit Bank, Director of the Canora Hospital Commission and the Canora Chamber of Commerce. In addition to holding public offices, they were active in Doukhobor affairs, serving as presidents and secretaries of various Doukhobor organizations.

Another well-known Independent was Norman Rebin who

---

* These group games resemble tag, "drop the hankie" and baseball, respectively.

graduated from the universities of Saskatchewan, Dalhousie and Stockholm. An expert in international law, he served as a Canadian diplomat in India.

Since the 1930s, the majority of Independents have taken part in Canadian government elections and some have stood for municipal election themselves.

The domestic life of the Independents is based on old Doukhobor traditions. The centre of their spiritual life is the prayer house, where they gather once a week, usually on a Sunday. The meeting begins at noon, with the ladies standing on the right and the men on the left. Some volunteers step forward and recite psalms by heart. Following prayers, the choir and congregation sing three psalms, The Lord's Prayer, and a hymn. The meeting ends with artistic performances (recitation or songs) or business discussions. Praying lasts one hour. When guests are invited, they are presented to the gathering on arrival and seen off on departure.

Doukhobor religious singing is unique. The spiritual psalms and hymns have been passed from generation to generation by word of mouth in line with the Doukhobor saying "record in the heart, proclaim in word". Although the hymns and psalms are of biblical origin, their meaning has been slightly altered to conform to the Doukhobor outlook. The interpretation is reminiscent of long, drawn-out Russian folks songs: a syllable may sometimes continue for as long as several musical phrases and the words, therefore, are hardly distinguishable. Some Doukhobors believe that in this way the words of the psalms were protected from being understood by outsiders during times of persecution of Doukhobors in Russia; others say that it is how one sang in the days of early Christianity.* The choir sings in unison, the soprano deviating occasionally to lead its "own" part. The choir has no conductor: the leading voice (a different person for each chant) starts the first syllables and the choir joins in. The singing is done in the manner of the Piatnitski folk choir. After the song is over, all the singers bow simultaneously. Doukhobors learn singing at an early age, memorizing the words and the melody while listening to the elders.

At their prayer house in Blaine Lake, Independent Doukhobors keep a collection of works by Tolstoy whom they hold in reverence. Pictures of him can be found at the prayer house and in their

---

* G. Fiala, a Canadian composer and musicologist, suggested in one of his Russian-language programmes on Radio Canada International in 1969 that this was Gregorian polyphony, the original, ancient style of Greek-Orthodox singing. Thus, the Doukhobors may be perpetuating a style of singing that existed centuries ago, and which has been forgotten by the rest of the Russians.

homes. In accordance with their tradition of committing knowledge to memory, they keep no other Russian books.

The Independents live among the Canadian population. Their houses usually have vegetable and flower gardens attached. In a modern house, one can often see a spinning wheel brought from Russia by grandparents. The Independents prefer Russian cuisine: borshch, vareniks, stuffed cabbage-rolls, noodles, pancakes, pies, vegetables, fruit, and, in remembrance of their exile to the Caucasus, watermelons.

Religious holidays, festivals, concerts, and picnics are part and parcel of Doukhobor life. A festival would draw people from all over the province. During the festivities, the visitors would roam from house to house to see their relatives and friends. The author of this article happened to witness two such events in 1969: St. Peter's Day (June 29) celebrated in all Doukhobor villages in memory of the day in 1895 when the Doukhobors in Russia burned their firearms in keeping with the commandment "thou shalt not kill" and, a week later, the 70th anniversary of the Doukhobors' migration to Canada. These two holidays give an interesting picture of Doukhobor life and provide, at the same time, a contrast in outlook between Independent and Community Doukhobors.

The first event took place at Petrovka, a former Doukhobor village now a provincial park, where the local Independent Doukhobors and their guests from Saskatchewan, Alberta, British Columbia and California were gathered.

An enormous tent inside which over 600 people were seated on freshly-cut plank benches still smelling of resin was set up in a field surrounded by hills and groves. In the air was the odour of freshly-cut grass. After prayers were over, the spiritual leader, N.A. Popoff, presented the guests to the public. There were speeches recalling the historical past of the Doukhobor movement, thanking Canada for according them the right to profess their religion freely and asking the younger generation to remember the teachings and spiritual values of their fathers. N.A. Popoff said simply and with deep feeling: "Religious convictions are weakening all over the world. Morals are on the decline. Honesty is vanishing. Happy people are difficult to find. A tranquil soul is a rarity today. Therefore, we must remember that Christ lives among us, in our hearts. And Christ knew how to love his fellow men. Therefore, let us, in the name of Christ, see to it that our sons will not attempt the life of another — this is the meaning of today's holiday".

Speeches alternated with performances of a religious nature and choral singing by choirs from British Columbia, Blaine Lake, Saskatoon and Langham. With the exception of some youth choirs, the female singers wore stylized Doukhobor attire: long pleated skirts with long-sleeved blouses over them, all in pastel colors, their heads covered with white silk or lace kerchiefs embroidered with floral patterns. I.I. Verigin, the Community Doukhobors' leader, expressed his concern about the widening generation gap. Then, Mr. I.G. Bondarev, a Doukhobor activist and a good public speaker began his captivating speech with the words "Praise be to God: Christ is risen!" ("Christ is risen" is said all the year round). He told the legend about Tsar Alexander I who was alleged to have joined the Doukhobors, instead of dying at the town of Taganrog.

After the speeches and performance, there was a lunch in the open air. According to Doukhobor custom, the tablecloths were spread on the grass and enormous amounts of meatless food served, including the traditional watermelon on each "table". As a rule, Doukhobors do not drink alcoholic beverages but prefer various "kvasses": raspberry, guelder-rose and dandelion.

The author was also invited to a typical Doukhobor banquet at a Canadian restaurant. The celebration, however, was family-style: the entertainment alone lasted six hours with only two short breaks and ended with choral singing.

Secular Doukhobor singing is quite distinctive. The Independents have preserved a variety of old folk songs, especially Cossack ones (the Community Doukhobors hardly remember any folk songs, as P.V. Verigin had imposed a ban on them). The tunes, however, have been changed significantly and resemble those of spiritual verse.

Lately, the young people are beginning to learn to sing as soloists, singing mostly Russian folk and English popular songs. Contemporary songs are learned from records. Some families have musical instruments: guitars, accordions and pianos. Although dancing is not encouraged, the young people enjoy contemporary dancing. They do not know any Russian dances as these had been forbidden in the past and, hence, long forgotten.

Today, the young generation of Independents is losing the Russian language and many of them cannot speak it at all. This can be explained partly by the reluctance of the young people to be different from their Canadian counterparts and partly by the parents' inertia, as well as the lack of Russian schools* affiliated with Doukhobor organizations.

The other holiday, that of July 6, was the 70th anniversary of the arrival of the first Doukhobors in Canada. It was held in the village of Verigino near the late P.V. Verigin's house, a beautiful three-storey wooden building that is now a museum. Under the coordination of I.I. Verigin, celebration was organized by the "Association of Canadians of Russian Origin", a small group of

---

* At the insistence of the Independents, the Russian language is taught at four Saskatchewan schools.

Doukhobors (put together by I.I. Verigin) and the "Federation of Russian Canadians" a pro-communist organization.

Because of the Federation's participation, the majority of Saskatchewan Doukhobors boycotted this event, explaining their decision as follows: "I.I. Verigin wants to mix a religious organization with a political organization that rejects God. That's why most of us would not accept it."[81] As a result, only 4,000 people gathered instead of the expected 20,000. In attendance were members of the Provincial government; Dr. J. Endicott — a Stalin Prize laureate and Chairman of the Canadian Peace Council; and Soviet representatives including the Chairman of the Committee for Cultural Relations Abroad, a Second Secretary from the Soviet Embassy and a married couple from the Caucasus representing the Soviet Doukhobors, all of whom made speeches. Many members of the press, radio and television were present as well.

The celebrations began with a general solemn prayer, followed by speeches and choral singing and concluded with an evening of performances. All speeches were devoted to recollections of Doukhobors persecutions in the 19th century and appeals to humanity not to make war. Dr. Endicott, Mr. Okulevich of the Federation, and the Soviet representatives, however, wandered from the topic of the day (i.e., the 70th anniversary of the Doukhobors' migration to Canada), denouncing aggression and American domestic and foreign policy. On the other hand, V. Chudskov, a Soviet Doukhobor, spoke only about the achievements of Soviet ballet, theatre and literature.

The Community Doukhobors

Some 5,000 Community Doukhobors are concentrated in British Columbia, the largest settlement being in Grand Forks, with a population of about 3,000. Many live in Brilliant, Nelson and other smaller towns. All Community Doukhobors are grouped into 17 communities which constitute the Union of the Spiritual Communities of Christ (USCC, or SDOKH in Russian). Communal houses, however, do not exist any longer as economic isolation ended in the late 1930s and assimilation has been going on for over 20 years.

Today, the average Community Doukhobor lives very much like an ordinary Canadian: he has a separate Canadian-style house, but with a vegetable garden; he supports his family himself, pays taxes and registers marriages, births and deaths; his children attend schools and universities; he takes part in Canadian social life. However, all Community Doukhobors obey their leader, Ivan Ivanovich Verigin. True, he is no longer a divinity to them, only a symbolic leader. Under him Community Doukhobors enjoy a freer life than they had under his predecessors.

Community Doukhobors are more conservative than the Independents; they fast during religious holidays and the ladies cover their heads with kerchiefs and wear traditional Doukhobor attire in prayer houses.

The teaching of Russian is well organized for Community Doukhobor children. Formerly, they had their own Russian schools; now, Russians is taught in certain Canadian schools* for thirty minutes a day from the third through to the twelfth grade. The teachers are of Doukhobors origin, most of whom have completed a short course for Russian teachers in the Soviet Union and who have Canadian teachers' training. Soviet textbooks have now replaced those from the USA.

The Union of Spiritual Communities of Christ (USCC) runs Russians schools for younger children,** weekly classes for school children in addition to Russian classes at Canadian schools and Sunday schools where they teach singing, psalm recitation and religious history.

Efforts are now being made to reopen the Russian schools because it is felt that the thirty minutes of Russian taught in Canadian schools are not sufficient. In addition, wishing to avert complete assimilation and preserve religious and cultural traditions, the Community Doukhobors have set up a so-called "Community of the Future".

As the principal organization uniting all Community Doukhobors, the USCC owns a number of public buildings, the newest being the Cultural Centre in Brilliant — an impressive structure of contemporary architecture, built with free labour at a cost of $750,000. Located on the ground floor is a 3,000 seat theatre with a large stage. The basement has office rooms and a dining hall for 500 people. The kitchen and utensils are modern, yet the ladles are made of wood and have Doukhobor designs.

A similar but smaller cultural centre at Grand Forks (1,200 seats) housing a library, archives and the Iskra Publishing House, was burnt down by the Freedomites in 1975.

The USCC has a Youth Union affiliated to it, and the com-

---

* Kootenay and Grand Forks Districts, British Columbia. Only the Kootenay District Doukhobor Russian School remained open after the introduction of Russian as a subject in Canadian schools in 1976. Here, the end of the school year is celebrated with recitals, singing and dramatic skits.

** At one time, all the schools were under the management of S.N. Petko, a non-Doukhobor and former displaced person. The teachers for these schools are trained by an experienced Soviet instructor.

munities have singing, literature, lecture, choir and drama groups, as well as a teetotal group (to prevent drinking, smoking and drug addiction). Because choir singing is exceptionally popular with the Doukhobors, each commune has its own choir. Some singers participate in several choirs and singers range from four-year-old tots to grandparents. In one instance, five generations of a family sang in the same choir.

In addition to annual amateur performances such as those at Grand Forks and Brilliant, festivals on a special theme are organized every year. In May 1979, the 30th festival was held in honour of the International Year of the Child. Lasting three days from early morning till late at night, it featured speeches and a multitude of choirs.

The young people go in for "healthy" sports: softball, baseball, hockey, and, occasionally, tennis. Sports such as boxing are unacceptable. Some handicrafts are quite popular in the Doukhobor community: older men can still carve spoons with fancy handles from various types of wood; women embroider kerchiefs, pillows and towels, weave, make small rugs on special machines and quilt. Quilts and pillows are usually given to newly-weds as a present which is why some old people like to ask the young one, "Well, is it time to make a quilt yet?".

The Community Doukhobors have a senior citizens' home and all are members of the Co-operative, which distributes goods among the Doukhobors population.

They also issue two periodicals: the Russian bi-weekly magazine, "Iskra" ("Spark") belonging to the USCC, and an English youth magazine called; "Mir" ("Peace").*

Community Doukhobors also have their own historians: V.A. Sukhorev, P.N. Maloff and K.J. Tarasoff. Novelist E.A. Popoff wrote "Tania", a historical chronicle of Doukhobor life[82] and N.N. Kalmakov gathered and published Doukhobor spiritual verses and songs.[83]

It is the Community Doukhobors' close contact with the Soviet Embassy and the Federation of Russian Canadians, however, which displeases the majority of Independents and draws open criticism and terrorist acts from the Freedomites.

In the opinion of one prominent Doukhobor, the rapprochement with the Soviet Union can be attributed to the fact that, for 68 years, the Doukhobors lived in Canada completely isolated from other Russians. In British Columbia, Canadians disliked and snubbed them. In addition, the Freedomites' terrorist activity and demonstrations in the nude brought unenviable notoriety to all Doukhobors; Canadians had no way of knowing that the terrorists

---

* Both magazines currently adopt a pro-Soviet line. (Ed.)

numbered only a few dozen. Over the years, the Doukhobors developed an inferiority complex. When a Doukhobor choir from British Columbia performed at Expo in Montreal, neither the Russian nor the Canadian public paid any attention, whereas the Soviet representatives got in touch with them and "gave them a hearty welcome, treating them like brothers, and rekindled their national pride that had been strangled by the Freedomite trials and the hostile attitude of some Canadian politicans."[84] After that, many Doukhobors maintained contact with Soviet representatives, thinking that the Soviet Union is striving for peace.

Woodcock and Avakumovic have the following to say on this matter:

> Criticism of Soviet policies among Doukhobors is noticeably mild. While they make forthright denunciations of militarism among the Western powers, the USSR is much more rarely called to order. This is not because Doukhobors are crypto-Communists. Only a tiny minority are or ever have been. It is rather because they still like to think of themselves as Russian, in culture if not in citizenship.[85]

The Soviet Union encourages Community Doukhobors to visit the USSR through the services of the tourist agency "Sputnik". The tourist pays for the transportation to Moscow but all other expenses are borne by the Soviet Government. The Soviet Society "Rodina"* provides scholarships to young people for two-year university courses in the USSR for teachers of Russian language and literature. Again, students only pay travelling expenses, with tuition fees, dormitory costs and meals paid by the Soviet government.

It must be emphasized that not all Community Doukhobors approve of the policy of close friendship with the USSR. For example, the late P.P. Lezhebokov, one of the Doukhobor leaders and an editor with the Iskra Publishing House for many years, left his post in 1973 because he objected to N.G. Kulikov, a Soviet representative and chairman of the Soviet Committee for Cultural Relations Abroad, meddling with *Iskra's* editorial work. In one of his speeches, Kulikov said that he "cannot understand the attitude of the Doukhobor magazine *Iskra*, which for some reason makes no mention of the Soviet Union's achievements in the building of a new life and its struggle for peace . . . shuts itself within the narrow confines of Doukhobor ideology . . . draws the reader's attention to outdated dogmas . . . that are below the level of thinking of Doukhobors and young people in particular."[86]

Being a religious Doukhobor himself, Lezhebokov could not

---

* "Motherland" in English.

support Kulikov's opinion that the Doukhobor ideology had its day and believed that "it would be a mistake to say we are fighting for peace hand-in-hand with those who fight for peace using weapons and violence. Trying to justify the fact that one could fight for peace using weapons and violence is tantamount to negating the true Doukhobor outlook . . ."[87] In response to Lezhebokov's speech, one of the Doukhobors wrote to him: "How is it possible to compare struggle for peace and brotherhood in the name of God to the struggle (allegedly for peace) supported by guns and bayonets and waged by the people who deny God?"

The Freedomites

The Freedomites number around 2,500. Their centre is the village of Krestovaya with another major settlement in Gilpin and a small community on Vancouver Island. The Freedomites assimilate rather slowly. They are gradually buying land back from the government and are building good houses rather than the type of shacks in which they used to live during the 1960s and which they repeatedly set on fire. True, at Gilpin the houses have no electricity, telephones, television or conveniences. But they are clean, though modestly furnished. The women wear Russian clothes at home (wide skirts and aprons) and Canadian clothes when going out. Children now attend Canadian schools, usually until the age of sixteen. Further education is discouraged. There are no Russian schools and Russian is learned from the parents. Agriculture and manual labour are the foundation of their ideology. They make their living chiefly from working in saw-mills and in construction.

After a quiet spell in the early 1960s, the Freedomites are once again engaged in arson. P.N. Maloff believes that the Freedomites consider arson the lesser of two evils, thinking that the burning of a school building is more pardonable in the eyes of God than the corruption of children's minds.[88]

Whereas, in the past, Freedomites used to protest against land purchase and sale (considering land common property such as water, air and sunshine), against education (schools are the main pillar of the State system), against the oath of allegiance or citizenship (which makes man a slave of the State), and against the registration of marriage, birth and death (which makes them dependent on the State), today, they set fire to Community Doukhobors' property, protesting against their friendship with the Soviet Union. In their memorandum "Axis Moscow-Grand Forks" published in 1973, the Freedomites reproached the Community Doukhobors: "Senior Brothers from Moscow have begun to pay frequent visits to the Society of USCC and to invite them — their 'younger brothers', the leaders of SPO[K]H*— to mutual visits. . ."[89]

The Freedomites believe that those faithful to the Doukhobor principles of labour and peaceful life should have "nothing to do with the Party authorities of Marxism and Leninism, no contact, no ties nor friendship of any kind. As it is said in the 'Synopsis', "Named Doukhobors" must remember that the spirit of Bolshevism and the spirit of Christ have absolutely nothing in common."[90]

Freedomites maintain that there can be no friendship between the Doukhobors, who consider it a crime to take someone's life and whose principal commandment is "thou shalt not kill" and the Soviet regime which . . . "executed tens of millions of innocent people, including Christians of various faiths . . ."[91] and accuse the Community Doukhobor leaders, and especially I.I. Verigin, of fraternization with the Soviet Union.[92]

As a result, Community Doukhobors sustained extensive damage from arson and have to keep watch over their public and private property, all adults taking turns as guards, although women only do so during the summer. One Community Doukhobor said with tears in his eyes: "Our grandfathers kept guard, our parents did, now it is our turn and our children's".[93]

* * *

After coming to Canada, the Community Doukhobors and the Freedomites made wide use of folk medicine, bone-setters, steam baths and the services of "babkas" — old women who charmed away illness. Today, Community Doukhobors go to a doctor rather than to a "babka" and use modern bathrooms instead of steam baths. In Freedomite villages, on the other hand, "babkas" still dispell fright and cure warts.

Many Doukhobors live in Vancouver as private Canadian citizens, outside of any community. There is no Russian Doukhobor school in Vancouver but Doukhobor students have organized a youth group which gives annual performances of songs, small plays and speeches.

Doukhobors give one the impression of unusual cordiality and hospitality, and of the cleanliness and cosiness in their homes.The women are extremely well-organized. Although Doukhobors make a point of considering themselves citizens of the world rather than of any particular country, the older and middle-aged generations have a marked Russian character. The young people, however, assimilate rather quickly, leaving their native villages to work as teachers, nurses, doctors, university professors, engineers, journalists, public

---

* SDOKH is the Russian acronym for USCC.

servants or office workers in various Canadian cities. Anxious to preserve their past, Doukhobors reminisce about it at gatherings on holidays as well as in the pages of Doukhobor magazines, and study it at Sunday school. This is supported by the Canadian Government's policy on multiculturalism: Doukhobor choirs travel on cultural exchange programs; the Russian language is now taught at a number of Canadian schools; three Doukhobor historical museums have been opened, the largest being in Castlegar, B.C. Among its exhibits is a restored communal house, workshops, steam bath and old furniture, clothes, utensils, photographs, home-woven fabrics and embroideries. Most of the Doukhobor archives are kept at the library of Selkirk College at Castlegar.

As for language, the old people (second generation), as a rule, speak only Russian; the middle-aged (third generation) speak both Russian and English with preference for the latter, especially in the Prairies; the youth (fourth generation) often cannot speak Russian at all. Because they have been completely separated from other Russians for 70 years, they speak Russian the way their forefathers did, which sounds peculiar today. Thus, they prefer to address a person by his first name using the "thou" form. Speaking in the third person, many use the words "brother" or "sister" ("Brother Petroff said . . ."). Men call each other either by diminutive names ("Petrunia" instead of "Piotr") or by full name and patronymic ("Piotr Ivanovich"). Women are addressed either by diminutive names ("Aniuta" instead of "Anna") or diminutive name and patronymic ("Aniuta Ivanovna").

Because of their isolation, Doukhobors have borrowed words from the English language and russified them (a "truck" became a "trok", a "pick-up" — "truchok", etc.) Quite often they have to invent new words for things that did not exist when they left Russia. For instance, their great-grandfathers did not yet have words for "camera" and "taking a picture". When cameras came into existence, they associated the new apparatus with the existing image "to draw a picture". As a result, a Doukhobor speaking Russian when standing ready with his camera may say: "Say cheese, I shall draw your picture".

The Doukobors' vocabulary is a treasure for a linguist: it is extremely rich in proverbs, sayings, folklore-type similies and parables. It is also very poetic. Obituaries in *Iskra* are sometimes reminiscent of ancient folk laments. Doukhobors use many obsolete expressions and others typical of the Ukraine, the Don area and the southern Russian provinces from which they came. Thus, as with Don Cossacks, neuter words become feminine, etc. Unfortunately, examples cannot be given as their beauty would be lost in the literal translations.

In conclusion, the author would like once again to cite Woodcock and Avakumovic who summed up the Doukhobor character of today:

> It now seems likely that the Doukhobors will maintain their separateness merely as one of the many small and picturesque religious groups of Canada: their dietary rules less complex than those of the Orthodox Jews; their theological concepts no more unorthodox than those of the Mormons; their economic organization far less radical than that of the still communitarian Hutterites; their pacifism no more rigorous than that of the Quakers. Only the strange chants of the Living Book, like an unsevered umbilical cord, will unite them with their increasingly remote past in the steppes and mountains of Russia.[94]

Notes

1. Sukhorev, V.A., *Istoriya Doukhobortsev* (History of the Doukhobors), North Kildonan, Manitoba, 1944, pp. 8, 29. (In Russian.)
2. Woodcock, George, and Avakumovic, Ivan, *The Doukhobors*, Toronto, New York, Oxford University Press, 1968, pp. 19-20, 22.
3. Sukhorev, V.A., *op. cit.*, p.29.
4. Maloff, Petr N., *Dukhobortsy, ikh istoriya, zhizn' i bor'ba*, (Doukhobors, their History, Life and Struggle), Thrums, B.C., P.N. Maloff (publ.), 1948, p. 22. (In Russian.)
5. Sukhorev, V.A., *op. cit.*, p. 35.
6. Woodcock and Avakumovic, *op. cit.*, p. 38.
7. *Ibid.*, pp. 43-46.
8. Novitskii, O., *Dukhobortsy, ikh istoriya i veroucheniye* (Doukhobors, their History and Beliefs), Kiev, 1882, pp. 143-144.
9. Maloff, Petr N., *op. cit.*, pp. 23-24.
10. Nikolsky, N.M. *Istoriya Russkoy Tserkvi*, (History of the Russian Church), Moscow, 1931, p. 269. (In Russian.)
11. Woodcock and Avakumovic, *op. cit.*, p. 66.
12. Maloff, P.N., *op. cit.*, pp. 25-26.
13. Woodcock and Avakumovic, *op. cit.*, p. 69-70.
14. Maloff, Petr N., *op. cit.*, pp. 26-27; N.M. Nikolsky, *op. cit.*, p. 317.
15. Sukhorev, V.A., *op. cit.*, pp. 65-67.
16. Woodcock and Avakumovic, *op. cit.*, pp. 80-83.
17. *Ibid.*, p. 89.
18. Verigin, P.V., Ustnaya peredacha cherez I.E. Konkina, (10 dek. 1833) (Verbal Testimony by I.E. Konkin, December 10, 1833), quoted by V.H. Sukhorev, *op. cit.*, p. 79.

19. Woodcock and Avakumovic, *op. cit.*, pp. 94-95.
20. Verigin, P.V., Speech addressed to Doukhobor delegates (1895), as quoted by V.A. Sukhorev, *op. cit.*, pp. 80-83.
21. Sukhorev, V.A., *op. cit.*, pp. 88-89.
22. Woodcock and Avakumovic, *op. cit.*, pp. 104-106.
23. Sukhorev, V.A., *op. cit.*, pp. 104-106.
24. Woodcock and Avakumovic, *op. cit.*, p. 118.
25. Sukhorev, V.A., *op. cit.*, p. 110.
26. *Ibid.*, p. 117.
27. Verigin, P.V., Letter to the parents, September 2, 1896, as quoted by P.N. Maloff, *op. cit.*, p. 59.
28. Maloff, P.N., *op. cit.*, p. 61.
29. *Ibid.*, p. 62.
30. *Ibid.*, p. 66.
31. *Ibid.*, p. 61.
32. *Ibid.*, p. 69.
33. Woodcock and Avakumovic, *op. cit.*, p. 177.
34. Maloff, P.N., *op. cit.*, p. 69.
35. *Ibid.*, p. 72.
36. Sukhorev, V.A., *op. cit.*, p. 126.
37. Maloff, P.N., *op. cit.*, p. 173.
38. Sukhorev, V.A., *op. cit.*, p. 140.
39. *Ibid.*, p. 141.
40. Woodcock and Avakumovic, *op. cit.*, pp. 198-199.
41. Tarasoff, Koozma J., *Traditional Doukhobor Folkways: an Ethnographic and Biographic Record of Prescribed Behaviour*, National Museum of Man, Ottawa, 1977, pp. 118, 120-125, 207, 223.
42. Woodcock and Avakumovic, *op. cit.*, pp. 222-223, 226-228, 266-267.
43. Maloff, P.N., *op. cit.*, pp. 100-101.
44. Sukhorev, V.A., *op.cit.*, p. 138.
45. Woodcock and Avakumovic, *op. cit.*, p. 232.
46. Maloff, P.N., *op. cit.*, pp. 106-107.
47. *Ibid.*, p. 109.
48. Woodcock and Avakumovic, *op. cit.*, pp. 240-241.
49. Sukhorev, V.A., *op. cit.*, p. 145.
50. Maloff, P.N., *op. cit.*, pp. 114-115.
51. Woodcock and Avakumovic, *op. cit.*, p. 254.

52. *Ibid.*, pp. 245, 251, 254-255.
53. *Ibid.*, p. 278.
54. *Ibid.*, pp. 260, 277-279, 280.
55. Maloff, P.N., *op. cit.*, pp. 153-154.
56. Sukhorev, V.A., *op. cit.*, p. 177.
57. *Ibid.*, p. 161.
58. *Ibid.*, pp. 161-162.
59. *Ibid.*, pp. 163-164.
60. Woodcock and Avakumovic, *op. cit.*, pp. 292-293.
61. Delegates of "Named Doukhobors" of Canada, Petition to the Politbureau of the Communist Party (Bolshevik), of the USSR, to Comrade Stalin, Moscow, as quoted by V.A. Sukhorev, *op. cit.*, pp. 182-184.
62. Sukhorev, V.A., *op. cit.*, p.184.
63. Woodcock and Avakumovic, *op. cit.*, pp. 297-301.
64. Sukhorev, V.A., *op. cit.*, pp.176-178.
65. Okulevich, G., *Russkiye v Kanade* (Russians in Canada) published by the Federation of Russian Canadians, Toronto, 1952, pp. 136-137. (In Russian.)
66. *Ibid.*, pp. 138-139.
67. *Ibid.*, p. 145.
68. Woodcock and Avakumovic, *op. cit.*, pp. 302-303.
69. Okulevich, G., *op. cit.*, p. 54.
70. Woodcock and Avakumovic, *op. cit.*, pp. 304-305.
71. Sukhorev, V.A., *op. cit.*, pp. 180,187,192.
72. Woodcock and Avakumovic, *op. cit.*, p. 309.
73. Okulevich, G., *op. cit.*, p. 63.
74. Woodcock and Avakumovic, *op. cit.*, pp. 323-324, 327-328, 331,333, 335-339, 341, 345-348, 350, 354-355, 357.
75. *Ibid.*, pp. 357-358.
76. *Ibid.*, p. 17; Koozma J. Tarasoff, *op. cit.*, pp. 348-353.
77. Tarasoff, Koozma J., *op. cit.*, pp. 1-3.
78. *Ibid.*, pp. 32-48.
79. *Ibid.*, p. 117-118.
80. *Ibid.*, pp. 347.
81. Author's personal notes.
82. Popoff, Elia, *Tanya*, Mir Publication Society, Grand Forks, 272 pages.

83. Kalmakov, N.N. (compiler) — *Spiritual verses and folk songs of Doukhobors in Canada*, privately printed in Richmond, B.C., 1973, 476 pages.
84. Author's personal notes.
85. Woodcock and Avakumovic, *op. cit.*, p. 360.
86. Kulikov, N.G., Speech cited in *Iskra*, No. 1322.
87. Lezhebokov, P.P., Paper of P. P. Lezhebokov and concluding remarks, (paper read at the Congress of SDOKH, 27.1.1973), Mimeographed Copy, Grand Forks, B.C., 8.2.1973, pp. 3-4.
88. Maloff, P.N., *op. cit.*, p. 183.
89. Member of Christian Community and Brotherhood of Reformed Doukhobors *et al.* (58 names), Axis Moscow-Grand Forks, Mimeographed Copy, [1973], p. 1.
90. *Ibid.*, p. 5.
91. *Ibid.*
92. *Ibid.*, pp. 4-5, 14-19, 22a-22b, 32-38.
93. Author's personal notes.
94. Woodcock and Avakumovic, *op. cit.*, p. 356.

C.V. Ponomareff

Three

RUSSIAN IMMIGRATION TO CANADA, 1917-1939

(Historical-Statistical Overview)

Problematics

The greatest problem that faces anyone attempting to write about Russian immigration to Canada between 1917 and 1939 and before lies in the fact that it is very difficult to come up with accurate immigration and census statistics for Russians.

Tables very often do not include Russians specifically but suggest their presence as a numerically vague or implicit percentage of general categories such as aliens or East Europeans. This lack of specificity in turn suggests a lack of interest and analysis in this area, which probably reflects a statistically confusing variety of "Russian" streams of immigrants.

One of these was the so-called "white" political emigration of Russians who came to Canada after, and in opposition to, the Bolshevik revolution of 1917; but one can never be certain that other groups of Russians who came to this country out of economic or religious rather than ideological motives might not be in fact included in a general statement such as the following:

> Political oppression of the intellectuals previous to the War, and antagonism to the Bolsheviks following on the Revolution of

1917*, have driven many Russians of culture and talent to Canadian shores.[1]

Probably because the Doukhobor groups were more visible and, therefore, statistically more verifiable, sociologists paid greater attention to them even though they made up only a minority of Russians in Canada. As a religious sect, they have been usually dealt with separately from other Russian immigrants[2] (see Chapter 2 on Doukhobors).

The description of Jewish immigration from Russia and from those western territories that were separated from Russia after the Treaty of Brest-Litovsk presents another problem. There is, for instance, a tendency when speaking about Russian Jewish immigration to North America to regard Russian Jews as distinct from Russians,[3] to lump them together statistically with all other Jews or only with Russian and Polish Jews[4] or, in effect, to list them with Russians.[5]

In like fashion, Ukrainians are sometimes regarded as part of the Russian alien group[6]; Byelorussians, we are told, are confused "with the larger Russian group"[7] and Mennonites (of German origin) are counted as Russians.[8]

Another cause contributing to statistical confusion was the Canadian Government's methods of compiling statistics. Immigration statistics were introduced in Canada only in 1900.[9] The Canadian Government, like its US counterpart, did not officially and statistically distinguish between "Great Russians", "Ukrainians" and "White Russians" until the post World War I period when only Ukrainians were put in a separate class.[10] To make matters worse, the official pre-1913 US and Canadian policy of classifying immigrants from Russia by linguistic groups rather than enumerating them in terms of "mother tongue" or country of birth did, as Obolensky's tables show, increase the margin or error. Classified linguistically, Russian immigrants were listed as "Hebrews, Poles Russians, Lithuanians, Finns, Germans"[11]** Such a statistical method could not reflect the actual figure of Russians in Canada, nor could the later Canadian official policy of establishing Russian nationality by country of birth altogether eliminate the problems because non-Russians born in Russia were recorded as Russian while Russians born outside Russia were not.[12] The above suggests the difficulty of arriving at an accurate statistical picture of Rus-

---

* At the same time also, there were groups of pro-Soviet Russians from the former Russian provinces of Poland, Volyn' and western Byelorussia. (Ed.)

** See also Chapter 1.

sians in Canada especially for the period 1917-1939 and should cast a healthy measure of doubt on statistics regarding this group.[13]

The Canadian Political Situation and Official Immigration Policy

Before embarking on a statistical analysis of Russian immigration into Canada and the population count of Russians for the year 1917-1939, a few words about government policy with respect to immigration to Canada might prove helpful.

A report of the Canadian immigration and population study for the years 1914-1945 has this to say: "World War 1 cut off virtually all emigration from the Continent . . .".[14] With Canadian demobilization and the "dislocation of conversion to a peacetime economy, heavy unemployment, labour unrest and a general recession ensued, and continued into 1922".[15] Restrictive legislation on immigration followed:

> Regulations in 1918 prohibited admission of people not possessing evidence of exemption from military service. Steps were taken the following year to prohibit the admission of enemy aliens (*such as Russian leftists and Communists*)* "skilled and unskilled labour" destined to British Columbia, and Mennonites, Doukhobors and Hutterites. The landing-money requirement was raised to $250 (except for farm workers, domestic servants and first-degree relatives of a person established in Canada). Amendments to the Act in 1919 made it possible for non-Canadian strike leaders (*such as members of the Russian Workers' Movement*)* to be found deportable and added, as new prohibited classes, alcoholics, conspirators (e.g. *Bolshevik spies or rabble rousers*)* and illiterates.[16]

"Normality" returned in 1922 and economic prosperity in 1923.[17]

The Canadian immigration policy in the 1920s, however, favoured the British, Americans and North Europeans:

> Emphasis remained on Britain, the United States and Northern Europe and on well-qualified immigrants, rather than numbers. This turning-away from eastern and southern Europe paralleled xenophobia in the United States which resulted in considerably more restrictive US immigration laws in 1921 and 1924.[18]

The restrictions on Doukhobor immigration, for example, were lifted only in 1926. Immigration of agricultural workers to Canada

---

* Author's comments in italics.

was jeopardized by previous immigrants who, instead of working the land, used Canada as a transit point to the USA or who settled in large numbers in urban areas. Then came the crash of 1929, followed by economic depression. "All promotional work was stopped in 1930" and "somewhat improved economic conditions in the late 1920s did not evoke any change in policy."[19]

Statistics on Russian Immigration

The following seem to provide the most convincing — though still approximate — statistics for Russians in Canada between 1917 and 1939.

As Russian immigration to Canada between 1900 and 1917 was 97,129,[20] and more than one researcher agrees that the population figure for Russians in 1921 was 100,064,[21] it follows that some 2,935 Russian immigrants came between 1917 and 1920. Only Willcox's distribution of immigration by nationality differs significantly; he tabulates only 135 Russians as having immigrated into Canada between 1917 and 1920.[22] But Willcox's figure of Russian immigration to Canada for 1916-1920 (i.e., 1,728)[23] based on immigration by country of last residence or nationality statistics, seems to contradict his low finding and brings it much closer to the 2,935 figure. A figure of 10,122 is arrived at by Willcox for the year 1921-1924[24]. If one ignores Willcox's low count for 1917-1920, the above statistics appear to indicate that some 13,057 Russians entered Canada between 1917 and 1924 (this figure varies from Willcox's for 1920-1925 which is 10,075).[25] Based on Gibbon's figure of 15,251 immigrants of Russian racial origin who came to Canada between 1921 and 1930,[26] — a figure corroborated by another official source,[27] we arrive at a figure of roughly 2,000 Russians entering Canada between 1925 and 1930 and a total figure of 18,186 Russians arriving between 1917 and 1930.

Russian immigration for the years 1930-1939 is difficult to gauge especially since, more than at any other time, there was no continuous increase but a *decrease* of Russians for these years, due most likely to emigration.[28] Thus, whereas there were 100,064 Russians in Canada in 1921, the count dropped to 88,148 in 1931, and 83,708 in 1941.[29] It is interesting, in view of the official Canadian policy giving preferential status to people of non-East European stock that, out of a total immigration to Canada of 252,044 between 1930 and 1939[30], Russian immigration was negligeable. Figures released by the Employment and Immigration Branch show 5,153 Russian immigrants admitted to Canada between 1926 and 1935 and only 560 between 1936 and 1945.[31] Taking into account the previous figure of 2,000 Russians as having entered Canada between 1925 and 1930, we get an approximate figure of around 3,000 as having probably entered the country between 1930 and 1939. Hence, we get an over-all total of 21,186 Russian immigrants coming to Canada between 1917 and 1939.

Russian Groupings

Although it is very difficult to isolate statistics for special Russian groups that made up the total, the different group types can be identified.

A.* The so-called "white" Russian émigrés (not to be confused with the ethnic White or Byelorussian group), members of various classes of Russian society — the aristocracy, the military, civil servants, the intelligentsia and other civilians who suddenly found themselves in the four corners of the world after the Communist take-over in Russia in 1917.[32]

B. Peasant Old Believers (religious schismatics who came to Canada between 1921 and 1930).[33]

C. The two groups of Doukhobors who came to Canada in 1920 and 1927 to escape religious persecution in the USSR for some of their "Tolstoyan" beliefs. These groups joined the Doukhobor communities in Western Canada. (Although it is accepted that the immigration of Doukhobors stopped before 1917, Gibbon's listing of over 15,000 in Canada in 1938[34] cannot be based solely on their pre-1917 immigration. In fact, although the 1899 immigration of over 7,000 Doukhobors to Canada "represented the largest single immigration of Russian-speaking people to Canada"[35] there seems to have been Doukhobor immigration up to 1920, followed by a smaller contingent in 1927.)[36]

D. Russians from Poland who also came to Canada for political reasons and joined the proletarian peasant-oriented groups. They did not share the monarchical views of the "white guard" immigrants. Essentially they were socially and culturally sympathetic to the Soviet Union.[37]

E. Russian peasant farmers and others who were attracted to Canada's generous offers and inducements for cultivating western Canada's vast tracts of land (Fig.9).

* See chapter 4.

F. There is also the question of how many of the "Russian" Ukrainians who identified themselves culturally with Russia could be considered to have made up yet another group thought of as Russians in Canada.*

Geographic Distribution

Among other reasons, Canada may very well have attracted Russians for its geographic parallels:

> Physically it (Russia) has areas that resemble Canada. The great plains or steppes of the southwest are not unlike the Canadian prairies; in the centre, Lake Baikal reminds the Trans-Siberian traveller of Lake Superior; and in the east a hilly country is drained by a great river (*the Amur River*)** which, as it approaches the Pacific, suggest the Fraser River Valley in British Columbia. Lumbering and mining have for many years been major industries in both countries. The Russian and Canadian winter again present a parallel.[38]

A brief statistical excursion will provide us with a vantage point from which to consider the social nature, size and spread of Russians across Canada between 1917 and 1939.

The 21,186 Russian immigrants who came to Canada during this period and who made up approximately one quarter of the Russian population in Canada according to the 1941 Census[39] were, of course, less urbanized than they are today.[40] We can conclude this from a descending order of urbanization as we follow statistics back into time. Thus, the 1961 census figure of 65% of Russians as urban dwellers drops in the 1951 census to 52%.[41] The predominantly rural distribution of the Russians during 1917-39 is further corroborated by Porter's findings that, between 1931 and 1951, the principal agricultural groups were German, Dutch, Scandinavian and East European.[42] Consequently, the greatest density of Russians would have to be in Western Canada, an area that had already been settled by Doukhobors.[43] This is backed up by statistics. Out of a total of 83,708 Russians recorded in the 1941 Census, the geographic distribution by province was as follows:[44]

---

* A small number of intellectual exiles from USSR in the 1920s, who are mentioned by Professor Pervushin in Chapter 4, also reached Canada. (Ed.)

** Author's comments in italics.

British Columbia	16,474
Alberta	19,316
Saskatchewan	25,933
Manitoba	6,571
Ontario	11,218
Quebec	3,433
Nova Scotia	534
New Brunswick	169
Prince Edward Island	2
Yukon	32
Northwest Territories	26

Gibbon corroborates this in 1938 by adding that "taking the Greek-Orthodox Russians as a guide to the distribution of this race throughout Canada, Montreal and the Province of Ontario are their chief centres in Eastern Canada and Saskatchewan and Alberta in Western Canada."[45] Another more concrete indicator of the rural trend in 1917-39 is Gibbon's reference to the 1931 Census according to which the Russian population figure of 88,148 is further broken down into 24,096 urban and 64,052 rural parts.[46]

Professions

It is impossible to give exact professional categories and figures for each of the Russian groups, but one can get a general picture. Porter provides us with figures and professional categories for 1931 which, although generalized, can be assumed to exemplify the Russian population.

As mentioned earlier, the majority of Russians prior to 1939 made up a rural farming population. According to Porter,

> in 1931, 34 per cent of the labour force was in agriculture. The German, Scandinavian, Dutch, Eastern European, Irish and French were all over represented in that order in agriculture. [47]

In the "professional and financial occupations" (4.8% of the labour force) all except the Jewish, Scottish, English and Irish were underrepresented. Compared to the Jewish and Scottish, who were tied at 7% and the English and Irish at 6.4% and 5.8% respectively, the East Europeans made up only 0.9% of this category, with Asians and other Central Europeans and Native Indians making up 0.5%, 0% and 0.3% respectively. But in the "low level, primary and unskilled" occupations (17.7% of the labour force) the proportions were reversed, the East Europeans being overrepresented at 30.1% (Asians, 27%, other Central Europeans, 53.5%, Native Indians, 63.0%) compared to an underrepresentation among the Jews of

3.2%, Scots 12.9%, English 13.3% and Irish, 12.8%. In the "clerical occupations" (3.8% of the male labour force), which are taken as an intermediate level, the Jews, British, Scots and Irish were again overrepresented, whereas all other were underrepresented.[48] The conclusions are obvious.

Life In Canada: Political and Religious Problems

As indicated earlier, the period after 1917 and through the 1920s was one in which restrictive legislation in Canada on East Europeans immigration affected Russians, among others. As the Bolshevik régime consolidated its power in Russia and extended it to other countries, there was an increase in the political distrust with which Russian émigrés were often viewed. Though such distrust must have been selective even at the worst of times, there is no doubt that some Russian groups such as those centered around the Russian Workers' Clubs which became especially active during the Depression, must have given valid political cause for such official suspicion. Reading Okulevich's history of the Russian Workers' Movement in Canada entitled *Russians in Canada*, there is no doubt of this organization's social and cultural identification with proletarian culture in Russia and a resulting political sympathy for the Soviet Union. It was, therefore, natural for this group to express hostility towards Russian "white" émigrés and intelligentsia alike. Inter-group conflict ensued. While it is difficult to measure the influence of the Workers' Movement on other Russians, there is no doubt that his group was led by activists who tried to promote their influence by establishing cultural societies and clubs, their own paper "The Canadian Whistle" (Kanadsky Gudok), special schools for Russian children — all bolstered by yearly conferences.[49] One should mention, however, that the difficulties with unemployment, strikes and demonstrations, and "forced" workers' camps during the Depression (1929-1939), while they may on occasion have been more aggravating for members of this group as a result of its pro-Soviet views, were, nevertheless, experiences shared with other immigrants and Canadians alike. The group's support of the republican side in the Spanish Civil War (1936-39) was also understandable but not limited to Russians alone, as demonstrated by the creation of the International Brigade of Spanish "democratic" supporters.* In a political context, the pacifist leanings of

* According to Okulevich, p. 171, there were about 80 "Russian" members of the Workers' Clubs, who joined the International Brigade. (Ed.)

the Russian Doukhobors, along with their inclination (like the German-Russian Hutterites) towards social segregation, was a contributing factor to Canadian suspiciousness of "aliens".

In addition to political stress, there was religious conflict between the Russian-Orthodox Church in Canada and the Presbyterian Church; between the Russian Church in North America and the Soviet Mother Church. There was friction within the Russian ethnic group in Canada and between Russian and Ukrainian orthodox believers fanned by a rising Ukrainian nationalism in Canada after 1919. Okulevich suggests, perhaps not without bias, that it was the Ukrainians from Galicia (Carpathian Poland) and Bucovina (Carpathian Romania), and not their "Russian" Ukrainian counterparts who indentified themselves culturally with the Russians and who were the most active religious supporters of the Russian-Orthodox faith (i.e., the Soviet Mother Church). It was consequently these Ukrainians who went on to create their own independent (autocephalic) Ukrainian Orthodox Church in the 1920s.[50]

The religious and spiritual tensions among Russians in Canada may suggest the reason why, from the 130 Russian parishes in 1911, only 65 remained in 1926.[51] Okulevich notes the turn to "white" émigré influence in Russian churches thereafter:*

> In the Orthodox parishes of the United States and Canada white émigrés became the most influential groups, persued their own political line in their churches, with the priests fully dependent on them.[52]

Life in Canada: Social and Economic Pressures

Although many Russians found a new home and freedom in Canada and were able, in time, to follow distinctive careers in the fields of medicine, electronics and engineering, ballet, radio and television, instrumental and choral music, the legal profession, academic pursuits, industry and business, painting, politics and international affairs,[53] there is no doubt that, for many Russians pioneering a new life in Canada, the period 1917 to 1939 brought a life of social and economic hardship.

As noted earlier, the Russians *as a group* did not find easy access to the professional and financial or clerical occupations of the time. Instead, most found themselves in the primary and unskilled

---

* In other words, the influence of the leftists' clubs of Workers and Peasants subsided, giving way to "white", anti-Soviet immigrants' views. (Ed.)

labour force which, for a large majority of Russians, meant railway construction and farming.

As recently as May 1979, the *National Geographic* published Ethel A. Starbird's account of "The People Who Made Saskatchewan", an account which may be taken as indicative of the kind of life immigrants to Canada led between 1917 and 1939.

Farming was the main occupation in the southern part of the province, with Slavic settlers comprising mainly Russians, Doukhobors, Ukrainians and Poles. The article dwells on the ultimate predominance of the Ukrainian settlers in "positions of political and professional prominence" due, for the most part, to their powerful drive to keep their ethnic and cultural identity intact and their ability to organize themselves. But, as a whole, the article does provide the reader with a feeling for the difficulties in the beginning, the struggle to survive during the Depression and the efforts to create a province in which Russian Doukhobors and other Russian immigrants had an important part. The geographic, social and economic climate is palpably brought home in the following passage:

> Despite the unpredictability of weather and the ability to grin and bear it, no one was prepared for the devastation and duration of the "Dirty Thirties". Plowed under by the Great Depression and ten consecutive years of futile, scorched earth farming, rural families by the hundreds fled elsewhere.[54]

This pioneering rural experience can be projected to other Canadian provinces where Russian immigrants, among others, lived and participated in the creation of one Canada.

Conclusion

If one were looking for a rationale for the inability of Russians in Canada to establish themselves as a successfully organized and tightly knit homogeneous group, the period 1917-1939 holds the key to the answer.

The group experienced a sense of individual freedom, happiness, achievement and other important, yet immeasurable, human qualities that undoubtedly tempered their difficult life in Canada.

However, practically all the cards seem to have been stacked against them from the very beginning. This may give a tragic quality to their pioneering experience in Canada. Still, only part of their difficulties lay in the historical and social conditions of the time. The root cause of their being unable to "find" themselves as Russians on a national scale came from the inner specifics of their ethnic situation.

The confusing "amalgam" of immigrant streams and strains of various shades of Russians militated against them as a whole from the start. Historical pressure and official bias contributed to their difficulties. The statistics for the period showed another problem that became endemic to the Russians: not only were they a minority at the best of times (such as in 1921 with a count of 100,000) which undercut their effectiveness as a group on a national scale, but they were also a decreasing minority. In fact, as can be seen from the statistics for the period 1917-1939, only slightly more Russian immigrants came to Canada than left this country.

The existence of a number of different groups of Russians further weakened their ethnic fibre. The tremendous distances separating Russians also undermined a cross-country "unification". To make matters worse, Russians had no real access to the power elites of the country, and other social and economic conflicts coupled with inner political and religious strife did the rest.

Notes

1. Gibbon, John Murray, "Russia and Canada", in *Canadian Mosaic, The Making of a Northern Nation* (Toronto, 1938), p. 367.
2. See, for instance, Morris Davis and Joseph F. Krauter, "The Doukhobors", in *The Other Canadians, Profiles of Six Minorities* (Toronto. London. Sydney, Wellington, 1971), pp. 73-86.
3. Liebmann, Hersch, "International Migration of Jews", in Walter F. Willcox, ed., *International Migrations* (Vols. 7-8; New York, London, Paris, 1969), VIII, 475 (First 1929 and 1931).
4. Obolensky-Ossinsky, V.V., "*Emigration from and Immigration into Russia*", Vol. VIII, pp. 507-8.
5. *Ibid.*, p. 546.
6. See "Ukrainians" in Joseph F. Krauter and Morris Davis, *Minority Canadians: Ethnic Groups* (Toronto, New York, London, Sydney, 1978), n.p.
7. *The Canadian Family Tree*, The Department of the Secretary of State, Ottawa, 1967, p. 51.
8. *Ibid.*, p. 273.
9. Obolensky-Ossinsky, V.V., *op. cit.*, p. 528.
10. *Ibid*, p. 547.
11. *Ibid.*, pp. 528-30.
12. *Kanada, 1867-1967*, "Vstrechi" Circle (London, Ontario, 1967), p. 13.
13. What renders research in this area more difficult is that no major works dealing specifically with Russians in Canada have appeared in English. See for instance the extensive bibliographies in Lyle E. Lar-

son, *The Canadian Family in Comparative Perspective* (Scarborough, Ontario, 1976), pp. 437-63; and in K. Ishwaran, ed., *The Canadian Family Revised* (Toronto. Montreal, 1976), pp. 671-705.

14. *The Immigration Program*, Manpower and Immigration, Ottawa, 1974, p. 11.
15. *Ibid.*, p. 12.
16. *Ibid.*
17. *Ibid.*, p. 13.
18. *Ibid.*, p. 14.
19. *Ibid.*, pp. 14-16. See also Victoria Dickenson, *Canada's Multicultural Heritage*, Ottawa, 1975, n.p.
20. Smith, W.G., *A Study in Canadian Immigration* (Toronto, 1920), Table 35; see also Employment and Immigration Canada, Jan. 15, 1973, Library Gov. Pubs., Tables of Immigrants Admitted to Canada, 1896-1915 as roughly equivalent with 97,816 Russians, n.p.
21. *Immigration and Population Statistics*, Manpower and Immigration, Ottawa, 1974, p. 10; see also R.H. Coats, "Canada", in Willcox, VIII, p. 134 (Table 45).
22. Willcox, Walter F., ed., *International Migrations*, New York, 1969. Vol. VII, p. 365, Table 6.
23. *Ibid.*, pp. 272-73.
24. *Ibid.*,
25. *Ibid.*, p. 367 (Table 8); see also Willcox, VIII, p. 507 (Table 221) where he records 18,000 Russian and Polish Jews immigrating into Canada in 1920-1924. This seems to be a separate figure from the Russians. Willcox's figure accords with the statistics for Russians in Employment and Immigration Canada, *op. cit.*, which shows 10,976 Russians as having come to Canada between 1916 and 1925.
26. Gibbon, J.M., *op. cit.*, p. 369.
27. *The Canadian Family Tree*, p. 273.
28. *Immigration and Population Statistics*, p. 8, where an emigration figure for the total Canadian population is given for the years 1921-31. See also Employment and Immigration Canada, *op. cit.*, which shows the Ukrainian immigration to Canada increasing after 1926, and Russian immigration as decreasing. Unfortunately, no official emigration records on separate ethnic groups are available.
29. *Immigration and Population Statistics*, p. 10.
30. Bonavia, George, *Focus on Canada Immigration*, Manpower and Immigration, Ottawa, 1977, p. 154. Victoria Dickenson's figure of 140,000 for the same years seems far off the mark.
31. *Employment and Immigration Canada*, n.p.
32. See also details on the "white" Russian émigrés in article by Prof. Pervushin.

33. Gibbon, *op.cit.*, p. 369
34. *Ibid.*, p. 379.
35. *The Canadian Family Tree*, p. 275.
36. *Ibid.*
37. See Okulevich, G., *Russkiye v Kanade* (Russians in Canada), published by the Federation of Russian Canadians, Toronto, 1952, pp. 23, 84-85, 91-94, and *passim*.
38. Gibbon, J.M., *op. cit.*, p. 365.
39. Okulevich, G., *op. cit.*, p. 322.
40. *The Canadian Family Tree*, pp. 237-74.
41. Porter, John, *The Vertical Mosaic, An Analysis of Social Class and Power in Canada*, (Toronto, 1970), p. 75.
42. *Ibid.*, p. 83.
43. *The Canadian Family Tree*, p. 275.
44. Okulevich, G., *op. cit.*, p. 322-3.
45. Gibbon, J.M., *op. cit.*, p. 367.
46. *Ibid.*, p. 366.
47. Porter, J., *op.cit.*, p. 80.
48. *Ibid.*
49. Okulevich, G., *op. cit.*, pp. 3-186.
50. *Ibid.*, pp. 303-21.
51. *Ibid.*, p. 307.
52. *Ibid.* p. 316.
53. *The Canadian Family Tree*, pp. 277-78; and Gibbon, pp. 367-70.
54. Starbird, Ethel A., "The People Who Made Saskatchewan", *National Geographic*, Vol. 155, No. 5 (May) 1979, pp. 651-78; here p. 665.

N.V. Pervushin

Four

HISTORIC PRECONDITIONS FOR THE POST-WORLD WAR I EXODUS FROM RUSSIA

The foregoing chapter described Russian immigration to Canada between the first and second World Wars. Here, we shall refer to the historical events causing the massive exodus from Russia after the Revolution and Civil War that had an important influence on Russian-Canadians in Canada, as well as on the Canadian public in general. This influence was significant despite the fact that only a relatively small number of people reached Canada, because these people formed the first wave of refugees that was political in its overall character. They were not ***emigrants*** *but* ***refugees****. In contrast to people who planned their departure from Russia and went abroad under normal conditions in search of work, land or, as it was in the case of Doukhobors, wishing to live their life outside an organized state and have religious freedom, the "whites" had no choice but to flee to save themselves after the fall of Russia.*

* * *

People started to flee the Russian Empire immediately after the October Revolution, brought about by the party of the Social-Democrats (Bolsheviks) in 1917 (in November by the Western calendar, as the "old" Russian Julian Calendar used at the time lagged behind the Gregorian by thirteen days). For this reason, the Russian emigrants were called refugees and many émigré organizations were called refugee organizations.

At first it was individuals who left Russia, and mostly families of well-informed and farsighted people who foresaw the approaching calamity. The civil war began in the summer of 1918, but even before that, in March, the German-Soviet Brest-Litovsk agreement had been signed. According to this agreement, vast territories of the former Russian Empire were ceded by Soviet Russia. Ukraine, Poland, Finland, Lithuania, Latvia and part of Georgia became either independent or fell under the German protectorate.

At this time, part of the Russian population started to leave the territory of Soviet Russia for other European countries. This departure intensified when, in 1917, troops of the Western Allies occupied the Russian sea ports of Arkhangelsk and Murmansk in the north, Vladivostok in the east and Odessa and Batum in the south. When these detachments of Allied troops were evacuated, a large number of Russians went abroad. The failures of the "white" armies in the south of Russia forced many Russians to leave their native land in 1919, and especially in 1920, when more than a hundred thousand people fled to Constantinople from Crimea alone.[1] Hundreds of thousands of Russians fled with the "white armies" through Siberia to Manchuria, settling down in Harbin and Shanghai, from where their children and those of the older generation who were still alive twenty years later, were once again forced to seek refuge in lands across the seas.

During the course of a few years, emigration continued across all the boundaries, with no regard for the rules and regulations forbidding it. People used whatever way they could to save themselves from persecution and death in the Soviet Union. In fact, right from the beginning, the Soviet regime announced that certain categories of Russians were "enemies of the people", enemies of the new order. These included the clergy, monks, and other "devotees of cults" as they were called in the Soviet Union, large landowners, merchants, manufacturers, nobility and other aristocrats, intellectuals, those who had participated at one time in the activities of political parties other than the radical left,* former tsarist officials — primarily policemen, gendarmes, army and navy officers, as well as prosperous peasants, who were in fact the most thrifty and enterprising of those who worked their own land—the very flower of Russian peasantry.

Of course, not all people in these categories were able to emi-

---

* Monarchists, Constitutional Democrats, Conservative, Liberal (right and left), Socialist Revolutionaries and moderate Socialists-Mensheviks.

grate or flee from the Soviet Union as it was nearly impossible. Those who remained in Russia after the triumph of communism suffered one way or another:

— the vast majority were "liquidated" either during the civil war (1918-1919), or during the famine induced by the period of "war communism";
— during the collectivization campaign in 1932-34 and the hunger resulting from crushing of the peasantry;
— during the terroristic "cleansing purges" and mass exiles of people to northern and east Siberian death camps; or
— later, before the war in 1941, when large groups of people were sent away from cities such as Leningrad because of their ethnic or social backgrounds.

One can say that those people who succeeded in emigrating during these years would have been potential victims of the new régime. Yet, among them only a small percentage was actively antagonistic to the Soviet régime — not more than 25%. They were soldiers and officers of the "white" volunteer armies, Cossacks who managed to escape from the Don, Kuban, Tersk and Amur Provinces (the Bolsheviks considered the Cossacks to be their most dangerous enemy), and active members of anti-communist organizations and parties who participated in the civil war against the Bolsheviks.

A large part of the emigrants settled in the Balkan Peninsula (Yugoslavia and Bulgaria), Slavic countries whose population and authorities were traditionally sympathetic to Russians and Russia. Some settled in Manchuria; other scattered throughout the world.

What distinguished the Russian emigration from all others was that it was massive in nature, included representatives of all classes of Russian society (Figs. 10, 11), and the most outstanding members of the intelligentsia.

Part of the intelligentsia (primarily representatives of the humanities) were exiled to Germany in 1922 by Government decree; they later settled in Western Europe, the USA and Canada.

It should be noted that a considerable number of Russian writers, scientists, journalists, artists, musicians, actors and dancers left Soviet Russia of their own accord soon after the revolution. They did not want to submit to an authority that did not recognize freedom of speech and creativity. Many of them joined different schools and universities and contributed greatly to the culture of their adopted countries (Fig. 12).

The position of Russian emigrants was particularly good in those countries where Russians had lived even before the revolution. That was the case in the former provinces of Imperial Russia that became sovereign states or part of other states after 1918.

According to the data of the League of Nations, about 1.6 million people left the Soviet Union by 1926. Moreover, many Russian

World War I prisoners-of-war and soldiers of the Russian Expeditionary Corps in France and Salonika (Greece) became emigrants. People living in territories that were ceded by Russia remained there. Among the emigrants were representatives of all the major nationalities (ethnic groups) that lived in the Russian Empire. Almost all spoke Russian and the majority considered Russian their native tongue. Most were Russians in the ethnic meaning of the word.

According to the 1920 census in Bessarabia, for instance, there were 42,000 people who declared themselves to be Russian (out of a total population of 2,686,000). The 1921 census in Poland indicated that there were 5,250,000 Russians out of a total population of 27,177,000. In Ugor Rus', there were 550,000 Russians; in Latvia, 231,000; in Lithuania, 55,000; in Estonia, 91,000; in Finland, 15,000; in China and the strip of territory along the Chinese Eastern Railroad, 200,000; in the USA, about 500,000; and in Canada, 100,064. Before the Revolution, there were 50,000 Russians in other countries of Western Europe.[2]

It is not possible to establish how many thousand "whites" of this number came to Canada during the period between the first and second World Wars because, as stated in the Introduction, statistical data do not include details relating to small ethnic groups, and it was frequently impossible to establish even the most essential figures.

Notes

1. *Encyclopaedia Britannica*, 1956, Vol. 19, p. 56.
2. Kovalevsky, P. *Zarubezhnaya Rossiya* (Russia Abroad), Librairie des cinq continents, Paris, France, 1971, pp. 11-13. (In Russian).

T.F. Jeletzky

Five

RUSSIAN IMMIGRATION TO CANADA AFTER WORLD WAR II

(Sometimes called "The Second Wave")

To The Late Fifties

Emigration from any country in the war zone was, of course, difficult at best and next to impossible in the case of the countries of Eastern Europe. Specifically, official statistics record a mere 426 immigrants as coming to Canada from the USSR during the six-year period of 1940 to 1945 and it is unlikely that more than a third of these people were Russians as defined in the Introduction. Because the term "Russian" was not clearly defined, this estimate may not be completely accurate.[1]

In the forties, however, the Canadian Government foresaw that the end of the war would usher in a period of heavy immigration from overseas. In anticipation, a new policy began to take shape, a policy that was both more liberal and more precise in placing emphasis on proper registration procedures.

At the end of the war, Canada was one of the first non-European countries to offer assistance in resolving the problem facing Europe caused by the migration of people and the accumulation of refugees in Germany and other countries of Central Europe. By the summer of 1945 Canada had already sent immigration officials, social workers, physicians and volunteers to help the refugees.

Shaped by economic conditions of the thirties, the government policy was still restrictionist at that time. However, a growing number of Canadian business leaders, the media and ethnic associations were anxious to sponsor close relatives and co-religionists from the Displaced Persons (DP)*[2] camps in Europe. Groups of ethnic communities who took part in parliamentary debates represented two opposing political attitudes: the anti-Soviet delegations urged that DPs be accepted as political refugees; the pro-Soviet groups, on the other hand, considered that the DPs should return to their states of origin to take part in the reconstruction of war-devastated areas.[3]

The debates over the desirability of a broadened immigration policy lasted for a long time and eventually resulted in the adoption of more liberal criteria for the admission of different groups of immigrants.[4]

As a result of these changes in Government regulations, the first groups of post-war immigrants classified as "Russians" began to arrive. From 1946 to 1951 people came in increasing numbers.** After that time, the "wave" of immigration declined as the refugees who were in Europe found permanent homes or resettled. Everyone who wished to emigrate and could do so, did. There was, however, no new influx from the USSR because the Soviet borders became as tightly closed as they had been before the war.

Who were these Russian immigrants who came to Canada in the post-war years? What made them emigrate instead of returning home?

One should note that the Russians who came at this time cannot be regarded as a homogeneous group.

Some of the immigrants were "old" or "white" émigrés, who found themselves as refugees for the second time. For them, the first stage of emigration was the flight from Russia after the civil war and the defeat of the "white armies" of Kornilov, Alekseyev, Denikin, Wrangel, Yudenich and Kolchak. Between the two World Wars, they were dispersed in different countries of Western Europe, the Middle East, the Far East and Africa. A considerable number of refugees had lived in China.

A brief review of the conditions that led to emigration from the Soviet Union between 1918 and 1924 is found in Chapter 4. According to League of Nations data, 1,160,000 people fled from Russia during that period. This number does not include many

---

* A "DP" is a person who was displaced from his original place of residence as a result of war which led to the mass migration of people from different countries. A "refugee" left the territory of the state in which he formerly resided either as a result of political events in that state or for other political reasons.

** See tables pp. 95-96.

prisoners-of-war who preferred to remain in Western Europe nor those who lived in countries that were part of Imperial Russia before the Brest-Litovsk Treaty[5] and who, subsequently finding themselves outside Russian borders, remained there as an ethnic minority. During the Second World War, many of those who did not wish to remain under the Bolsheviks fled to the West, to areas which eventually came under the control of Britain, the USA and France.

Many of these refugees belonged to the younger generation who had been born or had grown up outside Russia. They adopted the language and culture of the country in which they were educated and, in many cases, no longer regarded Russian as their mother tongue. The family and conditions of the host country played an important part in forming their attitudes. Thus, in Slavic countries such as the Kingdom of Serbs, Croats and Slovenes; Czechoslovakia; and Bulgaria, the state rendered moral and material support to Russian refugees.[6] In Serbia the government subsidized three Russian military schools and two Institutes in addition to many primary and secondary schools. Consequently, the preservation of the language, observance of traditions, "togetherness" and "Russianness" (the feeling of national identity and the desire to adhere to Russian culture) are much more pronounced in immigrants from these countries.

The second significant group of post-war immigrants consisted of former Soviet citizens who came to Germany during the Second World War. Some of them, predominantly young people, were transported by the Germans from the occupied areas of the USSR as forced labourers in industry and agriculture. They were the so-called "ostovtsy" or workers from the East. Others were actual or former prisoners-of-war who joined the ROA, Cossack and other units* to fight against Stalin's dictatorship.[7]

In addition to the "ostovtsy" and prisoners-of-war, a large number of civilians crowded into Germany. These were people who fled to the West rather than live under the Soviet régime again.

Not counting those deported from the territories occupied by the Germans before the armistice,[8] the overall number of DPs and refugees reached eight million by the end of the war.

Many of these were returned to their former homeland in the

---

* ROA — Russian Liberation Army. Units of Russian volunteers formed part of the German Wehrmacht. Towards the end of the war, however, ROA was formally put under General Vlasov's control, although *de facto* he had no influence on strategic decisions (see article on SBONR).

Cossacks — separate units under the command of Atamans Gen. Krasnov and Schkuro, who were under Wehrmacht control (see footnote No. 26).

first year following the war. It is impossible to estimate the number of Soviet citizens among them, to say nothing of the number of Russians. According to information given by N. Tolstoy,[9] more than 5 million people were either extradited to the USSR following the Yalta Agreement[10] or returned voluntarily.

UNRRA*[11] archives did not contain complete data on the number of Soviet repatriates as UNRRA officials were not admitted into the Soviet-controlled zone.[12]

Hundreds of thousands of people who refused to return to the Soviet Union or to the areas where they used to live before the war now had to be resettled.

How could it happen that these people, who often spoke no other language but their own, decided to risk staying in a strange land, taking a leap into the unknown in search of the phantom of happiness overseas?

The answer lies in the fact, little known in the West, that during the first months of World War II, many Soviet citizens were prone to feelings of defeatism.[13]

From the moment the Bolsheviks came to power, life at all levels of society was one of permanent terror. Contrary to the widely-held opinion in the West, terror was introduced not by Stalin, but by Lenin himself, and was formally legitimized as far back as 1918.[14] The denunciations, arrests and executions of innocent people, the misery of collectivization, the annhihilation of prosperous and middle-class peasants, the artificially-induced hunger of the early 1930s, the purges and trials of the "enemies of the people" during Stalin's time and the dread of prisons and "correctional-educational" camps from which people rarely emerged alive led to a reaction which is hard for free people to understand. The fact is that, during the first days of the war, the Germans were welcomed as liberators from the hated power of the Soviets. This happened not only in the Baltic States, which remembered their freedom, and in the Ukraine, which was fighting for its independence, but also in such Russian provinces as Novgorod, Smolensk and Orel.

> It was obvious that the army as well as the civilians did not wish to live under communism and saw in the war a chance to get rid of it . . . most significant, during the first stage of the war, was the enormous number of prisoners taken by the Germans . . . more than 4 million toward the end of 1941 . . .[15]

A rare phenomenon was observed: the conquered cheered the conquerors!

---

* United Nations Relief and Rehabilitation Administration.

But their joy was shortlived. The first units of the German army were soon replaced by the civilian administration, SS and Gestapo. Persecution and mass killings of Jews began less than one month after the occupation. Russian and other Soviet prisoners-of-war died daily by the thousands from enforced hunger conditions. The brief period of illusions soon ended . . . people realized that Hitler was by no means a saviour and that he had no intention whatever of creating a free Russian State . . .

Soon, people were being shipped to Germany as forced labourers for industry and agriculture. They were rounded up on the streets and in the market-places and peremptorily sent west. Partisan activity was countered by fierce reprisals: for every German slain by the partisans, the Gestapo shot hundreds of hostages, often innocent people who were arbitrarily detained.[16] Voluntary surrenders of Red Army soldiers stopped. People in the occupied territories were caught in a desperate situation — between Stalin and Hitler.[17]

The retreat of the Germans and the return of the Red Army brought new terror for the population of the zones that had been under occupation. In the eyes of the Soviet authorities, the mere fact of having lived under German occupation and being exposed to Nazi ideology was in itself a punishable crime. People began to flee west *en masse*.

The end of the war, which normally should have brought joy, liberation and homecoming, gave the Russian refugees that feeling of uncertainty that only an unpredictable future can engender.

> During the early days following the end of the war only the young people, taken to Germany by force and happy to be free from slavery gathered at the assembly points. Trains decorated with flowers and slogans took echelons of repatriates to the Soviet zone. However, news soon spread that families were separated at the border. People who managed to flee to the allied zones recounted how everyone was treated as an "enemy of the people" or as an "unreliable element" at best.[18]

Towards the end of 1945, the number of repatriates decreased drastically.[19] At that time, it became known that Stalin and the Western Allies had signed some kind of agreement in Yalta according to which all Soviet citizens had to be returned to the USSR "without regard to their individual wishes and by force if necessary".[20] Soviet repatriation officers showed up in Allied zones and the hunt for people began. Having no information from the radio or the newspapers, people lived by rumours and could not understand who was to be extradited. Soon it became known that the agreement included a clause defining those who were considered subject to extradition, namely all those who had Soviet citizenship before September 1, 1939.

> On this day . . . the first day of World War II, Hitler and Stalin who concluded a non-aggression pact a week earlier, ordered their troops to enter Poland.* The same day, Great Britain and France, according to their treaty with Poland, declared war on Germany.[21]

People who lived outside Soviet borders before that day (as for example, in Poland or the Baltic States), were not formally Soviet citizens and thus not subject to extradition under the terms of the Yalta agreement. This explains why September 1, 1939 became a crucial date in shaping the destiny of many people.

News of the agreement between the Allies produced panic among Soviet citizens; many refused to be repatriated and resorted to various tricks to avoid forcible extradition. Former Soviet Ukrainians, Byelorussians and Russians, the latter being particularly in the public eye, tried to become "lost" in the camps of Western Ukrainians, who were Polish citizens and, therefore not subject to repatriation by force. Some tried to "hide" among the Poles, Baltic people, Armenians and Germans — native or refugees. Some, pretending to be "white" émigrés, invented "proof" that on September 1, 1939 they were outside the Soviet borders and, therefore, not Soviet citizens.

There was a flourishing black market in false documents that were stolen or found on the dead. One could order any identity card or certificate from a craftsman or a special workshop. Driven by fear of forced repatriation, people changed their names; but by rejecting their own past in this way, they jeopardized their future by not being able to present proof of their education or work references.

No wonder that the first UNRRA registration of displaced persons in 1945 was, in many cases, based on misinformation. This later gave rise to a situation called "Berezov's disease" — life under false identity.[22]

Former Soviet soldiers were in a particularly vulnerable position. After World War I, the shaky Soviet régime was hardly interested in repatriating anti-communist prisoners-of-war and refugees from Western Europe who, at that time, were supporters of the monarchy (the officers in particular). As such, they only represented a threat to the Soviet régime.

After World War II the situation changed completely. The refusal of prisoners-of-war and civilians to return home was a blow to

* The German Army entered Poland on September 1, 1939, and the Soviet Army on September 17, 1939. (Ed.)

the prestige of the system, as these people were young and Soviet-educated and *not* aristocrats or members of the White Guard. To leave them in the West would embarrass the USSR. It would be simpler to condemn them as traitors and insist on their extradition on the grounds of "giving a lesson in this way to all anti-communists."[23]

Stalin did not consider himself bound by the International Conventions of the Red Cross.[24] The Western concept of a prisoner-of-war was not accepted by Soviet law according to which, if a man became a prisoner instead of committing suicide, it was reason enough to exclude him from Soviet society and punish him as a traitor. Stalin's own son Jacob was in that category, having been abandoned in a German prisoner-of-war camp where he perished.[25]

If ordinary prisoners-of-war knew that they could not expect decent treatment upon their return, then volunteers fighting against Stalin could surely not expect any mercy. The scope of this book does not permit a description of the history and aspirations of these people. Some joined the volunteer forces to save themselves from death by hunger in prisoner-of-war camps and only later became inspired by the ideas of the ROA. But most were anti-communist by conviction, united in their rejection of Bolshevism[26] which misused the name of Russia in its fight for international totalitarianism. These people wished to fight for the freedom of their lost homeland even if it meant temporary material support from the Germans.[27] Many were convinced that, after defeating Nazi Germany, the Allies would turn against the Soviet Union and deliver the world from communism. This confidence on the part of the members of the Liberation Movement* proved costly because, according to the provisions of the Treaty of Yalta, they were extradited to the USSR to face reprisals and death. The history of forcible repatriation and the treachery which preceded it is described in recently-published documents that were "frozen" for 30 years, only gradually becoming available for research purposes.[28]

Forcible repatriation *en masse* came to an end at the beginning of 1947. In July, UNRRA administration was taken over by the newly-organized IRO[29] and the refugee problem entered a new stage. The IRO became the custodian of about two million displaced persons, including those living in the camps (Fig. 18) and those in private quarters who received formal help from the IRO in the form of food, clothing, etc. It is impossible to account for the number of unregistered Russians who lived privately or hid behind a German identity. Fearing repatriation, they avoided all agencies dealing with refugees.[30] Some of them did not qualify for IRO assistance.[31]

---

* See Chapter 11.

In one American zone alone there were no less than 300 DP camps. T. Fessenko describes the life and atmosphere of the camps as follows:

> Usually the camps were organized in former army barracks where the *ostovtsy* used to live during the war. People were quartered according to ethnic groups. The camp provided shelter and rations, as well as the right to get parcels from different welfare organizations. Some camps had communal kitchens; in others, each inmate had to do his own cooking as best he could. Living conditions were very crowded; families with children had to be content with part of a room divided off by a blanket serving as a curtain. Despite the anguish of waiting for the unknown and the lack of a suitable occupation, there were nevertheless advantages to camp life. It was a refuge, offering rest for the weary, many of whom had lost all their belongings during their flight or bombing raids. Families who were separated found hope in registration procedures that could help to search for their loved ones. News spread by word of mouth and from one camp to another. Enterprising people became itinerant merchants and the most active could find a job with pay. In the big camps such as Munich, where the population reached several thousand, there were separate administrative offices, an IRO hospital (Fig. 19) and even a camp police force made up of DPs themselves. If there was a minister, a small church was organized, attracting people from adjacent camps, as well as those who lived in private quarters. The church was decorated by DP craftsmen: the iconostasis in Munich, for example, was beautifully decorated by strips of metal cut from American food cans. Workshops were formed where artists could meet, work and organize art exhibits. Cultural and political societies sprang up and concerts were held featuring the best artists.[32]

To a man, the immigrants considered life in Germany and in the other European countries as a temporary stage; only a few tried to settle down locally. Most people dreamed of going overseas to countries not devastated by the war where they would be far away from the threat of repatriation. The New World was thought of as a haven of happiness, prosperity and freedom.

Soon, Canadian recruiting committees appeared. in the camps along with representatives of different countries who were interested in labourers and who took upon themselves the responsibility for the rehabilitation of refugees.

As mentioned earlier, Canada was one of the first non-European countries to extend a tangible form of assistance. Between July, 1947 and February, 1952 Canada contributed $18,164,674 to the IRO fund.[33] The number of immigrants coming to Canada grew from 7,600 in 1942 to 75,719 in 1946 and to 125,414 in 1948. The big change came in May, 1947, when Prime Minister MacKenzie King opened the door to DPs and refugees.

The new immigration policy presented by the Prime Minister was based on a report of post-war economic growth which emphasized the necessity for increasing human resources. In his speech to Parliament, King stated that Canada needed immigrants and would accept them in numbers proportional to the rate of effective economic development in the country. The number of immigrants in every consecutive year was to be constantly monitored and controlled by Parliament. In selecting the immigrants, one had to ensure that the person accepted would never become a burden on Canadian society.[34]

Following MacKenzie King's declaration, the Ministry of Citizenship and Immigration took measures to create organizations whose officers would be specially trained to check, receive and resettle the immigrants.

In the camps of Europe, the Middle East and Far East, and wherever there were refugees, additional recruiting committees were formed.

Canada accepted refugees according to two categories:

1. group movement;[35]
2. sponsorship, where the sponsor could be a close relative or a prospective employer.[36]

Post-war immigration to Canada began as early as 1946 and was restricted to small groups accepted mostly on humanitarian principles. Following MacKenzie King's announcement, things shifted into high gear. Under the group movement principle, people were accepted who could be employed in agriculture, road construction or other manual jobs and as domestic help.[37]

Although these occupations consisted mainly of physical labour, even professional people accepted the offers just to go to that blessed land, Canada.

An immigrant had to pass an investigation commission and meet certain requirements regarding physical and mental health and political background. At first, only the young, strong and single, who were guaranteed work upon their arrival were selected. The Ministry of Labour had to verify the credibility of the employer, who had to prove his ability to provide pay and shelter to the sponsored immigrant.

The employer and the immigrant usually signed a contract for one year. After that time the latter was free of any obligations to the employer and could arrange his life as he saw fit. Such a contract ensured that the immigrant, once transplanted into new surroundings, would not have to worry about finding a job or shelter, in the first difficult times. It also eased the frustration and pain of having to work outside one's profession.

Several months could pass before the results of the screening commission were known. After that, the few days or even weeks of waiting in a transition camp seemed like nothing; it was already the beginning of a new life!

During the first two years, the majority of immigrants were transported to Canada by sea on three former American troop carriers. Later, several British ships were added and, in 1948, some immigrants were brought to Canada by air. The Government signed a contract with Trans-Canada Airlines which provided 10,000 seats for immigrants until the end of March, 1949. Every three or four weeks, the converted German trophy ship *Beaverbrae* carried about 770 relatives of DPs who had already come to Canada on a labour contract.[38] (Fig. 20)

Once on board, the immigrants felt secure for the first time since the war: the European shores had disappeared in the haze and, if the pitching was bearable, one could even enjoy the ship's cuisine — a luxury after the food rations in Germany. Moreover, there was entertainment on board and the captain occasionally gave a ball. A masquerade was arranged on the S. S. *Marine Swallow* and enthusiasts produced fancy dresses from virtually nothing.

Finally, there was Canada and the anticipation of a new life (Fig. 21).

People who left Europe after the war and the economic dislocation, were uplifted by the transition to life in the peaceful surroundings of a country that had not been devastated by war, where life seemed beautiful and too unreal for those who had known misery and hunger. At first, acclimatization proved difficult for many of the newcomers. City dwellers, for example, were not used to hard manual labour. Anxiety about the families left behind waiting for a visa, the lack of knowledge of the English language and the inability to communicate brought depression and dissatisfaction.

A worker assigned to a remote farm would be entirely at the mercy of his boss and situations developed where life seemed unbearable and contracts had to be broken. Sometimes disillusioned people would complain, requesting immigration authorities and private social work organizations to break their contracts. The majority, however, adjusted reasonably well. The sense of values is a relative thing — to a former Soviet citizen who experienced life under Stalin, all such difficulties seemed minor.

The Canadian authorities provided immigrants with a number of privileges: for example, medical expenses occurring within six months of arrival were paid by the Federal Government; provincial governments organized free language courses whenever six or more new Canadians lived in proximity.[39] In addition to instruction in one of the official languages of the country, the program included classes in Canadian history, geography, government, etc. Approximately 60% of the newcomers spoke neither English nor French.

The courses were also important from a social point of view. For many, it was the only chance to have a chat and exchange impressions after an entire week of isolation. The classes were like a club where people met and formed new friendships (Fig. 22).

Remote areas were served by travelling counsellors who spoke the language of the immigrant. Their task was to visit, give advice and information and direct an immigrant to the proper authorities for his particular needs. A counsellor would also be of help in the case of undesirable influences exerted on the immigrants by people who spoke their language, a situation of which the members of the Interdepartmental Coordinating Committee*, who supervised immigrants' affairs, were made aware.[40]

The role of the church was of utmost importance. Not everyone had access to one, however; people working in the Far North could attend services only occasionally, perhaps by going to the nearest city on holidays. The church attracted most of the immigrants — it was their own milieu where they could forget their unfamiliar surroundings.

Community life concentrated around the churches. Russian language and religious instruction schools were organized for children. Periodic meetings within the community sustained the hope that Russian traditions and culture would not be forsaken in their new homeland.

Towards the end of their first year in Canada, the majority of the newcomers were able to sponsor families from overseas and life started to settle down to normal.

Those whose English was still limited could, nevertheless, make themselves understood and even indicated a desire to become Canadian citizens. (At that time, the waiting period was five years.)

During the resettling period, once the work contract had expired, the New Canadian was able to look for a job that suited him better. The tendency was to concentrate in large cities or industrial areas; relatives and friends sought to move closer together.

In rural areas, where only single families were living, the assimilation process was faster. First the children, then their elders, switched to their neighbours' language and gradually became part of the indigenous way of life. Such cases were not numerous, however. In the cities, on the other hand, Russian ethnic groups developed closer ties through frequent social contacts.

---

* This Committee included the following Departments: External Affairs, Labour, Health and Welfare, and Citizenship.

It must be mentioned, however, that relations between the immigrants of the period after World War II and the previous "waves" were not always cordial either for political, professional or other reasons.

For example, Russians who came to Canada at the turn of the century were looking for jobs or land. These so-called "economic immigrants" were predominantly poor peasants from the south-western part of the Russian Empire (Volyn', Territories of Byelorussia and Eastern Poland). A few left Russia for political reasons, being afraid of reprisals for their part in anti-government activities.[41] They included representatives of the left-wing intelligentsia and revolutionaries who had fled Russia after the unsuccessful uprising of 1905.

Some immigrated to Canada looking for freedom of religious and social beliefs (Doukhobors, Old Believers, Mennonites and others). Most of them did not understand the emotionally negative attitude of the post-World War II immigrants towards the Soviet Government. Their animosity was directed against Tsarist Russia but not against the USSR. The diametrically opposed views of some old-timers and later immigrants were one of the obstacles to rapprochement.

Another obstacle was the difference in the professional make-up of the groups. The majority of the Russian population that lived in Canada at the end of the 19th and the beginning of the 20th century originated from rural areas and were agricultural workers. Among East Europeans, only 0.9% had qualified jobs, whereas unqualified workers accounted for 30.1%. There are no data specifically on Russians of that period as they were included in the East European group. Aside from administrative or professional personnel, there were hardly any white collar workers.*

The occupational make-up of post-World War II immigrants was completely different: the 7,709 people registered as Russians who arrived in Canada between 1946 and 1955 were broken down as shown below. More details are contained in Table 7, page 210.

Total number of workers	4,080
All dependents	3,629
Among these:	
— Administrative personnel	4
— Specialists	271
— Clerical workers	173
— Qualified workers in transport, communication, commerce, finance, agriculture, mining, mechanical fields, etc.	3,136
— Unqualified workers	485

* For comparison with the professional content of the groups between 1919 and 1939, see Chapter 3.

Within a political context, if Russian anti-communists came to a location where the "old-timers" were predominant, their mutual lack of understanding led to conflicts. As a result, they did not develop close ties and, in some cases, there were even strong animosities.

There were cases where newcomers came under the influence of pro-Soviet elements within the "old-timer" group*. In 1955, several organizations were formed in the USSR, such as the "Rodina" (Motherland) Society, "The Voice of Rodina" newspaper and the committee "Za vozvrashcheniye na rodinu" ("For the return to the Motherland"). Publicized by the FRC newspaper "Vestnik"**, these organizations conducted active propaganda campaigns directed mainly at newly-arrived immigrants.

The aforementioned committee, headed by Soviet General Michailov, had its main offices in Moscow and East Berlin, with many branches in various countries. It published newspapers and magazines in the languages of the USSR. In Canada, Ukrainian, Russian and Byelorussian editions were wide-spread; discretely-packaged newspapers were sent by mail or delivered to immigrants' homes. The committees were interested mainly in post-World War II immigrants.

Those who were disillusioned were taken in by the propaganda of a general amnesty and agreed to return home. There is no information on the number of these repatriates or on their fate in the USSR as, under pressure from Soviet authorities, they returned their Canadian passports and renounced their citizenship. After departure, they did not communicate with their friends in Canada. It is impossible to assess how many Russians were among them as they included Byelorussians and Ukrainians some of whom had come from the USSR (or Imperial Russia), others from Poland.

"Vestnik" gives its own version of the event: "... starting in 1955, when the committee *Za vozvrashchenie na rodinu* was founded ... many thousands of Soviet people were able, once more, to find their Motherland ..."[42]

The few "white" immigrants who reached Canada between the two World Wars and who succeeded in assimilating into the Canadian way of life, met the post-World War II immigrants with sympathy and understanding. This was especially noticeable in the rela-

---

* During World War II, when the Allies were on friendly terms with the USSR, many Russian emigrants in Europe, as well as in Canada, believed that the Soviet system would be changed after the war. This feeling, bred by nostalgia and pride in Soviet military successes, was termed as "Soviet patriotism" among the emigrants.

** Newspaper of the Federation of Russian Canadians, (FRC).

tionships between those who left Russia after the revolution and the civil war, but settled in Europe, and those who came to Canada only after 1945. Common religious, cultural and political interests helped to establish contacts despite differences in life-style outside Russia. These people were not only Russians, but European by culture.

On the other hand, the immigrants from the USSR who had never been exposed to the Western way of life and who had, in many cases, no religious education whatever, were people of a different world. Their adaptation was hindered by mistrust and suspiciousness, born during the years of terror. Eventually, most did fully adapt. Much credit for this must go to the church and its community life into which the newcomers were always welcomed.

History tends to repeat itself. The same mistrust that existed between the "old" and "new" immigrants, and between the "new" and "newest", can still be observed in relation to the immigrants of the 1970s. In that respect, there is no basic difference in attitude between successive waves of immigrants.

The Russian group, as a whole, does not have a common political outlook. For example, one would expect the Doukhobors to be more monolithic due to their social and religious beliefs; yet they too have serious fundamental differences.

The diversity of their roots is one of the causes of disunity within the Russian ethnic group which cannot be considered as an entity. Thus, there can be no agreement in matters of serious concern. Rapprochement between Russian Canadians and other Slavic groups is noticeable only at the level of individual friendships; this is partly caused by the extreme sensitivity of the immigrants to anti-Russian feelings which, unfortunately, exist on the part of others. One point of view is shared by most Russians*: they consider that the Russian people suffered *more* at the hands of the Soviet dictatorship and *not less* than other ethnic groups constituting the USSR. Yet, it is the Russians — the so-called "oppressors" — who tend to get blamed for the atrocities committed in their name by the communist government. There are too few Russians in Canada to counter this manifestly unfair opinion; those who venerate the culture of their forefathers, prefer to remain aloof rather than expose themselves to discriminatory remarks.

In general, assimilation into Canadian society proceeded at a reasonably quick rate. The Russians who came to Canada after the Second World War did not have the illusions of their predecessors thirty years earlier, who had expected that their stay abroad would

---

* This does not include representatives of Soviet sympathizer groups who use the expressions "Russian" and "Soviet" to mean one and the same thing. (Ed.)

be only temporary, that the Soviet dictatorship would soon fall and that they could then return home. The second-wave of immigrants knew that their decision to leave their country was irreversible and that they had to plan their lives accordingly. They were, therefore, determined to construct a new life in their adopted homeland and accepted a different set of rules for survival. They started from scratch. Not knowing the language, they learned "on the go" and quickly earned the respect of their neighbours.

Individually and collectively, the Russian ethnic group, although not as vociferous as other more numerous minorities, made its contribution to Canadian life and culture in all its aspects. It is this factor which is the key to evaluating their ability to assimilate.

Notes

1. Some errors produced by confusing the terms *Russia* and *USSR (Union of Soviet Socialist Republics)* can be seen in Table A 316-336, published in *Historical Statistics Canada*, M. C. Urquhart, editor, MacMillan Co. of Canada, Toronto, 1965, p. 28. Under the heading *The ethnic origin of immigrants to Canada from 1900 to 1960* one reads: *Immigrants who arrived from USSR, Poland and the Baltic countries.* This sentence can be applied only for the period of time starting after the revolution in 1917. Before that, the official name of the Russian State was Imperial Russia or Russia of which Poland and the Baltic countries were a part. The official declaration establishing the USSR on the territory of former Russia was proclaimed at the First Congress of the Soviets, December 30, 1922, after the civil war and the stabilization of the Soviet Government. USSR is a multinational state and Russia (Great Russia) or the Russian Soviet Federated Socialist Republic (RSFSR), is the largest of fifteen republics comprising the USSR. In turn, RSFSR, the first republic that was proclaimed October 25, 1917, includes in its structure sixteen autonomous republics and five autonomous provinces (oblast).

2. Vernant, Jacques, *The Refugee in the post-war world*, Geneva, 1951, Part I, Chapter I, the concept of "Refugee", pp. 3-14.

   Brownlie, Ian, editor, *Basic documents on human rights*, Clarendon Press, Oxford, 1971, Chapter I, General Provisions, Definition of the term "Refugee", p. 136.

3. Dirks, Gerald E., *Canada's Refugee Policy, Indifference or Opportunism?*, Chapter VI, "The Postwar Scene in Canada", McGill-Queen's University Press, Montreal & London, 1977, p. 132.

4. *Debates, House of Commons*, Dominion of Canada, 1946, pp. 224-229, 239-240, 524-545; 1978-1979, pp. 5, 492-5, 496-5, 506-5, 518.

   Canada Yearbook, 1948, Chapter V, Immigration and Emigration.

5. The Treaty of Brest-Litovsk was signed by the Soviet Government and Germany on March 3, 1918. According to the Treaty, Germany received

the Ukraine, Lithuania and Latvia. Finland and part of Transcaucasia separated in 1917. After Germany's defeat, Poland and the Baltic States were recognized as independent sovereign states. See G. Vernadsky, *History of Russia*, Yale University Press, Mass., USA, 1962, p. 301.

6. Kovalevsky, P., *Zarubezhnaya Rossiya* (Russia Abroad), Part 2, "The Cultural-Educational Work of Russians outside of Russia", Librairie des cinq continents, Paris, 1971, p. 347. (In Russian).

7. Thorvald, Jurgen, *The Illusion, Soviet Soldiers in Hitler's Armies*, A. Helen and Kurt Wolff Book, Droemer Knaur Verlag, Schoeller and Co., USA, 1975.

8. United Nations, Department of Public Information. *What the United Nations is Doing for Refugees and Displaced Persons*, New York, 1948, p. 2.

9. Tolstoy, Nikolai, *Victims of Yalta*, Hodder & Stoughton, London, 1978, pp. 408-409. Nikolai Tolstoy gives the following information: According to an official Soviet account, 5,236,130 people were liberated and repatriated in 1945. Of these, from an estimate of a former officer of the NKVD who had access to that organization's files:

   20% received the death sentence or 25 years in concentration camps; 15-20% received sentences of five to ten years; 10% were exiled to frontier regions of Siberia for a period of not less than six years; 15% were sent as work conscripts to Donbas, Kuzbas and other devastated areas. These were not allowed to return home after the expiration of their sentence; 15-20% were allowed to return home, but could rarely (as registered labour) find work. These estimates do not add up to 100%. Possibly the missing 15-25% can be assigned to "wastage": people who . . . died in transit, or escaped.

10. The Yalta Agreement between the Soviet Union and USA was signed in Yalta, Crimea, February 11, 1945. It concerned the treatment of liberated prisoners-of-war and was made public on March 8, 1945. Similar agreements were signed by representatives of Great Britain and France on another date. (As cited in Julius Epstein, *Operation Keelhaul, The Story of Forced Repatriation*, the Devin Adair company, Old Greenwich, Conn., USA, 1972, p. 21.)

11. United Nations Relief and Rehabilitation Administration (UNRRA) was established by forty-four nations (including USSR) on November 9, 1942 as an operational and temporary UN specialized Agency . . . Its objectives were "to plan and administer a relief program, additional to the Allied armies" and "to prepare and undertake measures for the return of prisoners and exiles to their country of origin."

    UNRRA, The History of the United Nations Relief and Rehabilitation Administration, prepared under the direction of George Woodbridge, in three volumes, Columbia University Press, New York, 1950, Vol. III, Appendix Three, Article I, p. 23.

    The direct (physical) repatriation was the function of SHAEF (Supreme Headquarters Allied Expeditionary Force), which had its own DP Branch, (Resolution 10, "*The History of UNRRA*", p. 111).

12. Holborn, Louise, *Refugees: a Problem of our Time*, The Scarecrow Press Inc., Metuchen, N.J., 1975, p. 24.
13. "Defeatism" — a term used by the Bolsheviks and by Lenin, during the 1914-1917 World War. At that time, Lenin considered that Russia's defeat in the war would disrupt the base of the Tsarist régime and because of that it would be to the benefit of the revolution. It is a paradox that the same term was used by those who saw in the defeat of the Soviet system by the Germans the salvation of Russia from Communism.
14. Vernadsky, G., *op. cit.*, p. 297. ". . . the policy, named the Red Terror, was formally proclaimed on 5 Sept. 1918. Lenin himself made the following statement: 'Dictatorship of the proletariat is impossible without terror and violence.'"
15. Byelopolsky, A., *USSR on the Background of Russia's Past*, Washington, 1973, p. 391 (In Russian).
16. Kuznetsov, Anatoly, *Babi Yar*, Jonathan Cape Ltd., London, 1970, pp. 25, 150. Text of the leaflets signed by General-Commandant Eberhardt that were posted around the city of Kiev at that time read as follows:

> As a repressive measure against the committed act of sabotage, the death penalty was inflicted on 100 inhabitants of the City of Kiev. This is a warning. Every inhabitant of the City of Kiev will be held responsible for any act of sabotage.
>
> Kiev, 22 October, 1941
> City Commandant

17. Plivier, Theodore, *Moscow*, (first part of the Trilogy: *Moscow-Stalingrad-Berlin*), Love and Malcomson Ltd., Redhill, Surrey Pantherbooks, London, pp., 246-255, 309, 317.
18. Bohatirchuk, F.P., *My Life's Path to Vlasov and the Prague Manifesto*, Globus Publishing House, San-Francisco, 1978, p. 214 (In Russian).
19. Holborn, L., *op. cit.*, p. 26.
20. According to the agreement, the US authorities had to separate all Soviet citizens and hand them over to Soviet authorities. The original text of the Yalta Agreement contains no reference to the use of force for the purpose of repatriating people not wishing to be repatriated. The Handbook of July 7, 1945, amended through September 20, 1945, issued by the Headquarters, United States Quarters European Theater, includes a passage that deals with "Treatment of US, British and Soviet nationals", which reads as follows:

    Liberated Soviet citizens, including those who were former members of German Armed Forces (Vlasov's forces uncovered or captured after February, 1945) . . . will be returned . . . to the control of the USSR without regard for their individual wishes", as cited by

Epstein, *Operation Keelhaul, the Story of Forced Repatriation,* the Devin Adair Co., Old Greenwich, 1973, pp. 23-38.

Also: *Debates, House of Commons,* 1945, p. 229, address of Mr. A. Hlynka on the following order: HQ 30 Corps District, 219/DP, December 29, 1945, British Zone, Subject — Ukrainians.

21. Mogiljansky, M. I., *History of Canada*, Sovremennik, Toronto, 1976, p. 222.

22. Epstein, J., *op. cit.*, p. 150, Appendix 6, pp. 219-221. The Russian writer Akulshin, using the name Rodion Berezov, immigrated to the USA. Soon he felt that he could no longer bear the false situation he had put himself in and revealed to the Immigration authorities that his papers did not correspond to his true identity. The verdict of the law was: deportation. A long legal process followed. Berezov who, by that time, had become a Baptist preacher, explained the reasons behind his action and finally won the case, creating a precedent and clearing the way for many who were in the same situation.

23. *Ibid.*, pp. 20-21.

24. *The Law of War*, A Documentary History, Vol. I, Random House, New York, Convention on treatment of Prisoners-of-War, Geneva, July 27, 1929.

25. Alliluyeva, Svetlana, *Twenty Letters to a Friend*, Harper & Row, New York and Evanston, 1967, pp. 161-163.

    "How Joseph Stalin's Son Died", *The Gazette*, Montreal, March 1980, p. 25.

26. Solzhenitsyn, A. I., *The Gulag Archipelago*, Harper & Row, New York, 1978, Vol. III, Part 5, Chapter I, pp. 27-36, "The Doomed."

    Krasnov, Nikolai, *Nezabyvayemoye* (The Unforgettable), New York, 1957, p. 348 (in Russian).

27. Steenberg, Sven, *Vlasov*, A. Knopf, New York, 1970, pp. 154, 157-160.

28. Bethell, Nicholas, *The Last Secret, Forcible repatriation to Russia*, 1944-47, André Deutsch, 1975, London, p. 224.

    Tolstoy, Nikolai, *op. cit.*

    Epstein, Julius, *op. cit.*

    These books are but a few of many written on the subject, some of them in the Russian language.

29. The International Refugee Organization (IRO) took over the responsibility of UNRRA on July 1, 1947. Canada was one of its 18 members (the USSR did not take part in it). At that time, the Third Committee of the General Assembly prepared its views on the Refugee Problem. Following debate, the General Assembly, in a resolution of February 14, 1946, laid down the following three principles: 1) The refugee problem should be considered international; 2) There should be no forced repatriation; 3) Repatriation for displaced persons should be pursued and assisted. The function of the IRO was: temporary care and

maintenance of refugees; the movement of refugees either through repatriation or resettlement; and the establishment of the refugee as a person, possessing full citizenship. As cited by Louise Holborn, 1975, p. 29.

30. Vernant, Jacques, *op. cit.*, Geneva, 1951, p. 150.
31. IRO Constitution (December 15, 1946), Annex II, Part I, Sections A, B and C.
32. Fessenko, Tatiana, *Tale of the "Crooked" Years* (Povest' Krivykh Let), Novoye Russkoye Slovo, New York, 1963, pp. 180, 188-190 (in Russian).
33. Holborn, L., *op. cit.*, Annex 2.3, p. 48.
34. *Commons Debates*, 1947, pp. 2, 644-2, 646; Right Honourable MacKenzie King's speech, May 1, 1957.
35. *Annual report of the Department of Mines and Resources*, year ending March 31, 1948, Ottawa, p. 243, contains the following table:

Group Movements Approved by the Immigration Committee

March 31, 1948

Miners	2,222
Railway Workers	2,100
Steel Workers	375
Aluminum Workers	3,622
Foundry Workers	50
Hydro Construction Workers	64
Clothing Industry Workers	2,000
Domestics	2,316
Farmers	4,500
Fur Workers	2,000
Shoe Workers	500
Textile Workers	100
Others	50

36. *Commons Debates*, 1947, pp. 2, 475-2, 485.
37. *Ibid.*, pp. 3, 566-3, 567.
38. *Debates of the Senate*, June 24, 1948, p. 664, Transportation.

    Commons Debates, 1947, pp. 2, 121-2, 122.
39. New Canadians, *Argosy of Commerce*, 25th Anniversary Issue, Toronto, 1954, pp. 54-61.
40. *Debates of the Senate*, June 1948, p. 665.
41. Simpson, G.W., *People of Russian Origin*, Encyclopedia Canadiana, Vol. 9, Toronto, 1961, pp. 116-117.
42. "A Quarter Century of the Society 'Rodina'", *Vestnik*, Toronto, May 31, 1981, p. 4.

Immigration in the Late Fifties and Early Sixties

Towards the end of the 1950s, the stream of immigrants ebbed considerably. The Russians who remained in Europe were either the old and sick or those who had adapted to their communities. With the erection of the Berlin Wall, the last opening in the Iron Curtain was closed. This accounted for the low rate of immigrants until the end of the sixties. Small numbers of Russians continued to arrive from various countries of Europe and Asia. Some were people of the so-called "illegal" category of immigrants many of whom were defectors; some were members of visiting delegations who had planned their escape from the USSR during an official trip abroad.

It is difficult to make generalizations about this latter category. Each case is unique and often reflects a personal tragedy, a broken family, loss of rights and property in the USSR. Not knowing the laws of the new country, the "fugitive" sometimes fell victim to forced deportation. For obvious reasons there are no statistics on people who have received political asylum and political refugee status. The situation can sometimes be discerned through scattered newspaper articles, interviews, etc. One example is the statement published in the 1968-69 Annual Report of Manpower and Immigration, which states: "The desertion of seamen who seek a quick and easy entry into Canada, generally in search of freedom, has continued. During 1968, a total of 682 seamen deserters were located and 344 were ordered deported." The report, however, does not specify their nationality.

Once the immigrant obtained political asylum, he was unlikely to seek an audience for his story; rather, he would try to "lose himself" in the population. His contacts with the people around him would be superficial and, as far as the Russian community was concerned, practically nonexistent.

The so-called "legal" immigration from the end of the sixties to the present can be divided into two unequal parts:

1. persons who found themselves abroad, sometimes against their will, as exiles of the Soviet Government—the so-called "dissidents";
2. a mass wave—the so-called "third wave", discussed in the next chapter.

Dissidents

The group of people who left the Soviet Union legally or who were banished by the Soviet government includes those who were in conflict with the Soviet authorities and had acquired the name "dissidents".

Numerically, this is a small category, but it is the one that is most frequently discussed by immigrants of earlier waves, drawing the attention of those circles where the development of events in the Soviet Union is monitored. The statements of dissidents are taken into account and, in some cases, have an influence on public opinion in the West.

On the other hand, it should be noted that the phenomenon of dissidence *per se* is not clearly defined and may consequently be subject to ambiguity. What follows are excerpts from the personal reminiscences of a scientist/dissident* who had spent many years in Soviet concentration camps.

"People who escaped Bolshevik terror during Stalin's time find it hard to understand why a totalitarian government does not destroy its enemies as it did before, but lets them out, thus giving them an opportunity to "slander" the socialist order. Some old immigrants see in it a sign of democratization and weakening of the communist régime; others suspect a 'dirty trick' explaining it approximately as follows:

> Since exit visas from the Soviet Union are controlled by the authorities (Fig. 23), it means that the new emigrant has passed through a government filter. In that case, only those people are let out who, on finding themselves outside the borders of the USSR, will bring benefit to that state. So, is this not a spy? Or is it possibly a 'fifth column'?

Indeed it is true that the Soviet government no longer carries out a policy of mass liquidation of its citizens. But this does not mean that it has become more liberal. There has simply been a change in tactics. Apparently, it is more beneficial for the government to let some dissidents leave the country rather than put them in prisons or camps. But why?

> Among the dissidents one can find people of the most varied opinions. If one were to take a collective letter signed by dissidents, one would find atheists, believers, Ukrainians, Jews and representatives of other ethnic groups, "back to the land" adherents, "westerners" and Slavophiles, etc.

They are united by one factor: a negative attitude towards the actions of the Soviet government—in this case, in the area of the violation of human rights. Outside the USSR they lose this negative

* S.G. Mugué, private publication, 1979.

pivot point and, as particles bearing some charge, they begin to repel one another. There are as many different opinions as there are dissidents. At times, this leads to sharp discussions in the press, resulting in a negative attitude towards dissidents as a whole—they are suspected of over-indulging in exhibitionist behaviour or pathological vanity. This reduces their impact in the eyes of western society and consequently plays into the hands of the Soviet Union.

It is a different matter inside the country. For the Soviet government, the opinions of one person do not have the same significance as does dissidence *per se* which sets an example of disobedience, of not accepting ideological doctrines emanating from "above". Active defenders of human rights annoy the administration not only when they are at liberty, but also in detention, and it is no wonder, therefore, that such "trouble-makers" are exiled at the first opportune moment. In exile, they immediately become objects of attention.

The media publicize sensational cases and forget about them just as quickly. A dissident who becomes an expatriate without uniting with other emigrants does not present a direct danger to the USSR.

On the contrary, Soviet ideology could even be served by a dissident who is disillusioned but who remains a communist by conviction. In the USSR, such a person may consider that the Central Committee of the Communist Party of the USSR has deviated from Lenin's principles, has protested against it, and has thus contributed to discord in Party unity. In Canada, however, by defending the very idea of communism, under the halo of a "combattant against party deviations" in particular, he is adding grist to the mill of local communists. To the Kremlin ideologists, of course, it is important to destabilize the existing order in the West."

The number of "dissidents" in Canada is not as great as in the USA. For obvious reasons, it would be impossible to determine their number. The few who remain in our country, who are not engaged in political, activities are busy establishing a new life for themselves.

F.J. Yaroshevsky

Six

IMMIGRATION IN THE 1970s

*(The so-called "Third Wave")**

The early 1970s marked the beginning of mass emigration from the USSR. Essentially, it comprised Jews going to Israel. There had, of course, been earlier isolated cases of Jews leaving the country. Many, if not most, were people who, despite censorship and mail interference, had established contact with relatives abroad and managed to get permission to leave the Soviet Union.

In 1972-73, some immigrants who left the USSR on a Jewish visa came to North America. The first families to arrive in Canada settled in Toronto and Montreal. Towards the end of the 1970s, approximately 5,000 Soviet citizens immigrated to Canada through Vienna, Rome, Paris and Brussels, where they received assistance from Jewish and Christian (Orthodox and Catholic) organizations and from the UN Refugee Committee.

The historical and technical details of the interim peregrinations of the so-called "third wave" deserve separate research. This article provides a description of the process of adaptation and the analysis of the composition (as related to nationality, religion, age, profession, etc.) of this new Russian-speaking group that arrived in Canada.

Some relevant data (Tables 1, 2, 3, at pages 95-96) have been provided by Mrs. R. Markus of the University of Toronto, who compiled a study sponsored by the Multiculturism Directorate of the

---

* This chapter by F.J. Yaroshevsky is based on the author's personal experience and observations.

Department of the Secretary of State. The information obtained was based on a questionnaire sent to over 2,000 immigrants.

The statistics available cover only a portion of the group but there is no reason to doubt their being fairly representative.

Reasons for Leaving the USSR

The "third wave" emigration can be ascribed to national, religious and socio-political factors characteristic of Soviet life. As stated earlier, the majority of these immigrants were Jewish; only an insignificant number was otherwise definable, owing mainly to mixed marriages.

Until 1967, national identification was regarded as a negative factor in the Soviet Union*. Jewishness was not instilled through education; on the contrary, it was officially suppressed and to call oneself a Jew was to declare oneself a member of a persecuted group.

Then another factor came into play: the Six-Day War in the Middle East stimulated Jewish self-consciousness and made attractive the idea of emigration to Israel which, in turn, led to a more determined effort on the part of Jews to emigrate.

It is important to point out that, in general, a Soviet Jew is educated in Russian culture, speaks Russian and does not actively profess Judaism. Nevertheless, a national stigma hangs over him which is based not on religion, but on racial grounds, according to which Jews are separated from non-Jews.

This explains the fact that, under the harsh conditions of a police state such as exists in the USSR, the children of mixed marriages were inclined, and, indeed, encouraged by their parents to declare themselves as belonging to the more advantageous nationality when obtaining their passports at the age of 16 (except in the case of both parents' having the same nationality, when the young citizen has no choice). Conditions vary in the different republics of the Soviet Union but from a socio-political point of view, it is considered better to register as a Ukrainian, Russian, Tartar or Kalmyk, than as a Jew. Some, however, decline to do so out of a feeling of protest and a sense of dignity. At heart, many Jews who left Russia consider themselves Russian inasmuch as their national and personal traits are formed by a language and culture rooted in tradition which, in this case, is Greek Orthodox Christianity. Upon their arrival in Canada, their dual identification is maintained by the fact

---

* See "Birobidzhan Autonomous Oblast: Jewish State within the USSR", page 98.

that they are listed according to the country of origin as immigrants from Russia and are, therefore, called Russians.

A few actually profess Christianity but most, as already mentioned, have succumbed to Soviet atheistic propaganda and are not interested in religion. Many identify themselves with the Jewish community and, in a certain measure, observe Jewish religious rites. This, however, is done more on a secular than on a religious level; psychologically, they are guided by group instinct. The older, established groups make definite demands on the new arrivals, who, in turn, have to conform to receive social, economic and psychological support.

As regards their reasons for leaving the USSR, the "Third Wave" can be divided into the following categories:

1. Those who left because they wanted to and who had to struggle to get permission. This group makes up the majority and includes those who were persecuted in an indirect fashion (lack of freedom, religious or national discrimination) and/or those who were attracted by the higher standard of living of the non-Communist world and wished to start life anew. The sense of protest and the concealed or manifested identification with Jewishness was often related to limited educational and professional opportunities or concern for their children's' future.

2. Those who were exiled by the KGB. Unable to reconcile themselves with the political regime of the USSR, many took part in distributing "samizdat" literature or participated in other illegal activities, thus placing themselves in danger of being arrested. By leaving the country, they escaped persecution by the KGB. It should be noted that a large number of those who were actually persecuted do not wish to leave but are forced to apply for an exit visa due to strong pressure (deprivation of the means of livelihood, isolation and threat of arrest). Some are simply "turfed out" by force.

3. Those who escaped persecution by the militsia* (OBKHSS — Department of Combatting the Embezzlement of Socialist Property and Speculation). Even people in the professions or those who have a high position can fall victim to the militsia. This includes such persons as doctors or engineers who have, in some way, violated the law in the course of their duties. Let us take the example of a doctor to see how he can get into such a situation. As there is a shortage of hospital beds in the USSR, a patient is normally placed on a long waiting list. If the patient wants to speed things up, he may seek an acquaintance who will arrange for him to be admitted "through the back door". By tacitly sanctioning this, the doctor can see to it that the hospital will benefit: for example, he can request a favour from the organization that employs the patient. Chronic shortages of simple essentials naturally lead to "trade-offs" of this kind; the practice is called "blat" (backdoor influence) and is, of course, illegal. Thus, almost any citizen may

* Militsia — police dealing with criminal offences.

find himself, at some point in his career, a criminal, subject to arrest, indictment and maybe persecution. The person who engages in any type of private enterprise is especially vulnerable. Also, many seek escape out of fear of arrest, especially if they had already been in such a situation. They are then mortally afraid of being sentenced once more to forced labour camps. To a certain extent, this motivating factor coincides with the interests of the OVIR (Visa and Registration Department) which has to declare in its statistical accounts that a certain number of "criminal elements" was permitted to emigrate, thus benefitting Soviet society.

The foregoing can be called the "push out" forces, which complement the "pull in" forces, that is, the attractions of life in the West, with its greater freedoms and high standard of living.

It should be emphasized that the so-called "third wave" differs markedly from the former waves of immigrants. Those who left Russia after the Revolution and Civil War, or after the Second World War, escaped under conditions of acute political and economic instability, often to save their lives. The new immigrants, on the other hand, were plagued by personal problems, lack of food and consumer items, ever-present political repression and blatant violations of elementary rights. Their lives, however, were not endangered as there was no threat of the Great Terror as was the case with their predecessors. Even though they lived under the constant fear of arrest or loss of work, they were not subject to death by firing squad or hanging.

Application for an exit permit, which brings the potential emigrant closer to his goal, is at the same time a dangerous step, opening the door to persecution on the part of the authorities. Should an exit permit be refused, the applicant often loses his job and risks lifelong suffering as friends may avoid him so as not to compromise themselves.

Having finally achieved their goal, many emigrants were inevitably disappointed at first; their dreams clashed with reality. In the past, they had led a settled life, some becoming relatively prosperous and achieving high social status. Their new life, on the other hand, was full of uncertainties.

The most active and gifted succeeded in reaching Canada and established a prosperous life-style. Before 1979, only 5,000 arrived in Canada. This is not a large number, particularly when one considers that 170,000-180,000 people left the Soviet Union between 1971 and 1979.

Adaptation to Canada

Even highly-qualified professionals found life difficult at first. Re-adjustment could take from two to five years. Learning a new language, adapting one's profession to new standards, obtaining a licence to practise medicine, law or engineering was often an insurmountable task for those who found themselves in new surroundings, especially the older people. It was difficult to begin from the bottom — to learn anew, to write exams on subjects in which one was already a recognized specialist. Doctors, for example, had to do night-duty along with interns half their age. This applied to all the professions and particularly to those involved in the humanities which require an intimate knowledge of the language of the new country.

Tradesmen and administrators were more successful in establishing themselves. Salesmen found their fortunes in more or less adventurous enterprises. Restaurants opened and closed; the most long-lived restaurant in Toronto is, for some reason, called "Barmaley", named after the terrible cannibal made famous in one of Kornei Chukovsky's children's stories. But, the owner of the "Rasputin" restaurant did not last long in this business. Nor did the "Doctor Zhivago", a dark place where a candle burned at each table and where prices were said to be exhorbitant. The restaurant soon closed and the sign was taken down much to the delight of those Torontonians who respect Russian literature.

Musicians fared better than most, making up to 10% of the Toronto Symphony Orchestra. Others became insurance agents, salesmen of real estate, shoes, vacuum cleaners or food. Still others found niches as auto-mechanics, house-painters and plumbers. Sportsmen and trainers established professional connections in the congenial world of Canadian sports. In addition to those who do an honest day's work, there are those who have skillfully adapted themselves to the social welfare system offered by a generous Canadian society, sometimes taking advantage of social assistance, cheap government housing, pensions and subsidies. The Soviet citizen is well-trained in being "wise" as far as social aid is concerned.

Some unlucky, socially-isolated single men who broke their symbiotic relationship with their mothers, developed psychoses of paranoia and hallucinosis. They were obsessed with the idea that the police and KGB were still relentlessly pursuing them. For them, this obsession compensated for the feelings of loneliness and abandonment; it was a desperate attempt to draw attention to themselves, to create the illusion of being objects of great concern to the all-powerful state of Canada.

Many fell victim to "émigré" depression, often nostalgic in nature. The psychology behind the development of such a depression can be described as follows:

> For a long time, a person living in the USSR was subject to the influence of two types of forces: the "push out" forces, (trials and

tribulations in the USSR) and those of "attraction", both real and imaginary (the appealing aspects of life in the West).

In the new country, these forces are no longer at work: no pressures, no rush. All an immigrant feels is emptiness and disappointment; he had left behind his friends and relatives, the moral support in this life. All this leads to depression which, in most cases, is fortunately not long-lasting.

At the other extreme, there were a few suicides and attempted suicides, but they were probably no more frequent than those in the population at large. Most immigrants got over their blues, made new friends, formed social ties and got on with the business of living. Many, indeed most, prospered. The children adapted easily and were soon speaking only English. The teenagers, dutifully trying to speak Russian, used anglicized forms of speech and spoke an appalling mish-mash of the two languages.

Still, the old-timers and new arrivals of the Russian-Canadian community maintained contact, assuring cultural continuity. Organizations have been formed from time to time. In Montreal, a Russian-Jewish Society was founded, but did not flourish. The Chekhov Society of Ottawa is open to all who treasure Russian culture. In Toronto, the Corporation of New Canadians from the USSR maintains ties with other Russian societies, organizing lectures and concerts.

Unfortunately, a certain degree of mutual misunderstanding and mistrust sometimes exists between the newly-arrived immigrants and those who came earlier. This feeling consequently leads to alienation or a complete lack of communication. Such attitudes are due to a number of factors — sociological and national/racial*, as well as attitudes toward aspects of everyday life.

The newcomers also exhibit other traits common to all immi-

---

* One obstacle to normal relations between the new immigrants and those who lived abroad for a long time is anti-semitism among some groups of the latter category. These pople hold the view that Jews begot the revolution and that they founded the Soviet régime. It is a fact indeed that among the active participants of the revolution during the first years of Soviet power, there were many Jews in Government positions. What is forgotten, however, is that the dependent and oppressed state of the Jews in Russia prior to 1917 led to their seeking a solution by participating in the revolution. The same was true of other national minorities such as the Latvians, Poles and others. By the end of the 1930s, the Jews once again became scapegoats. Naturally, anti-semitic feelings are not held by everyone and one hopes that they are in a minority. It must also be noted that xenophobia, as any other form of prejudice, is mutual and some recent immigrants have exhibited a distinct tendency to Russophobia.

grants: spy-mania, dissension, distrust and a penchant for informing or gossiping. Such gossip, unfortunately, has a habit of reaching the Soviet Union, causing misunderstandings and arguments between friends and relatives, a fact which only plays into the hands of the Soviet authorities.

TABLE 1

ARRIVAL BY YEAR (Toronto)

Year	Number of People	Percentage
1970	4	0.2
1971	3	0.1
1972	29	1.4
1973	185	9.0
1974	337	16.4
1975	708	34.5
1976	386	18.0
1977-78	356	17.3

Total (1970-78): 2,008

TABLE 2

AGE OF IMMIGRANTS UPON ARRIVAL IN CANADA

Number of People	Age	Percentage
90	1-4	4.4
197	5-11	9.6
108	12-15	5.3
109	16-19	5.3
128	20-25	6.2
419	26-35	20.4
435	36-45	21.2
267	46-55	13.0
128	56-65	6.2
74	65-70	3.6
63	over 70	3.1
31	unknown	1.7

TABLE 3

LAST ADDRESS OF IMMIGRANT

Country	Number	Percentage
Israel	150	7.3
Italy	1,476	71.9
Austria	69	3.4
Belgium	106	5.2
Germany	43	2.1
France	69	3.4
USSR	50	2.4
USA	41	2.0
England	2	0.1
Switzerland	1	0.0
Greece	3	0.1
United Kingdom	38	1.9
Others	4	0.2

TABLE 4*

DISTRIBUTION BY CITY, IN CANADA (1973-1978)

City	Number of People
Toronto	2,470
Montreal	554
Winnipeg	362
Edmonton	204
Calgary	104
Halifax	155
Vancouver	117
Ottawa	59
Regina	34
Windsor	22
London	10
Saskatoon	14
Kitchener	6
Pembroke	4
Sydney (N.S.)	3

* Source: Author's data.

TABLE 5

JEWISH EMIGRATION FROM THE USSR, 1968-1976*

	Number of Jews (1970 Census)	Number of Visas Issued for Isreal	Percentage of Visas Issued in Relation to Jewish Population
USSR total	2,150,700	132,500	6.2%
RSFSR	807,900	15,500	1.9%
Ukraine	777,100	42,100	5.4%
Byelorussia	148,000	2,300	1.6%
Uzbekistan	102,800	8,450	8.2%
Moldavia	98,100	12,300	12.5%
Georgia	55,400	28,700	51.8%
Azerbaijan	41,300	3,000	7.2%
Latvia	36,700	8,100	22.0%
Kazakhstan	27,700	190	0.7%
Lithuania	23,600	9,600	40.7%
Tadzhikistan	14,600	1,600	1.2%
Kirghizia	7,700	200	2.6%
Estonia	5,300	240	4.5%
Turkmenia	3,500	110	3.1%
Armenia	1,000	40	4.0%
Others	—	130	—

Note: Percentage of emigrants who arrived in Vienna and chose to go to the USA or other Western countries:

1973	4.2%
1974	18.8%
1975	37.2%
1976	49.1%

* Source: *The Jews in Soviet Russia since 1917*, edited by Lionel Kochan, Third Edition. Institute of Jewish Affairs, Oxford University Press, London, 1978, pp. 370, 372-3.

Recommended Reading

Kochan, Lionel (ed.), *The Jews in Soviet Russia since 1917*, Institute of Jewish Affairs, Oxford University Press, Third Edition, London, 1978, 431 pages.

Markus, Roberta, *Some Data on Recent Jewish Immigration from the USSR*, unpublished materials, University of Toronto, Toronto, 1978.

Bush, Robert, *Research on Materials of Immigration of Jews from the USSR in Alberta*, Paper presented at the University of Alberta, Edmonton, 1979.

Birobidzhan Autonomous Oblast: Jewish State Within the USSR

Jewish ethnic identity in the Soviet Union has had a strange, convoluted history, and one of its strangest manifestations deserves mention here. Initially Jews were "emancipated" and then encouraged to become assimilated and, like everyone else, at least in theory, irreligious.

In 1928 a sort of Communist Zion was created in eastern Siberia; it eventually became the Jewish Autonomous Oblast, with Birobidzhan, on the Amur River, as its capital city. (The choice of location is said, plausibly enough, to have been influenced by the desire to have a solid Soviet population base close to China and Japan.)

In 1934, Mikhail Kalinin, Chairman of the Presidimum of the RSFSR, acclaimed the new political region as the "first Jewish National State in 2000 years." Nevertheless, the number of Jews who settled there (with, according to one source,* "free transportation, free housing, and free land") had even then passed its peak of about 40,000 persons, and the non-Jewish population was much in the majority. The later 1930s were characterized by an exodus. At the outbreak of the Second World War in 1941, the Jewish settlement was down to 20,000.

Evacuation of the civil population from those parts of European Russia that had been occupied by the Nazis or were so threatened, increased the population east of the Urals. At the beginning of the 1950s, the Jewish population of the Birobidzhan Oblast once more approached 40,000 (out of a total of about 170,000). Then the thrust weakened again, and another exodus took place, one that was to halve the Jewish settlement. Subsequently, the total population seems to have steadied at about 180,000, whereas the Jewish component fell to less than 10%. The Oblast became as unimportant to the mainstream of Jewish life as it was remote geographically.

The mass Jewish emigration from the USSR in the 1970s apparently had no impact. Were they reported or discussed in the Birobidzhan press? We do not know. An American in Moscow at the time stated that the Oblast "is regarded by most Jews as an irrelevant farce". (Years earlier, Khrushchev, in his blunt way, had publicly called it a "failure".)

On the other hand, the settlement has retained its name and identity as a Jewish National State, and it still has radio and newspapers in (*nota bene*) Yiddish. In 1967 the Oblast was awarded the

---

* Lord Marly, *Soviet Culture*, March 1934, p. 5, as quoted by S. Webb.

Order of Lenin for progressiveness. Over the long difficult years there must have been many interesting human stories concerning the settlers and emigrants. No doubt, among the Soviet Jews who have migrated to Canada, there are a few with first-hand knowledge of this remote Jewish state within the USSR.

Notes

The story of the Jewish Autonomous Oblast is not well documented. The above sketch is based, for the most part, on the entries in the principal English-language encyclopedias, in the *Great Soviet Encyclopedia* (Moscow, third edition, 1970; English translation, MacMillan, New York, 1973), and in the *Encyclopedia Judaica* (Israel and New York, 1972). Statistical information varies among the sources; the figures used here are the "most likely" from among all those available. Two books that provided ancillary material are *The Russians*, by Hedrick Smith (Quadrangle/New York Times Book Company, 1976), and *Soviet Communism: A New Civilization?*, by Sidney and Beatrice Webb, 1935, Charles Scribner's Sons, New York, 1936, pp. 149-153.) But the most comprehensive review can be found in Lionel Kochan, *The News in Soviet Russia since 1917*, Institute of Jewish Affairs, London, Oxford University Press, Oxford/London/New York, 1978, Third edition, Biri-Bidzhan, pp.; 7, 70-76, 35-6, 154, 159, 385-6, 389.

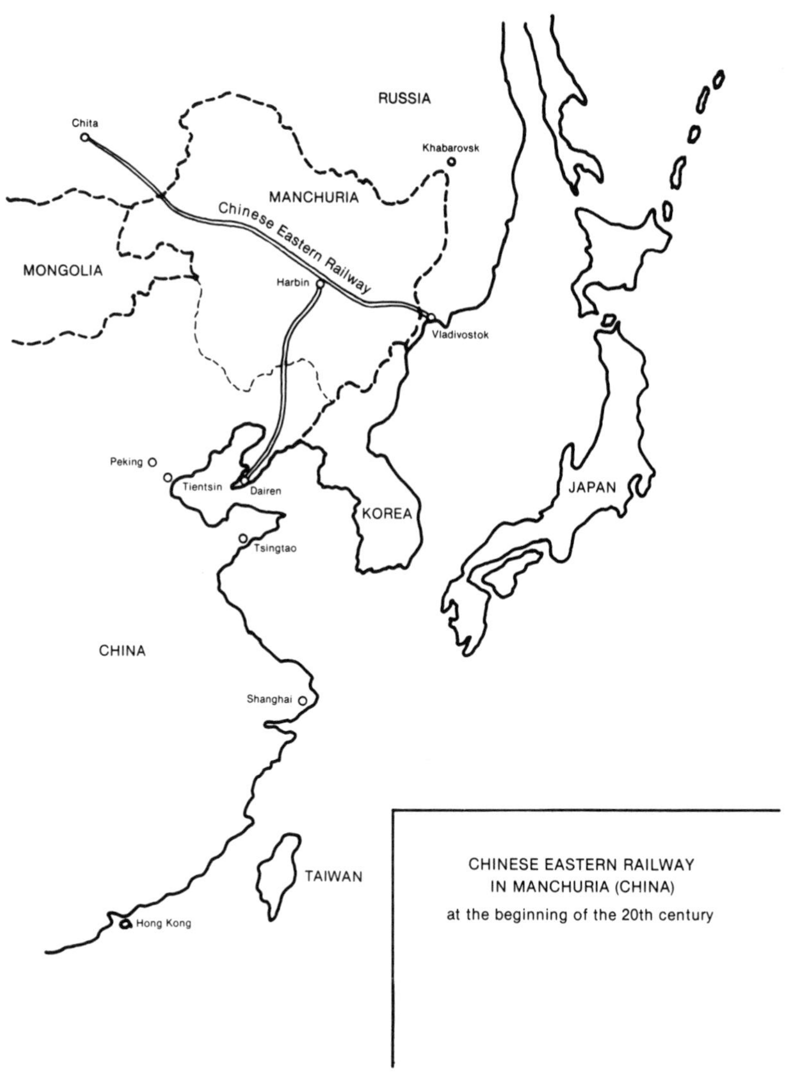
RUSSIA
Chita
Khabarovsk
MANCHURIA
Chinese Eastern Railway
MONGOLIA
Harbin
Vladivostok
Peking
Tientsin
Dairen
KOREA
JAPAN
Tsingtao
CHINA
Shanghai
TAIWAN
Hong Kong
CHINESE EASTERN RAILWAY
IN MANCHURIA (CHINA)
at the beginning of the 20th century

R.F. Piotrovsky

Seven

RUSSIANS FROM CHINA

The Arrival of Russians in China

In the 19th century two countries, Russia and Japan, were interested in penetrating into Manchuria and the Liao-tung Peninsula in Northern China. According to the Treaty of Peking of 1860, which was prepared by the Russian diplomat N.P. Ignatieff, Russia was given the territory between the right bank of the Ussuri River and the Sea of Japan (Primor'e)* and the right to joint navigation along the Sungari River in Manchuria. In addition, trade tariffs at the Chinese border were eliminated.[1]

Immediately after the Sino-Japanese war of 1894-1895, the Chinese Imperial Government, fearing Japanese more than Russian expansionist plans,[2] made a secret pact with the latter[3] and in 1896 signed a second agreement giving Russia the right to build the Chinese Eastern Railroad and to operate it for 80 years.[4] According to this agreement, a strip of land, 25 kilometres to each side of the line running the full length of the railroad, was recognised as Russian territory, giving Russia extra-territorial rights such as the right to maintain its own police, monetary and postal systems, courts, city administration, etc.[5] The railroad was to be built from the city of Chita in the west, through Manchuria to Vladivostok in the east, and from Harbin, the administrative centre of the road, southward to the Liao-tung peninsula.[6]

---

* Primor'e is the maritime region running north of the Korean and Chinese borders to about 48′ N., just south of the Amur River.

In addition to providing protection from Japanese aggression, the railroad insured rapid and intensive development of Manchuria which was the most under-populated and under-developed part of the Chinese Empire.

The first large groups of Russians headed for the construction sites of the Chinese Eastern Railroad began arriving in China between 1897 and 1903.[8] During the construction period, the Russian population grew rapidly to several tens of thousands. The high rates of pay and excellent working conditions made working in Manchuria very attractive.

From 1917 through 1922, a civil war raged in Russia between the Red Army of the Communists and the White Army defending the old system of government. The civilian population of Siberia* and the Russian Far East, following the retreating Far Eastern White Army, rushed into Manchuria to save themselves from the Bolsheviks. A much smaller number of refugees reached Sinkiang (Eastern Turkestan). Some went by water to the cities of central China: Dairen, Tienstin, Shanghai and others. As there was no census in China at that time, there are no precise data on the Russian population but it is estimated that in the 1920s there were about 250,000 Russians in China.[9] After the establishment of the Soviet régime in the Priamur'e** territory in 1922, there was a small but steady flow of refugees from that area which continued until 1945.

Living Conditions of Russians in China

The unexpected incursion of Caucasian foreigners, and refugees at that, did not exactly delight the Chinese Government. Up to that time, foreigners had come to China with money and ambitious plans. The Russian refugees had neither and they found themselves on the lowest rung of the social ladder. In 1922, after the fall of the Omsk Government,[10] the Chinese Eastern Railroad lost its extra-territorial rights and all Russians in China became stateless, politically unprotected apostates whom no one wanted.

The Russians' living conditions were to a large extent determined by their place of residence. Two trends developed: life in Manchuria, and life in the cities of central China. In Manchuria, where there was practically no industry, no system of taxation and

---

* Siberia is the Russian territory from the Ural Mountains east to the Pacific Coast.

** Priamur'e: the basin of the middle and part of the lower reaches of the Amur River.

extremely cheap labour, all sorts of enterprises blossomed and the Russians gradually adapted themselves to their new environment. In the 1920s, there were about 150,000 Russians, several thousand other Europeans and 350,000 Chinese in Harbin, a city built in 1898 by the Russians for the central administration of the Chinese Eastern Railroad.[11] The remaining 100,000 Russians lived in towns and villages along the railroad and in the cities of central China. Between 1920-1940, dozens of churches and schools, thousands of workshops, stores, factories, restaurants, hospitals, recreation facilities, cinemas, libraries, technical schools, universities, and printing houses for books, magazines and newspapers were built in Harbin alone. There were Russian operas, operettas, symphony orchestras and theatres. Smaller towns and villages provided moderate amenities and a secure life. Everywhere was the old life-style of pre-revolutionary Russia with all its traditions, world outlook and customs.[12] (Figs. 13, 14.)

In the cities of central China, however, and in particular in Tientsin and Shanghai, there were large foreign concessions with a typical Western European, mainly Anglo-Saxon, life-style. Here there was no Manchurian "life in clover" or freedom of action but, instead, a lot of snobbism and intolerance, and the new immigrants had to endure a great deal of badgering and persecution.[13] But even here, after several difficult years of adaptation to the new conditions, the Russians emerged as victors in the arena of life. They established various types of offices, beauty salons, restaurants, cafes and shops. Many found good positions in large American, British or French companies. Medical doctors, dentists and lawyers obtained recognition of their credentials from the authorities and started their practices. Shanghai became the cultural centre for the Russian population of central China. While retaining their "Russianness", they acquired some Western European traits.

A characteristic of all Russians in China, and in Manchuria in particular, was their complete lack of assimilation. This can be simply explained by three factors:

1. The great gap between the Chinese and Russian cultures;
2. No need to adopt another culture;
3. The large size of the Russian population.

This, of course, applies to the majority. Those Russians who, because of their work or vocation, had to learn the Chinese language, folklore and way of life, did so without difficulty.

It is interesting to note, as a paradox, that all the Chinese who provided services for the Russians (sales people, hairdressers, police officers, taxi-drivers, office workers) spoke Russian fluently, though with an accent, and some young Chinese even learned to speak Russian perfectly.

Gradually, the Chinese people and authorities saw that it was easy to get along with Russians, that they did not cause trouble but provided work opportunities thus facilitating the economic development of Manchuria. It seemed that this symbiosis could continue forever, but a twist in history disrupted this newly-born equilibrium.

The Japanese Occupation

In 1931 the Japanese occupied Manchuria.[14] In 1932 they found a person named Henry Pu-yi living in Tientsin who was the last offspring of the Manchurian Ching dynasty. They declared him chief ruler and, in 1934, Emperor of the new state of Manchukuo.[15] In fact, however, all aspects of the new state were controlled by the Japanese military clique. The capture of Siberia was the next stage in their plans of aggression in which the Russian immigrants were to play a particular role.

To control the Russian population, the Japanese forced them to join an organization which, in addition to carrying out a census of the population, supervised employment, food supplies, resettlement, charitable institutions, jurisprudence and education of the youth. Information regarding all activities of this organization had to be presented daily to the Japanese military mission.[16] Russian youths were forcibly recruited to attend special military schools, to be later sent on reconnaissance and sabotage operations in the USSR. Students and adults were forced to learn the Japanese language and attend meetings.

From the beginning of the War in the Pacific in 1940, the living conditions of the Russians deteriorated. They had to wear a numbered identification badge when leaving their house and failure to observe this rule led to unpleasant consequences and punishment. A list was made of American and English gramophone records that had to be destroyed as "enemy music"; the opera, "Madame Butterfly" was banned because it showed a Japanese woman humiliated by an American. Shortwave reception was prohibited and this band was removed from radios. Listening to such broadcasts was punishable by death, but only after the offender was tortured to find out who had readjusted the radio, who else listened to the broadcasts, etc.

Everyone in the country was supervised by two organizations: the military mission and the gendarmerie, whose operations could be compared to those of the Gestapo or the KGB. Japanese spymania turned every white person into a real or potential Soviet or

American spy. People were sent to torture chambers without any reason; a simple report would be sufficient. Torture was used during interrogation, people were forced to become informers and recruited into military units.[17]

From the beginning of the war in the Pacific all food products went to meet military requirements: meat, flour, groats, fats and milk products disappeared from the market. Essential food items were rationed. Rice was reserved for the Japanese and bread, in limited quantities, was available only for Europeans; sugar was rationed to one pound a month, vegetable oil, a half-pound, etc. Everyone hated the Japanese, took delight in each rumour of a Japanese defeat and waited for the end of the war, expecting a return to a peaceful life in Nationalist China. Events turned out to be quite different, however.

The Soviet Occupation

On August 9, 1945,[18] following a seven-day war with an already-defeated Japan, the Soviet Army occupied Manchuria. As the Soviets always considered the Russian emigrant to be "Enemy No. 1", their military authorities began to arrest people either because their names appeared on special Soviet lists, acting on information from informants, or simply for no apparent reason. They were accused of co-operation with the Japanese, Americans, Germans or British or charged with anti-Soviet activities, statements or attitudes, as well as former participation in the White Army or in anti-Soviet partisan groups. So as not to miss anyone, the Soviets operated on the principle that it was better to have ten innocent people "in the hand" rather than one guilty one "in the bush".

There was no order whatsoever: what was decreed by one commandant was contradicted by another. Mostly men were arrested, but women and even children were not excluded. Robberies and rape were rampant. All those arrested were sent in freight cars to the Soviet Union where, after a trial was staged, all were sentenced to slave labour in camps for terms of ten years or more.[19] Most of them died before the end of their term and those who were fortunate enough to survive, remained in the Soviet Union to die of natural causes. No-one ever returned to their families in China. The Soviet Government, of course, does not publish statistical data on the number of Russians taken to camps from China. The author estimates that these numbered from 20,000 to 30,000 people.

Stripping Manchuria of all its plants and factories, which were dismantled, disassembled and sent to the Soviet Union under the guise of reparations from Japan,[20] the Soviet "liberation" army left Manchuria on April 6, 1946, handing the territory, now completely barren, to their "younger brothers", the Eighth Chinese Peoples' Army.

The Chinese Communist Army was highly disciplined and life began to return to normal. The mass arrests of Russians ceased. Only a few Russians were sent from Manchuria to the USSR between the end of the Soviet occupation and 1957. People no longer feared walking in the streets at night and robberies and rape ceased completely. The Chinese began to restore the industries looted by the Soviets and the Russians started to work on reconstruction in shops, offices and factories as specialists who knew the local conditions.

Soon, however, a new wave of arrests began, this time affecting the Chinese. Property was confiscated and people were made to repent all sorts of political, economic and ideological sins. They had fallen victim to the excesses common to all totalitarian regimes. For a while the Russian population was left alone but everyone soon began to understand that there would be no future for them in China. In the meantime, Soviet Consulates let it be known that all Russians who had not taken out Soviet passports would be forcibly sent to the USSR and that non-Soviet citizens would not be accepted for work. Thus, the greater majority was obliged to take out what was for them, hated Soviet passports. These passports were, in fact, fictitious, since they could not be used for entry into the USSR even if anyone wanted to go there.[21] In fact, it was necessary for the Soviet Government to keep such Soviet citizens in Manchuria, to be used at some convenient time to provoke an incident which would permit the USSR to reoccupy Manchuria under the pretext of defending its citizens. The Chinese understood this very well and this was one of the reasons that later led to a cooling of the "great friendship between the two fraternal people".

After the war, when Russians in Manchuria were being arrested and sent to the Soviet Union, those living in the cities of central China were subjected to repression by the Kuomintang authorities who did not like the fact that, during the Sino-Japanese War, Russians, being dependent on the Japanese occupation forces, had to carry out the latter's orders. Arrests took place though not on the massive scale seen in Manchuria.

By the end of the forties, Russians from other Chinese cities gathered in Shanghai. In all, there were about 40,000[22], most of whom were unemployed, leading a miserable existence, being maintained at first by UNRRA (UN Relief and Rehabilitation Administration) and then by the IRO (International Refugee Organization). The few who had relatives or friends abroad obtained visas and left China. The rest awaited their fate.

Here, Soviet authorities did not have the physical or economic power to force the Russians to take out Soviet citizenship as they had done in Manchuria. The Soviet Consulate, therefore, took a different approach. They let out the rumour that those who did not take out Soviet passports would be forcibly deported, that life in the Soviet Union had changed, that there was no longer punishment for past political sins and that all those who wished could go to the USSR, where they would be employed in their particular fields of endeavour. As a result, in 1947, several thousand "new" Soviet citizens were transported to the USSR on five ships. That ended the matter.[23] There were no more volunteers.

On the eve of the Communist capture of Shanghai in 1949, the IRO evacuated 5,500 people to a small uninhabited island called Tubabao which was offered as a temporary refuge by the Philippine Republic.[24] After that, the fate of the Russians who remained was comparable to that of the Russians in Manchuria, except that they remained in China under the care of the IRO. Those who got to the island had to endure a harsh tropical climate, typhoons and moral depression for four years until they dispersed among the countries that granted them visas — Australia, Paraguay, the USA, Canada and Brazil.

In the meantime, the free world learned about the Russians in China and attempts were made to help them out of their disastrous situation. Russian organizations in Europe, Canada and the USA awakened public opinion and appealed to their respective governments. As a result, the World Council of Churches opened an office in Hong Kong and started to obtain visas for Russians in various countries.

Wishing to rid themselves of the Russians, particularly those with Soviet citizenship, Chinese Communists readily agreed to such an arrangement. They did not care where the Russians went as long as they left China. By this time, Sino-Soviet relations were such that the Soviets could not simply order China not to let the Russians migrate to the West; on the other hand, China could not directly refuse such a request either. In all probability, the question was resolved through compromise whereby the Chinese agreed to keep the Russians from leaving for a while. The aim of the Soviet authorities was to create the impression of a hopeless situation for Russians in China. At the same time, all Soviet Consulates announced that those who wanted to go to develop virgin lands in the USSR were free to do so. Although this was not the Soviets' initial aim, given the situation that had developed, they considered that it was better to let the Russians go to the Soviet Union than have them migrate to the West. Many families, driven to despair and not seeing any way out of their situation, left for the Soviet Union against their wishes and found themselves on virgin lands under conditions much worse than they had experienced in China.

A larger number of Russians who remained endured adversity,

unemployment and deprivation; but they waited. Although they were deliberately misinformed, they knew that the Soviets did not have the power to send them to the Soviet Union as they had done in 1945. Nor could they stop them from leaving China. They knew that time was on their side.

In the meantime, the Soviet Consulates began releasing names of small numbers of people from their consular lists, to whom the Chinese readily gave exit visas. Finally, the time came, in 1957, when the Chinese police, no longer seeking permission from the Soviet Consulates, started to issue exit visas to all those going to the West. By this time, most of those who wished had entry visas to various countries (mainly Australia and Brazil); elderly people went to Belgium and Switzerland where they could find accommodation in establishments for the aged.

Thus, by the beginning of the "Cultural Revolution" in 1965, when China was completely isolated from the rest of the world, almost all the Russians had left. The several thousand who remained were subjected to humiliation and violence from enraged mobs who vented their anger and hatred against all foreigners, and Soviets in particular.

After all the changes in the political course of China, the few Russians who were still alive were able to apply for visas in the newly-opened foreign consulates. According to information published in the Canadian press,[25] they all had to leave China for any country that would give them refuge, thus leaving forever the country that had once been their second homeland.

So ended the unprecedented history of a nation within a nation that lasted for 80 years and produced several generations of Russians among whom were many writers, scientists, musicians, poets and stars in the performing arts. Some of them, like Yul Brynner from Harbin, are well known throughout the world.[26]

Pre-War Immigration To Canada

The first immigration of Russians from China to Canada started in 1924, owing to the coincidence of a number of factors that must be elucidated in order to have a correct understanding of the event.

Before 1917, there were several tens of thousands of prosperous Russian employees of the Chinese Eastern Railroad living with their families in Manchuria. After the October Revolution of 1917, there was an annual flow of thousands of refugees who wanted to avoid the terror of the Red Army. These were primarily civilians from Siberia and the Far East. After the fall of the last anti-communist

IMMIGRATION OF RUSSIANS FROM CHINA
from 1924 to 1971
(including offspring born outside of China)

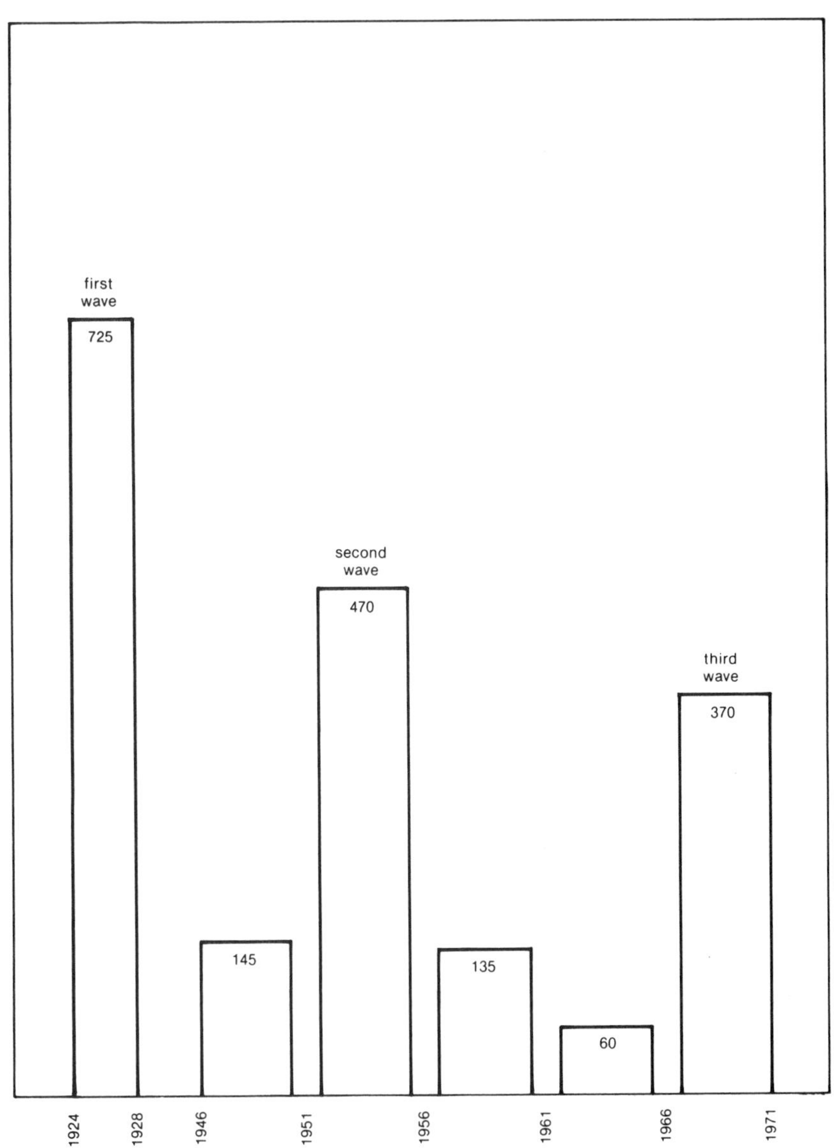

Omsk Government in 1922, the number of refugees increased owing to the disbanding of units of the Far Eastern White Army. As a result, about 250,000 Russians had gathered in Manchuria by 1923, more than half of whom were in Harbin.[27] Only a small number were employed, primarily on the C.E.R. After the establishment of the joint administration of the railroad, one of the terms of the agreement was that Russian employees would have to take out Soviet citizenship.* As a result, many Russians who did not want to accept this provision left their work.[28]

The situation was difficult: there was overpopulation and unemployment; life was precarious, even to the point of starvation; there were no prospects for the future. In addition, Chinese-Soviet relations had become stretched to the limit and the worst possible consequences were expected, even the occupation of Manchuria by the Red Army.

During approximately the same period, Canada was experiencing a labour shortage in agriculture, particularly in seasonal harvest work in Manitoba, Saskatchewan and Alberta.[29] Up to 1923, this shortage was made up by cheap, modest and "convenient" Chinese immigrants. That year, however, the House of Commons adopted a bill[30] to terminate Chinese immigration; it was given Royal Assent on October 2, 1923.[31] The highly-desirable British immigrants were more expensive and did not show much enthusiasm for coming to Canada at that time.[32] The Canadian Pacific Railroad, which was entrusted with recruiting immigrants, opened offices in Europe and other parts of the world. Such offices already existed in China, and because Canada decided to try letting in Russian immigrants, there was no shortage of those wishing to leave China for Canada.

In fact, the presence of Colonel Orest Dmitrievich Dournovo of the Russian Imperial Army among the Russian refugees in Manchuria could be considered an important factor in the success of the whole enterprise. Dournovo was a member of one of the most prominent aristocratic families of Russia, a grandson of the tutor of Tsar Alexander III and director of the first Russian Cadet Corps. A talented mathematician and author of a philosophic religious work, entitled "Thus spoke Christ", Dournovo also had a talent for organization and an unquenchable drive for activity. He was fair and just in his relations with everyone[33] and was well-known outside the boundaries of his native land.

An important role in Canada's decision was played by the organizations and private individuals who persistently petitioned Ca-

* Chinese-Soviet agreement of 1924 on the joint administration of the C.E.R. According to this agreement, employees of the Railroad had to be Chinese or Soviet citizens.

nadian authorities to permit the immigration of Russians from China. They included the Salvation Army, the YMCA, the Methodist pastor R.E. Fairbairn, the Russian-Orthodox priest V. Gindlin, Prince Alexander Golitzin and Captain Robert MacGrath. Of particular significance was the Russian Refugee Relief Society of America which gave a great deal of financial aid without which immigration would not have been possible.[34] At that time, as Canada was afraid of the penetration of communist agents into the country, only organizations of non-Russian origin were trusted. The exceptions were Russians such as Prince Golitzin and Colonel Dournovo who, because of their origins and past performance, could in no way be suspected of being communist sympathizers.

The C.P.R. showed great enthusiasm in recruiting future Russian immigrants from Manchuria. Its agency in Harbin placed large advertisements in local newspapers stating that all those who wished could apply for immigration to Canada through this agency. According to documents presented by the Commissioner of the Russian Red Cross in Harbin, Prince Alexander Golitzin and the executive secretary of the Russian Refugee Relief Society of America, Captain Robert P. MacGrath, sixteen thousand Russians registered to immigrate to Canada and the United States. According to biographical data, however, only one thousand five hundred of them had the required minimum of two hundred dollars in Canadian funds.

Their scandalous poverty, however, did not protect them from abuse by greedy entrepreneurs who, seeing opportunities of turning a fast buck, began selling them so-called farmland in remote areas. The conditions of sale were extortionate: sight unseen and a five-hundred dollar down-payment. Fortunately, these activities were exposed in Harbin newspapers and in correspondence addressed to Colonel Dournovo and to Mr. Colley, an official of the C.P.R.[35]

Before the immigration of Russians to this country, the Canadian government did not have any experience with political refugees. Apparently the very concept of a special status for refugees did not exist at the time. This can probably explain the cold and completely indifferent attitude towards Russian refugees from China. All Russians in Manchuria were regarded as ordinary individuals applying for admission to Canada. One need only recall the treatment of recent political refugees from Chile or the "boat people" from Vietnam to see how things have changed in the past half century.

To avoid any chance of the immigrants becoming a financial burden on the government, the Canadian Minister of Immigration and Colonization, W.J. Egan, established the rule that, on arrival from China, all Russians had to work in agriculture for two years and to have at least four hundred dollars in cash to acquire the necessities of life in Canada.[36] (This was a lot of money by Canadian standards at the time and completely unattainable under refugee conditions). In general, the arrival of the Russians, as a group, into Canada was considered undesirable; the Ministry, therefore, preferred to examine requests on an individual basis. The suggestion of guarantors that at least the fathers of the families be allowed to work in cities was not accepted by the Ministry.[37]

Finally, after several months of negotiations between the employers and the government, Ottawa approved visas for a group of thirty families on the condition that the behaviour of all members correspond to established intellectual, moral and physical requirements, that they agree to work two years in agriculture on land belonging to the Canadian Pacific Railroad in Alberta and that, on arrival, they could show a total of twenty-five thousand dollars.[38]

In addition, the Russian Refugee Relief Society of America undertook not to burden the government with any requests for financial assistance for the immigrants and, to ensure greater success, obligated each member of the group to bear the responsibility for the entire group.[39]

The fact that the majority of refugees who fled to Manchuria came from Western Siberia and the Volga Valley, which supplied wheat not only for all of Russia but for Europe as well, apparently led the immigration authorities to believe that all the refugees were former farmers.[40] This was not so. Apart from a group of "Old Believers"*, the majority of refugees did not have the slightest idea about agriculture.

The screening and selection of future immigrants in Harbin was entrusted to V.H. Dmohovsky, the representative of the Russian Refugee Relief Society of America in Canada and to Colonel O. Dournovo.[41] According to the latter's daughter, he was the only one who carried out this task.[42] He was also to head the first group on its journey to Canada.

That group was to be an experiment for Canada and the fate of the Russians who were left behind and who wanted to escape the desperate situation in Manchuria depended on its success. Being well aware of the situation, Colonel Dournovo, for that very reason, selected Old Believers who were really grain farmers, unpretentious and obedient.

Because of domestic problems, nine families who were supposed to go with the first group were delayed. The others, twenty-one families comprising 116 people, arrived in Vancouver on June 16, 1924 on the S.S. *Empress of Russia* (Fig. 15). Their first day in Canada was clouded by an unpleasant incident. The immigrants

* A religious group which recognizes only the unrevised Old and New Testaments.

could muster only $7,500. As the remaining $17,500 promised by the Russian Refugee Relief Society of America had not been deposited on time with the immigration authorities, debarkation was denied. The situation was saved by the timely arrival of a representative of the colonization department of the CPR who convinced the authorities that the above-mentioned Society was in a position to deposit the required sum of money. Everything went smoothly, and the New Canadians left by train for Alberta.[43]

Upon their arrival in Wetaskiwin, the first Russian colonists from China were given a friendly welcome by the local population. The ladies prepared a luncheon at which welcoming speeches were given by the mayor of the City (Mr. Moan), a member of Parliament (Mr. E.E. Sparks), members of the Kiwanis Club and others. The Kiwanis Club undertook to transport the settlers to their new place of residence, a camp located on the Battle River where tents had already been erected.

After prayers in the main tent-cafeteria the settlers went to work on constructing houses,[44] but on the fourth day after their arrival, there was a snow fall. That was on July 3 and although the old-timers maintained that this had never happened before and the snow did melt quickly, the occurrence did arouse some fear[45] and five people fled to the city. The rest went to work. After several months, the tents were replaced by wooden houses, work shops and a large central building of 3,360 square feet (Fig. 16). It served as a cafeteria and recreation hall and was also intended to be the home of the next group of immigrants.

Life in the camp proceeded under the scrutiny of Dournovo who was at the same time selecting people for the groups to come. He knew that the impression created by the first group would be the key to further immigration. The impressions were good. Headed by Commissioner Donald, the supervisory commission of the Canadian Pacific Railroad reported to the Immigration Department that the enterprise was completely successful. Finally, even the Canadian Government began to change its views of Russians and willingly let them into the country, on condition that they come under the patronage of the CPR and the Russian Refugee Relief Society of America.

Between 1924 and 1926, sixty-two families, comprising 625 people, came to Canada. The majority were screened, selected and organized by Dournovo and his trusted people in Harbin.[46] In addition to the commission of Dournovo and the Canadian Pacific Railroad, which had been approved by the Canadian Government, other organizations became involved with the immigration of Russians from China. These were the Canadian Pacific Railroad (without Colonel Dournovo), its eternal competitor, the Canadian National Railroad, the League of Nations and the Ukrainian Immigration Association. It started to look as though the main criterion became the number of immigrants to be brought in and not their individual selection.[47] The last group of 11 families left China for Canada in July, 1928.[48] All were transported to Alberta to work on farms where, after the expiration of the two-year term of the contract, some remained in agriculture, owning their own farms (Fig. 17). Others headed for the city. During the Depression, those who bought farms were forced to sell them and move to Vancouver, Calgary, Winnipeg and other cities. It is interesting to note that none of them came to Eastern Canada.

In addition to the above-mentioned groups, there were individual cases of immigrants who, during the 1920s, came to stay with relatives or friends who were established and could guarantee to support them. These immigrants were likely no more than several dozen.

When the war in the Pacific began, there was no way for Russians to emigrate. Thus ended the first (pre-war) wave of Russians immigrating to Canada from China.

Post-War Immigration

Statistics Canada records the following information on all residents: country of birth, ethnic origin, citizenship, religion, mother tongue and language used at home. It is quite obvious that none of these indicators, taken alone, could identify Russians from China. By country of birth, some would be identified with the Chinese; by ethnic origin and language, with Russians in general; by citizenship, they would not fit into any group as most of those coming to Canada were stateless. Religious affiliation and language used at home are not always specific and, therefore, could not be used as indicators.

The most reasonable approach, under the circumstances, would be to consider two indicators: the country of birth and the mother tongue, thereby extracting information using the key words: "foreigners, born in China, mother tongue — Russian." In conjunction with other information, such data could be used to establish accurately the total number of Russian immigrants who had, at one time, lived in China, starting from the time of their first arrival in Canada in June 1924 up to the last census in Canada in 1971. During this 48-year period, a total of about two thousand people came to Canada from China. They did not come in a continuous stream, but in three distinct waves,[49] the first of which has already been described.

The second wave began to arrive after the end of the war in the Pacific. In contrast to the first, it consisted of Russians who were in the non-communist parts of central China (not from Manchuria, in northern China). For most Russians who were living in communist-occupied Manchuria, there was not the faintest hope of going anywhere. By 1949, the first families from Shanghai, the city where all Russians in China wanted to live, were heading for Canada sponsored by relatives or friends. During the next two or three years they were joined by refugees from the camps on the island of Tubabao in the Phillipines where 5,500 Russians had been transferred from Shanghai in 1949.[50]

The second wave (1949-1957) numbered more than 700 people; about half of them settled in British Columbia, the rest divided equally between Ontario and Quebec. However, many of those who went to the last two provinces soon moved to British Columbia. By that time, Canada had acquired a great deal of experience with Russian post-war immigration from Europe, and the question of political refugees from China was no longer the problem it had been during the period of the first wave. Moreover, the second-wave immigrants differed greatly from those of the first. They all spoke English, many of them very well, and were "westernized" to a considerable degree since they had spent many years in close contact with the people inhabiting the international concessions of Shanghai, Tientsin, and other cities of international significance in China. Because of this, they readily acquired work in their special fields. Among them were dentists, accountants, medical doctors, actors and actresses, engineers and businessmen. Those who were not specialists found work as waiters, sales people, or organized guilds of house painters, opened hairdressing shops and confectioneries. In time, they fused with the immigrants of the first wave.

The third wave of Russian immigrants from China began to arrive in Canada in the middle sixties. Some came from Australia, Brazil, Paraguay, Argentina and Chile to which they had immigrated earlier. The school-aged children of these families were born in those countries. Beginning in 1966, Russians who were still in China during the "Cultural Revolution" could not even dream of coming to Canada directly from China. Basically, immigrants of the third wave came to Canada as a result of the immigration policy of the time which admitted people who had the professions required by Canada. By 1971, about 350 such people entered Canada. After China renewed its relations with the West several years ago, not a single Russian came to Canada from China or such an occurrence would have become known to the Russian community.

An interesting group in this wave are the Russians from Sinkiang province who belong to the Pentecostal sect. They live in a strongly cohesive and closed society. There are about 150 members in London, Ontario and another 150 equally divided between

Vancouver and Vernon, British Columbia. Their history deserves to be told in greater detail.

To save themselves from Stalin's terror and hunger during the early thirties, the people of the Soviet Union living in the region bordering on the Chinese province of Sinkiang began to cross the boundary and settle in the towns of that province. Sinkiang, the westernmost part of China, is bordered by Mongolia, Kazakhstan, Kashmir and Tibet and includes part of the Tien-Shan mountains and the Gobi Desert. Several tens of thousands fled to this region, many of whom settled in the town of Kul'dja. They lived well, working in trade, handicrafts, in shops and factories.

During the summer of 1952, however, the Chinese government started a policy of oppression. As a result, some Russians who lived in Sinkiang fled back across the border to the Soviet Union, although most of them were deported to China. By 1956, the Soviet government began to force these same Russians to go and develop virgin lands in Kazakhstan. Many went, and found themselves under inhuman conditions. Others, including the members of the Pentecostal sect, did not return to the Soviet Union hoping somehow to get to the West. Secretly, and in small groups, they started to make their way to Shanghai. In the late fifties and early sixties they moved to Australia and other countries. Slowly, they started coming to Canada, family after family, having found out that there were Russian Pentecostals and prayer houses. In Canada, they are now all employed in the production sector and are satisfied with their puritanical morals and their non-association with people of other faiths.[51]

All people have a basic and unvarying aspiration — to provide the most reliable and comfortable living conditions for their families and themselves and to satisfy their spiritual requirements. The latter include the performance of religious rites, observation of customs, various forms of entertainment and the opportunity to meet with others of the same faith. For the immigrants, these needs are first satisfied by the ethnic community which brings together its members on the basis of a common language, origin and interests. If one also keeps in mind that, before their arrival in Canada, Russians from China, with few exceptions, were either white or blue-collar workers living in large cities, it is understandable why, in Canada, most of them settled in urban areas. The development of industry provides opportunities for employment and the gathering of compatriots facilitates social contacts.

Almost all of the first-wave Russian immigrants who arrived from Manchuria during the twenties settled in Vancouver and became the first large group of Russians in that city. They formed the core of a Russian community which subsequent Russian immigrants, from China and other countries, simply joined. In contrast to this, Russians emigrating from China during the fifties and sixties settled in such cities as Toronto and Montreal, joining earlier "non-Chinese" Russian communities. Thus, as a result of emigration from China, Vancouver, where, before 1924, there were only several dozen political refugees and revolutionaries from Imperial Russia who were considered by both the Russian and Canadian governments as "undesirable elements", now has the largest Russian population.

As a rule, the social life of Russians in the free world begins with the organization of an Orthodox Church. In 1925, Father Anton Pokrovsky, a Russian priest from China, organized a parish in Vancouver and, in the same year, a small house was bought with donations from the community. The parishioners soon converted it into a house of worship. A parish school, a ladies' aid group and a choir were also established. As there were outstanding singers from major theatres in Russia, an experienced choir director was not hard to find. As there was not enough space to accommodate the ever-increasing parish, a large new church was built in 1928. In 1954, after the arrival of the second wave of immigrants from Shanghai, an even larger church was built, which still exists as the Church of the Holy Resurrection, the largest of the three Russian-Orthodox churches in Vancouver today.

In 1925, the Russian community established a program of cultural and educational activities. Concerts, meetings, lectures and plays were organized in a building associated with the church; performances were put on by amateur orchestras and the choir. In 1956 a Russian Community Centre was formed. Three years later an old cinema was bought with money borrowed from members of the Community Centre. Modified to meet the needs of the society, the centre is still in operation today and has a balalaika orchestra, dance group, choir and Russian-language school for children and adults.

In addition to the above, a Russian-Orthodox Society was established in 1935 to take care of the legal and financial responsibilities for the Church of the Holy Resurrection. A member for many years and now a president of this society, Mrs. I.A. Rozvalyaeff, gave the author data concerning the life of the Russian colony in Vancouver, thus rendering an inestimable service.[52]

Based on many years of observation and personal contacts with representatives of Russians living in various countries before they immigrated to Canada, it is the author's opinion that the Russians from China have a number of typical characteristics. They are enterprising but not pretentious, neither snobs nor money-grubbers, generous and relatively independent. They hold values that transcend the material and have a highly-developed sense of personal sacrifice for the benefit of the collective group. In their political views, they are confirmed anti-communists.

Although it is not within the scope of this book to provide a detailed account of all those who made a contribution to the culture and development of their adopted homeland, a few names stand out among the Russians who emigrated to this country from China.

Of the Dournovo clan alone, one daughter, Sophia Orestovna Grand-Maison, is a sculptor whose eight-foot statue of Sir John A. MacDonald decorates a square in Regina. Another daughter, Maria Orestovna von Rosenbach, is the author of the book "Family Kaleidoscope" which describes the experiences of her entire family during their flight from the Bolshevik regime. A grandson, Professor Orest Kochkanov, is the dean of mathematics at Dalhousie University. Another, Orest Grand-Maison, is a painter who enjoys considerable popularity throughout Canada. A third grandson, Bob Pickle, was a member of Canada's basketball team at the Olympic Games.[53]

The Opera Association of Vancouver was the offspring of a small group founded by the bass, A.M. Ustinovich. Many contemporary Canadian singers such as Milla Andrew (daughter of the precentor E.A. Andreyev) studied at the studio of music and opera of Anna Ivanovna Nickols in Vancouver. A number of well-known ballet dancers graduated from the ballet school directed by Lydia Karpova (formerly with the Russian Imperial Theatre); another ballet school offered classes by Svetlanov.

In the academic field, Sergei Rozval founded the Slavic Department at the University of Alberta.

An interesting personal history is that of Dr. G.M. Volkoff who, as a boy, lived with his parents in Canada for three years. In 1927, they took him to China. After finishing his secondary education he returned to Canada in 1930 and registered at the University of British Columbia where he was awarded a gold medal on graduation. In 1940 he received a doctor's degree from Berkeley University in California after working for four years under the supervision of Professor Oppenheimer. Since then, he has taught mathematics at the University of British Columbia, retiring in 1979 with the rank of dean. He participated in the preliminary theoretical work to establish the Crown Corporation, Atomic Energy of Canada Limited.[54]

Notes

1. Walsh, W. B., *History of the Modern World*, University of Michigan, pp. 266-268.
2. *Encyclopaedia Britannica*, "Manchuria", 1973/74 ed., Vol. 11, p. 437.
3. Harcave, Prof. Sidney, *Russian History*, State University of New York, p. 381.

4. Vernadsky, George, *History of Russia*, Yale University, 1968, p. 238.
5. Balakshin, Peter, *Finale in China*, Sirius Press, 1958, Vol. 1, p. 92.
6. *Great Soviet Encyclopaedia*, 1973 ed., Vol. 12, p. 243.
7. Vernadsky, G., *op. cit.*, p. 238.
8. *Great Soviet Encyclopaedia*, "Chinese Eastern Railway", 1973 ed., Vol. 12, p. 243.
9. Balakshin, P., *op. cit.*, Vol. 1, pp. 102, 103.
10. *Idem*, Vol. 1, pp. 99, 100, 102.
11. *Idem*, Vol. 1, p. 105.
12. Petrov, Victor, "City on the Sungari", *Russkaya Zhizn'*, San Francisco, October 14, 1978, p. 6.
13. Balakshin, P., *op. cit.*, Vol. 1, pp. 325-327.
14. *Encyclopaedia Britannica*, *loc. cit.*, Vol. 11, p. 438.
15. *Idem*, Vol. 1, pp. 201, 202.
16, Balakshin, P., *op. cit.*, p. 181.
17. *Idem*, pp. 201-202.
18. *Encyclopaedia Britannica*, "Manchuria", Vol. 14, p. 761.
19. Balakshin, P., *op. cit.*, Vol. 2, p. 143.
20. *Idem*, Vol. 2, p. 191.
21. *Idem*, Vol. 2, p. 270.
22. Petrov, V., *op. cit.*, October 21, 1978, p. 6.
23. Balakshin, P., *op. cit.*, Vol. 2, pp. 289, 290.
24. *Idem*, Vol. 2, p. 312.
25. Fraser, John, "Russian Exiles prepare to leave China", *Globe and Mail*, Toronto, Sept. 1, 1978.
26. Zhiganov, "Russians in China" (In Russian), *Polytekhnik*, Anniversary Issue, 1969-79, No. 10, Sydney, Australia.
27. Balakshin, P., *op. cit.*, Vol. 1, pp. 103, 105.
28. *Idem*, Vol. 1, p. 134.
29. *The Canadian Annual Review of Public Affairs*, 1923, p. 266.
30. *Idem.*, pp. 45, 46.
31. *Idem.*, 1924/25, p. 195.
32. *Idem.*, 1923, p. 267.
33. Balawyder, A., "Russian Refugees from Constantinople and Harbin", *Canadian Slavonic Papers*, April 1972, p. 24.
34. *Idem.*, p. 25.
35. *Idem.*, p. 28. Also "Speculation on Immigration Sentiments", *New Word*, Harbin, China, 1926 (in Russian); *Letter to Col. Dournovo* from

Beliakoff who was involved in recruiting immigrants to Canada, April 5, 1926; *Memorandum to Mr. Colley*, C.P.R. official, Calgary, Alberta, May 4, 1926. These three documents are available through the of Archives, Glenbow Museum, Calgary, Alberta (Canadian Pacific Railways Papers, BN/.C212G, File 676).

36. *Canadian Slavonic Papers*, April 1972, p. 26.
37. *Idem.*
38. *Idem.*
39. *Idem,.*, p. 27.
40. *Idem.*, p. 25.
41. *Idem.*, p. 26.
42. von Rosenbach, M., *Family Kaleidoscope*, Vancouver, B.C., 1976, pp. 149, 153.
43. Balawyder, A., *op. cit.*, p. 27.
44. von Rosenbach, M., *op. cit.*, p. 149; also "Russian Immigrants Settle in West Country" in *Falun Historical Society*, 1973, p. 118.
45. von Rosenbach, M., *op. cit.*, p. 150.
46. Balawyder, A., *op. cit.*, p. 27.
47. *Idem.*, p. 29.
48. *Idem.*
49. Based on information supplied by Statistics Canada for the years 1924-1971.
50. Balakshin, P., *op. cit.*, Vol. 2, p. 309.
51. Personal interview with Mr. M. Popov, member of an active family of the Russian Pentecostal community in London, Ontario.
52. Personal interview with Mrs. E. Rozvalyaeff, chairman of the Russian Orthodox Society of the City of Vancouver, B.C.
53. Personal interview with Mrs. M. von Rosenbach, daughter of Colonel Orest Dournovo in Vancouver, B.C.
54. Personal interview with Dr. G. Volkoff, Dean of Faculty of Mathematics, University of B.C. in Vancouver, B.C.

Among the recent immigrants from the Soviet Union, are many Russian-Germans of different religious denominations. Categorized according to their place of birth and former citizenship, they are sometimes erroneously regarded as Russian immigrants. Indeed, they have lived in Russia for many years and, in many cases, intermarried with the native population. For these reasons we have included, in Chapters Eight and Nine, brief descriptions of Russian-Germans and of Mennonites.

[Editor]

Tova Yedlin

Eight

GERMANS FROM RUSSIA IN CANADA; AN OVERVIEW

Germans from Russia who immigrated to Canada had a history two centuries apart from that of the Germans who came following the emergence of the German Empire in 1871. Although allowed much freedom to preserve their own culture, in particular in the first century of their settlement, they were influenced by their environment in one way or another.

It is the author's contention that the influence of the Slavic (Russian and Ukrainian) culture, character and way of thinking left a mark on the *nemetskie kolonisty* (German colonists) as they were officially designated by the Russian authorities.

The story of the Germans from Russia began in the eighteenth century when close to 100,000 Germans immigrated to Russia and settled, for the most part, in three areas: the Volga, the Black Sea region and, following the partitions of Poland in 1772-1795, in the Volhynia *guberniya* (province).

After a period of adjustment, the colonists established themselves in their adopted country and, by 1870, their numbers had grown to 450,000. They were mainly farmers and, given the freedoms which were first outlined in Catherine's Manifesto of July 1762, were able to preserve their language, religion and traditions. For over a hundred years the German settlers in the Russian Empire enjoyed preferential treatment and were able to prosper both economically and culturally. The situation changed in the period of the Great Reforms inaugurated by Alexander II (1855-1881). First, many of the privileges were taken away. The local governments or *zemstva* as they were called, were entrusted with the construction and administration of schools; the German colonies were to be controlled by Russian authorities, district or provincial. In 1874, part of the Great Reforms included the introduction of compulsory military service, one of the causes that motivated the Germans to leave their adopted country. Further deterioration of their status came in the last decades of the nineteenth century when Tsar Alexander III embarked on a policy of forced Russification.

Because of their cultural and physical isolation, the German group was particularly vulnerable. By 1897, Russian-language instruction became mandatory and the German schools came under the jurisdiction of the Russian government.

All these developments motivated a great number of Germans to seek a new homeland. The road led to the Americas, and, within the North American continent, to Canada where Germans, who were mainly from around the Black Sea, began arriving after 1885.

Western Canada received the bulk of these immigrants for two reasons: the immigration policy of Clifford Sifton, the Minister of the Interior in Sir Wilfrid Laurier's government, and the soil and climatic conditions of Western Canada which made for an easy adaptation. Black Sea Germans of Catholic faith settled in Saskatchewan, Alberta and Manitoba. They were the first of thousands who settled in Saskatchewan between 1886 and 1914, primarily around Regina and Yorkton. The Volhynia Germans arrived later, and, in addition to the large settlements which they established in Alberta, were to be found in Manitoba and Saskatchewan as well.

The Germans from Russia started arriving in Alberta during the last decade of the nineteenth century. Some came directly from Russia; others via the United States. Only a small number of settlements was founded by those who belonged to the Catholic church. These were in Pincher Creek where they settled in 1896, and in Spring Lake, where a community was established in 1902. The Black Sea German Catholics built settlements near Grassy Lake in 1908, and in Schuler, northeast of Medicine Hat, in 1910. Another group settled near Beiseker, north of Calgary. The Rosenheim colony near Provost was founded by Volga Germans who named the place after their village on the Volga. In the Peace River area, German Catholics from Russia founded Friedenstahl near Fairview and Battle River.

Of the immigrant communities, the Lutherans were both more numerous and better organized. In 1889 they established a settlement near Dunmore, in southern Alberta. Two years later, in 1890-91 were founded the colonies of Hoftmangsau and Rosenthal (better known as Stony Plain) and Friedenthal in the Rabbit Hills, west of Nisku. North of Nisku, the Volhynia Germans built Lutherort in

1892-93. The two colonies, Friedenthal and Lutherort merged in 1897, to found the Lutheran community of Ellerslie.

The Stony Plain community grew due to the number of immigrants that kept arriving from Volhynia and, by 1894, three years after its founding, they had their own church and spiritual leader. In 1892, the Lutheran Russian-Germans founded the settlements of New Norway, Bashaw and Stettler, south-east of Wetaskiwin.

Another group that arrived in Alberta in the 1890s was that of Moravian Brethren or Herren-Hutter who came from Volhynia and, in 1894, founded the colonies of Bruderheim, Bruderfeld and New Sarepta.

From 1895 to 1905 the number of Germans from Russia who settled in districts south of Edmonton increased constantly. These settlers were, in the majority, in the Edmonton-Wetaskawin-Camrose triangle.

By 1911, there were 105,490 Germans in Alberta and Saskatchewan more than half of whom had come from Russia. In Manitoba, in addition to a large Mennonite community, Germans from Russia settled in the area west of Lake Manitoba. British Columbia, too, received a number of these immigrants.

The war that broke out in 1914 interrupted the process of immigration of Germans from Russia. The ravages of war, revolution and civil war, and the establishment of the Soviet régime, contributed to renewed efforts on the part of the Germans to leave. Their efforts did not cease even when, after 1930, the government forbade all emigration.

The total number of Germans from Russia who came to Canada in the inter-war period did not exceed 10,000; half of that number settled in the Prairie provinces in the years 1926-29. By 1939, according to Heinz Lehmann's study published in Berlin in 1939, 44% of the immigrants of German ethnic origin who settled in the Prairie Provinces were Germans from Russia.

The final wave arrived after World War II. The Russo-German war that had started on June 22, 1941 brought significant changes to the situation of the German population in the Soviet Union. The Volga German Autonomous Republic, which had been in existence since 1924, was liquidated in October 1941, its entire population being sent into exile to Siberia and Central Asia. In the western parts of the Soviet Union, due to the rapid occupation of the territories, close to 300,000 Russian Germans found themselves behind Nazi lines. As Germans, they were treated preferentially by the Nazis and when their armies began the retreat in 1943-44 some 100,000 Russian Germans left with the Wehrmacht and, through Poland, arrived in West Germany. When the restrictions against the immigration of Germans were lifted, it is estimated that close to 100,000 Germans entered Canada, one quarter of whom were from the Soviet Union.

At this point it is difficult to establish the exact number of Germans who came from Russia in Canada. According to Adam Giesinger, 300,000 of them came to the Americas since the 1870s. The number of their descendants is estimated at close to a million and a half, of whom 350,000 are in Canada.

The census of 1971, in which the question of ethnicity was asked, lists a total of 1,317,000 as belonging to the German group. Of these, 732,580 live in western Canada. If one accepts Giesinger's figures, then the per cent of Germans from Russia in Canada is about 26.6 per cent of the total German minority. Given the earlier estimate by Heinz Lehmann, the percentage would be higher for Western Canada.

The question of the impact of the Slavic culture and environment on the Germans from Russia, where they lived for close to a century and a half, as well as an analysis of the economic, social and cultural aspects of their life in Canada require further study.

Notes

1. Giesinger, Adam, *From Catherine to Khruschchev: The Story of Russia's Germans*, Winnipeg, 1974.
2. Lehmann, Heinz, *Das Deutschtum in Westkanada*, Berlin, 1939.
3. Heier, Edmund, "The Immigration of the Russo-German Catholics and Lutherans into Canada." *Canadian Slavonic Papers*, Vol. 4, 1960, pp. 160-175.
4. Pisarevskii, *Iz istorii inostrannoi kolonizatsii v Rossii v XVIII veke*, Moscow, 1909.
5. Stumpp, Karl, *The German-Russians: Two Centuries of Pioneering*, New York, 1967.
6. Williams, Hattie Plum, *The Czar's Germans: With particular reference to the Volga Germans*, Lincoln, Nebraska, 1975.

Frank H. Epp

Nine

MENNONITES FROM RUSSIA

According to the 1971 census, there are about 168,000 Mennonites in Canada.* In terms of the European origins of the vast majority, they represent two cultural streams: the Swiss-South German stream, which first arrived in Canada via Pennsylvania in 1786, and the Dutch-North German stream, which started coming via Russia beginning nearly 100 years later.

The majority of Mennonites in Canada are of Dutch background, most of whom once knew Russia as their homeland. About 40,000 Mennonites from Russia came to Canada in three major and several minor migrations since the 1870s.

In that decade, about 7,000 of the 58,000 Mennonites then in Russia settled in Manitoba on lands reserved for their exclusive use by the Dominion Government. Another 11,000 made the plains of the USA mid-west their home at that time.

In the 1920s, a major migration, actually the largest Mennonite mass movement in history brought 20,000 Mennonites to Canada from the USSR, or about one-sixth of the total Mennonite population in the Soviet Union at the time. They settled in all the provinces from Ontario to British Columbia. A third movement of over 12,000 Mennonites took place in the late 1940s and early 1950s from the refugee camps of Western Europe. Most of these were former citizens of the USSR who had been swept out of their Ukrainian colonies in 1943 by the retreating German armies.

The minor movements, which did not involve Mennonite immigration agencies and, therefore, for which no accurate records are available, occurred around the turn of the century and in recent decades. Most of the Mennonites leaving the USSR in the 1970s

* The 1981 Census shows 189,370.

came to West Germany under that government's *Umsiedler* (resettler) program and number over 10,000 to date.

The experience of the Mennonites in Russia parallels that of the German Catholics and German Lutherans in many ways. They entered the country from Prussia starting in 1789 and generally enjoyed the privileges outlined in the Catherine Manifesto. The Mennonite Privilegium, concluded under Paul, also included perpetual exemption from military service.

The Mennonites were unique also in the sense that they boasted a Dutch cultural heritage in addition to the German one acquired after several centuries in the Vistula Valley, to which they had fled, as persecuted Anabaptists from the Nederlanden in the sixteenth century. When the German identity became a problem, as it did in the two world wars, the Mennonites of Russian background indulged in "Hollanderei", meaning a doting on their Dutch heritage.

The several migrations from Russia were motivated by the termination of special privileges as well as by considerations of general security and well-being. The reforms of the 1870s, including the Russification of the schools and the introduction of universal military service, albeit with alternate provisions (such as medical orderly, batman, kitchen helper, etc.), prompted the exodus at that time.

In the 1920s the exodus was spurred on by physical devastation as well as cultural and religious deprivation resulting from the revolution, civil war and policies of the new régime. Many more would have come to Canada had emigration from the USSR not been cut off at the end of the twenties.

The migrations following World War II would have been much greater but for the fact that two thirds of the 35,000 Mennonites who retreated with the German Army were later repatriated by the victorious Soviet armies of occupation.

These three major migrations resulted in varying settlement patterns. The immigrants of the 1870s reestablished in the east and west reserves of Manitoba colonies and villages they had left behind in Russia. When these were populated to capacity, additional resevations were settled in Saskatchewan.

These *Kanadier*, as they came to be called, to differentiate them from the *Russlaender* who came in the 1920s, were determined to maintain their separate way of life as well as their own schools. When this became impossible under the new school legislation of Manitoba and Saskatchewan in the 1920s, about 7,000 migrated to Mexico and Paraguay.

Further movements since that time have led to Kanadier settlements in Belize and Bolivia, as well as isolated communities in northern Alberta and British Columbia.

The immigrants of the 1920s would also have preferred compact settlements, but these were no longer possible. Thus, a great number of communities of Russlaender came into being, 17 in Ontario, 89 in Manitoba, 108 in Saskatchewan, 43 in Alberta, and 51 in British Columbia, totalling 6,127 households.

The immigrants who came after World War II joined existing Russlaender communities, though mainly in such urban or urbanizing areas as Kitchener-Waterloo, the Niagara Peninsula, Winnipeg, Saskatoon, Calgary, Vancouver and the Fraser Valley.

Their common life in Canada is centred on the Mennonite congregations, organized in conferences and nurtured by several networks of educational institutions (Bible schools, high schools and colleges) as well as periodicals and a variety of cultural events. The common Mennonite organization is the Mennonite Central Committee Canada, an agency for immigration, relief, service, peace and development.

Notes

1. Epp, Frank H., *Mennonite Exodus*, (Altona: D.W. Friesen & Sons, Ltd., 1962).
2. ——————, *Mennonites in Canada, 1786-1920: The History of a Separate People* (Toronto: Macmillan of Canada, 1974).
3. Francis, E.K., *In Search of Utopia: The Mennonites of Manitoba* (Altona: D.W. Friesen & Sons, Ltd., 1955).
4. Smith, C. Henry, *The Coming of the Russian Mennonites* (Berne, Indiana: Mennonite Book Concern, 1927).

V.I. Grebenshikov

Ten

THE EASTERN-ORTHODOX CHURCH AND THE RUSSIAN COMMUNITIES IN CANADA

In their book *Religion in Canada*[1], Kilbourn, Forrest and Watson examine the history and activities of sixteen communities in Canada. They break them into six well-defined groups, as follows:

1. the Roman-Catholic Church, comprising about 46 per cent of Canadians;
2. the major Protestant Churches (Anglican, United Church and the other members of the Canadian Council of Churches), totalling about 45 per cent;
3. the Eastern Orthodox Churches, with about 300,000 members or roughly 1.5 per cent;
4. the conservative Evangelical and Fundamentalist Churches;
5. minor Christian sects (Doukhobors, Jehovahs Witnesses, Mennonites, Hutterites and others); and
6. non-Christian religions (Hebrews, Muslims, Buddhists, etc.).

This article deals primarily with the third group.

Who are the Russian and the Orthodox People?

Russian culture is intimately bound up with Eastern-orthodox theology and philosophy. These bounds are eloquently described in Russian literature by such widely known writers as Tolstoy, Dostoevsky, Soloviov and others. Yet, when we study the lives of Russians in Canada, we do not find a similarly harmonious rapport between the concepts "Russian" and "Orthodox".

For example, according to official statistics, in February 1974 there were 64,165 persons of Russian origin in Canada, or 0.3 per cent of the total population.[2] Their religious affiliations were as follows:

Table 1

Religious Affiliations of Russians in Canada

Eastern-Orthodox	10,085	15.6%
United Church	10,870	16.8%
Doukhobors	9,170	14.2%
Roman-Catholics	8,505	13.0%
Lutherans	3,455	5.3%
Anglican	3,130	4.8%
Mennonites, Hutterites	2,950	4.5%
Baptists	1,985	3.0%
Other denominations	5,855	9.0%
No religion	8,460	13.0%

This breakdown is surprising. Even if we take into account the obvious and inevitable process of alienation resulting from mixed marriages, pressures of the social environment, etc., such a large number (nearly 85%) of "non-orthodox" Russians is truly strange.

According to the same official statistics,[3] only 23,435, or 36 per cent of all "ethnic" Russians claimed Russian as their main language. It is well known that the loss of a mother tongue frequently furthers the breaking-away from traditions, culture and the church, although the intensity of this process has not yet been studied.

But a closer examination of statistics reveals certain discrepancies. Consider, for instance, the following table:[4]

Table 2

Membership in the Orthodox Church in Canada, by Ethnic Group

Greeks	112,000
Ukrainians	116,700
Asian Nations	13,020
Russians	10,065
British	9,910
Poles	5,565
Germans, Austrians	2,425
French	1,575
Czech, Slovaks	1,570
Hungarians	1,260
Italians	455
Finns	185
Jews	320
Dutch	335
Portuguese	300
Scandinavians	555
Other Europeans	37,795
Total (approximate)	316,000

These figures are hard to understand. Germans, French, Hungarians, Italians, Portuguese, Scandinavians — all Orthodox?! Even less comprehensible is the number of Jews. It may be assumed that some people in these ethnic groups claimed their religion to be "Orthodox Jewish" or "Orthodox Catholic" or even "Orthodoxal Evangelism" none of which has any relation to the Eastern Orthodox religion or Church.

Moreover, we see in the table that, in Canada, there are 112,000 Orthodox Greeks while in the ethnic statistics for the same period[5] we find only 91,530 Greeks. How does it happen that there are more "Orthodox Greeks" than "ordinary" Greeks?

Furthermore, the official statistics do not include Orthodox Copts, Serbs, Bulgarians, Romanians, Byelorussians — all of whom have active communities with their own churches, schools and social activities. One may argue that the Slavs and Romanians have been included in the number of "other Europeans"; even so, Copts could not be included either with the "Europeans" or the "Asians".

The Orthodox Church and the Russian Ethnic Group

The most important fact not reflected in the data is that only the Orthodox Church and the Doukhobor communities could be considered as true representatives of Russians in Canada. Only these two religious movements have consistently gathered around them significant numbers of the Russian population and looked after their cultural, spiritual and even social needs.

In other religious organizations, Russians constituted only a minor part of the whole and, therefore, the preservation of the cultural heritage, language or ethnic traditions of the Russian members was never a priority and seldom a necessity. On the contrary, these organizations promote linguistic and cultural assimilation.

That is why this chapter will focus on the life and role of the Russian-Orthodox Church.

At the present time there are about one hundred Russian-Orthodox churches, communities and small monasteries in Canada.[6] Interestingly, in 1911 their number was 130 whereas in 1926 there were only 65.[7] It would, however, be wrong to consider all these centres of Russian Orthodoxy as integral parts of a centralized church. From its establishment in Canada to the present, the Russian-Orthodox Church in Canada was subject to strong social and political influences. As a result, three distinct juridictions are active, striving to expand their constituencies. Today, 54 parishes belong to the Orthodox Church in America (OCA — Fig. 24), 30 recognize the authority of the Holy Synod of the Russian-Orthodox Church Abroad (ROCA — Fig. 25), and 22, mostly in Alberta and Saskatchewan, belong to the Edmonton Diocese of the Moscow Patriarchate (MP — Fig. 26).

In describing the Eastern-Orthodox Church in Canada, Kilbourn, Forrest and Watson stress the fact that most Canadians could not understand the rivalries and animosities existing under the Byzantine domes, nor could they appreciate the majesty and richness of the historical and spiritual traditions preserved in the Orthodox churches as inherited from almost two thousand years of religious experience by 150 million Eastern Christians. Saturated as they were with these rich traditions, the Eastern-Orthodox Churches in Canada remained somewhat aloof from the mainstream of Canadian religious and social life; their priests continued to worship in their traditional or national languages and endeavoured to serve their flock from Eastern Europe or the Near East with no concern for proselytizing or spreading their faith among other people.[8]

These general observations are applicable to the Russian Orthodox Church in Canada as well.

The major causes for the split within the Russian Orthodox Church can be properly explained only in a retrospective review of three historical events: 1) Russian missionary activities in Alaska in the 18th and 19th centuries; 2) the Russian revolution and Civil war of 1917-20; 3) the World War II.

The Russian-Orthodox Mission in Alaska

At the time when English and French tradesmen, adventurers and missionaires from Quebec, Montreal and Hudson Bay were moving west to the prairies of Manitoba and north up the MacKenzie River towards the Pacific shores, Russian tradesmen, Cossacks and missionaries were moving through Siberia and the Aleutian Islands eastward to the Alaskan coast (Fig. 27).

On a dark day in October 1794, the Russian ship *The Three Saints* reached the island of Kodiak. Along with the other passengers who came ashore was the reverend Joasaph Bolotov who headed a group of ten Russian-Orthodox monks from the Valaam monastery.[9] This was the first Russian mission to the American continent sent to provide spiritual comfort to the first Russian settlers and also to Christianize the Aleuts and Indians of the region. (Fig. 28). In the first two years of its activities, the mission claimed to have converted over 12,000 of the local "Americans". The Russian-Orthodox Church has kept growing ever since. In 1799, a bishop was appointed to Kodiak; in the same year the entire administration of the Russian colony as well as the Mission were transferred to Sitka. In 1841 a seminary was opened there to train new indigenous priests. The missionary work expanded the most under Rev. Ivan Veniaminov, who was soon appointed Bishop of Siberia and Alaska, and subsequently elected Patriarch of Moscow. He devised the first alphabet for the Aleuts and translated some of the Holy Scriptures into their dialect. In 1872, the Mission was transferred from Sitka to San Francisco and, in 1905, to New York.

After Alaska was sold to the USA in 1867, the Russian-Orthodox Church continued work both in Alaska and in the United States. By 1916, the Russian-Orthodox Church administered over 350 parishes in North America and about 500,000 parishioners.[10] Being the sole Eastern-Orthodox Church on the continent, it served the spiritual needs of various ethnic groups: Russians and Ukrainians, Greeks and Armenians, Syrians, Albanians, Serbs and Bulgarians, Romanians and others. Their numbers increased with the influx of immigrants from Central and Eastern Europe (Slavic minorities from the Austro-Hungarian Empire, religious sects from Russia, Greeks, Slavs and Armenians escaping religious persecution in the Ottoman Empire).[11]

Russian Canadians

As for Canada, the number of people of Eastern-Orthodox faith was growing steadily towards the end of the 1890s as a result of the immigration of Slavic minorities from the Austro-Hungarian Empire (Galicians, Bukovinians and Ruthenes from the Subcarpathian regions) and the arrival of religious sects, members of which endeavoured to avoid military service in Russia (Doukhobors, Mennonites, Baptists and others). This was almost exclusively an immigration of farmers who settled on lands put at their disposal by the Canadian government in the prairies of Manitoba, Saskatchewan and Alberta.

By 1907, a new wave of Slavic immigrants appeared, mainly from Byelorussia and Bessarabia. This was essentially a so-called "economic" immigration consisting mainly of unskilled workers in search of wages who settled in industrial centers and cities such as Windsor, Timmins, Toronto, Hamilton and Montreal.[12]

The ethnic origins of the immigrants at the turn of the century were not precisely determined or recorded; they came from various countries but called themselves "Russians" or "Ruthenes" and, in their religious activities, they adhered to the traditions of the Eastern-Orthodox rites, although nominally they belonged either to the Russian-Orthodox or the Greek-Catholic churches. Both groups came to Canada without priests or any established church organization.

The Russian-Orthodox Church which was already established and in full operation in North America endeavoured to provide these newcomers with spiritual and social assistance. New Orthodox missionary schools were established in Seattle and Minneapolis, and Orthodox priests began to visit the new immigrants in Canada.[13]

At the turn of the century, this crowd of Slavs, clad in sheepskin coats, speaking an incomprehensible language and practising strange customs provoked not only curiosity but frequently hostility among the local Anglo-Saxon population. The newcomers got the reputation of being "rough", "strange" and "godless", and were referred to as "sheepskins". In many places, the old-timers refused to allow the burial of "strangers" in their cemeteries and the immigrants had to bury their dead on their own land. Later, they pooled their lots and created their own cemeteries, built Orthodox chapels and even churches. That, indeed, is how the first known Russian-Orthodox church was built in 1901 in the village of Limestone-Lake (now called "Vostok").[14]

Later on churches were also built in Skrada, Victoria, Beaver Creek, Rabbit Hills, Kiselevo, Serediaky, Star, Sifton (all in Alberta) and in Stuartborn (now Gardenton), Emerson, Yorkton, Ounz River, Tetlak, Moose Jaw, Krudun Lake, Julik, Bibel-guer, Nard, Minitonas, Sandy Lake, Stenner, (in Saskatchewan and Manitoba).[15] In 1904 the Holy Trinity Cathedral was built in Winnipeg. It was consecrated by Bishop Tikhon of Alaska, who subsequently became the Patriarch of Moscow; he was later repressed by the new Soviet government.

In 1916, in Winnipeg, Bishop Alexander was the first Orthodox bishop to be appointed for Canada. That year there were about 150 Russian-Orthodox parishes in that first Diocese.[16] All these parishes, however, were serviced by a dozen or so travelling priests and missionaries, who periodically visited the parishes to hold divine service and perform other church rites.[17]

The shortage of priests and missionaries prevented the appointment of permanent pastors even in the larger agglomerations of Orthodox people. No wonder then, that this great mass of faithful Christians became the object of special attention from other religious organizations and sects. However, each of the other Canadian Christian churches developed its own approach to Slavic immigrants. The Catholic church established an information centre for newcomers in Vancouver and a Society of Assistance to Immigrants in Winnipeg.[18] The Lutheran, Presbyterian and Congregationist Churches concentrated on serving immigrants of their respective faiths, whereas the Methodists and the Baptists began proselytizing energetically among the Slavic immigrants. The Anglican Church preached among the Slavs as well, although the main thrust of their missionary effort remained directed toward the local Indian and Eskimo populations.[19]

The intensity of the proselytic efforts of some Protestant churches may be illustrated by the adventure of Ivan Bodrug in Manitoba who, with the help of the Presbyterian missionary Carmichael, organized an "Independent Orthodox Church". It was based on Presbyterian canonical principles but retained a somewhat simplified Eastern-Orthodox rite and liturgy.[20] This "church" achieved a certain degree of success and at one point had 51 missionaries of its own. However, after the death of Carmichael in 1913, the Church fell apart leaving a number of "converted Slavs" in the Presbyterian Church, including Ivan Bodrug himself.

In the cities, the Orthodox population came under the influence of Catholic and Protestant welfare organizations such as "Houses of Friendship", "Missions for the People" and centers of the Salvation Army. The aim of these organizations was to help poor people in the city slums where a substantial number of Slavic immigrants usually lived. These were mostly farmers and workers who came to Canada to earn higher wages, and who had neither education nor skills.[21]

The acute shortage of Orthodox clergy and the active proselytizing of the other Canadian churches and sects combined to bring about a substantial reduction in Russian-Orthodox parishes; by 1926 their number had fallen to 65.[22]

Meanwhile, in the aftermath of World War I, the Russian Revolution and Civil War events led to changes that influenced the lives of Russian Canadians.

The Russian Revolution and the Russian-Orthodox Church in Exile

As a direct result of the revolution of 1917 and the civil war of 1917-1920, the Orthodox Church in Russia found itself geographically partitioned so that communication between the Patriarch and the Central Church Administration in Moscow and the many peripheral Dioceses was difficult and sometimes completely disrupted. Patriarch Tikhon himself was under surveillance and strong pressure from the revolutionary government; he was finally arrested. On November 20, 1920, shortly before his death, the Patriarch issued Decree Number 362, by virtue of which Dioceses or groups of Dioceses that were outside Moscow obtained the canonical right to organize local Church Administrations for the coordination of local ecclesiastical activities. Thus, a "Church Administration of South-West Russia" was created on territory still under anti-communist control. After the end of the civil war, this church administration was evacuated to Constantinople (Istanbul) together with the remaining anti-communist forces. A conference of Russian bishops who were outside the Soviet government's influence was convened. Thirty-four bishops attended this conference coming from scattered Dioceses of pre-revolutionary Russia and from several countries with Russian-Orthodox populations: Latvia, Finland, Manchuria, Japan and Jerusalem; in attendance also was the Archbishop of Alaska and America. A "High Administration of the Russian Orthodox Church Outside Russia" was formed. In 1921 the High Church Administration moved to Yugoslavia at the invitation of the Serbian Patriarch Dimitry, and, in August 1922, it was reorganized into a Synod of the Russian-Orthodox Church Abroad (ROCA).[23]

From the end of the civil war in Russia to the beginning of the German-Soviet War, that is, from 1920 to 1941, the Russian Orthodox Church Abroad carried out an intensive programme creating new parishes, building new churches, opening schools for children and even institutions of theology and servicing the spiritual, cultural and social needs of Russians scattered all over the free world, from China and Japan, through North Africa, Iran, India, Turkey, the Balkan States, Greece, Central and Western Europe, to Australia, South and North America. All these Dioceses were nominally administered by the Synod of the Russian-Orthodox Church Abroad.

From time to time, however, there was friction, conflicts and even splits occurred within this Church, particularly within the richest and the most active Dioceses such as those in Western Europe and North America. Conflicts and quarrels alternated with compromises and reconciliations but the life of the Church continued unabated.

As for Canada, the effect of World War I and especially of the revolution in Russia upon the Russian Canadian population was considerable and complex. The Orthodox people in Canada began to split into groups according to their attitudes to the events in Europe, and this fostered the growth of a national and ethnic consciousness and a search for identity. Thus, in 1918, the Greeks in North America segregated into an American Greek-Orthodox Church with direct allegiance to the Ecumenical Patriarch of Constantinople. In 1919, an independent Ukrainian Orthodox Church was formed and, in 1920, an independent Serbian Orthodox Church formed in the USA and Canada.[24]

Among the Russian Canadians, a differentiation took place essentially depending on the attitude people adopted toward the new Communist republic that emerged in Russia. A substantial part of the Russian workers in Canadian cities acclaimed the revolution and, with the help of exiled Russian revolutionaries who came to Canada following the unsuccessful first revolution of 1905-06, they formed "Associations for Technical Assistance to Russia" which, among other activities, assisted people wishing to return to the USSR.[25] Other Russian Canadians took part in the activities of the radical workers' movement in Canada and organized a number of active "progressive" and "workers" Clubs, libraries and "Maxim Gorky Societies". In 1931, all these leftwing clubs were united in a "Federation of Russian Workers' and Farmers' Clubs" which achieved their maximum expansion by 1935-36 when they had a total of 60 clubs and about 2,500 members all across Canada.[26] Thus, this radical stratum of the Russian Canadian population made up about 3.5 percent of the total number of Russian Canadians at that time. Even if we accept Mr. Okulevich's statement[27] that the influence of these organizations touched 10,000 people, this constituted, at most, 12.5 percent of all Russian-Canadians.

The mainstream of Russian Canadians manifested no particular attachment to the new order in Russia. They continued to organize their lives in Canada, building new churches and schools for their children observing old Russian customs and being, at that time, loyal Canadian citizens (Fig. 29). In those years, new Russian-Orthodox churches were opened in Toronto (1915), Windsor (1916), Sydney (1917) and Vancouver among others.

The churches benefitted greatly from the arrival to Canada of a new wave of immigrants from Europe. These were the participants and supporters of the anti-communist struggle in Russia who went into exile after the end of the civil war in 1920. This was the beginning of the so-called "white immigration" for whom the Russian-Orthodox Church had a particular significance as a symbol of spiritual, national and cultural survival. For these people, who had tragically lost their homeland, the Church remained the witness of fidelity to the history and traditions of their anscestors (Figs. 30, 31, 32). With great zeal they took an active part in the life of the Church, trying to strengthen the existing Russian-Orthodox Churches and building new ones. Thus, after the 1920s new churches were opened in Montreal, Quebec, Toronto, Hamilton, London, Windsor, Niagara Falls, Ottawa, Winnipeg, Edmonton, Calgary, Lethbridge, Vancouver and Victoria.

In most cases, due to cultural conservatism and acute anti-communist feelings of the "white immigrants", these new churches chose to belong to the Russian Orthodox Church Abroad. Sometimes conflicts occurred in the parishes where the "old-timers" opposed the newcomers and, occasionally, churches passed from the fold of one jurisdiction to another.

At the beginning of World War II the three jurisdictions of the Russian-Orthodox Church that we know today were already in place in Canada. However, the American Metropolia was the only one to designate a special Bishop for Canada. Bishop Alexander was followed by Bishop Arseni in Winnipeg (1925); in 1927 a second Bishop, Emmanuel, was nominated in Montreal to minister to the Syrian members of the Orthodox Church.

World War II and the Nomination of a Patriarch in Moscow

Internal conflicts within the Russian-Orthodox Church became acute at the beginning of the war in Europe. In particular, in 1941, when the German-Soviet war started and stirred great excitement among Russian exiles everywhere, many were gripped by hopes for internal changes in Russia. Extreme optimists expected the rapid collapse of Communist power and some of the Orthodox clergy shared these hopes and expectations.

On the other hand, many Russian exiles who were worried about the fate of their homeland were dismayed by those who wished for the defeat of the Soviet government; in its extreme form, this feeling expressed itself in active "Soviet patriotism", and this sentiment, too, found some sympathizers among members of the Orthodox clergy.

In 1943, when Stalin decided to play on the religious feelings of the Russian people during the harsh years of the war, he allowed the "election" of a Patriarch for the Russian Orthodox Church in the

USSR. At this point, internal conflicts in the entire church (both inside the USSR and abroad) became sharper because the church's canonical and religious problems were amplified by the political overtones. In particular, the Synod of the Russian-Orthodox Church Abroad refused to recognize the canonical legitimacy of the new Patriarch because he was thought of as a captive, an instrument of the Soviet government and of the Communist Party. Yet at the same time, the West European Diocese and the American Metropolia established communications with the new Patriarch of Moscow with the intention of restoring canonical order in the Russian-Orthodox Church. Following a number of controversies, interruptions and reconciliations, the negotiations with Moscow ended with the granting of independence to the Russian-Orthodox Church in America, which was then converted into the Autocephalous Orthodox Church in America.

The Thomos issued by the Patriarch of Moscow in 1970 established a new canonical order for the American Church but made little change in the status of the Russian-Orthodox Church in Canada. The text of this Thomos excluded from the conversion process 43 parishes in the USA, which remained in direct subordination to the Patriarch of Moscow, as well as "all parishes and clergy in Canada belonging to the Edmonton Diocese".[28] The Thomos also stipulated that, when a parish belonging to the Moscow Patriarchate in the USA or Canada wished to leave the Patriarchate, the only canonical option was to join the Orthodox Church in America.

So it came about that all Russian-Orthodox parishes in Canada today are distributed among three jurisdictions, as mentioned earlier. The 54 parishes of the OCA are headed by Archbiship Sylvester Garuns, whose Chair is in Montreal, and the 30 parishes of the ROCA are headed by Archbishop Vitali Ustinov, also in Montreal. Both Churches are administered from New York. The 22 parishes of the Edmonton Diocese are administered by the Patriarch of Moscow. (Fig. 33).

As for the Russian Canadian population, the beginning of World War II was greeted with both excitement and anxiety, a mood which was widely shared in the Russian-Orthodox parishes. It must be noted, however, that the radical members of the Russian Canadian population, as represented by the Russian Workers' and Farmers' Clubs, reacted to the war in a more active way and in a mood which was more consistent with Soviet ideological precepts than did their "brothers" in Moscow; while the Soviet government participated with Hitler in the new partition of Poland, the Central Executive Committee of the Russian-Canadian Workers' and Farmers' Clubs in Winnipeg published, as early as September 4, 1939, an appeal "to the entire Russian population in Canada" which read in part:

> Russian Canadians, united in the Russian Workers' and Farmers' Clubs, are deeply democratic and hate Fascism and its agents . . . We support the struggle of the peoples of Poland and other countries, who rose against German Fascism. The parents and brothers of the majority of our members are still living in Poland and now they are menaced by direct annihilation. Our fathers and brothers in Western Byelorussia and Volynia will support, together with the other peoples of Poland, their struggle against Hitler.[29]

Notwithstanding this appeal, the Canadian government, perturbed as it was by the German-Soviet agreement and alliance of 1939-41, outlawed all fascist and communist organizations and newspapers in Canada, including the Russian Workers' and Farmers' Clubs and their paper, "Kanadskii Gudok" (The Canadian Whistle).[30]

However, at the beginning of the German-Soviet war in the summer of 1941, "Russian Committees for Assistance to the Homeland" were formed in Montreal and Toronto, and began to spread to other cities. These Committees initiated vigorous campaigns for collecting money for medical assistance for the Soviet Union. By May 1942, a total of $73,960 had been collected. Such a campaign, aimed at humanitarian assistance to an ally, appealed to Canadians and attracted support for the Committees. By the end of 1942, about $100,000 was collected for assistance for wounded Soviet soldiers. A new campaign produced over $75,469 for the delivery of 12 ambulances to the USSR; at the end of 1943 another $102,033 was collected to purchase 1,000 beds for the hospitals in Briansk and Kharkov. All in all, these Committees collected over a half a million dollars for assistance for the Soviet Union.[31]

Besides their purely humanitarian operations, the Committees for Assistance to the Homeland developed cultural, political and educational activities as well: schools for children, choirs, dancing groups, reading halls and libraries reopened all over the country. Doukhobors and several Russian-Orthodox churches associated themselves with these activities.

The first convention of the Russian Committees for Assistance to the Homeland took place in May 1942 in Toronto. Its major decision was to combine all activities within the framework of one organization, the Federation of Russian-Canadians (FRC). Particular attention was given to enlisting the Orthodox churches in the activities of the new Federation. In the minutes of the newly-elected executive committee of the Federation, the following statement occurs: "The Central Executive Committee believes that the participation of our church organizations in the activities of the FRC is of great importance . . . The participation of the Orthodox parishes in the work of assistance to the Soviet Union will neutralize the main objections of Canadian fascists and neo-fascists, who strive to arouse Canadians against the USSR".[32]

Some members of the Orthodox clergy occasionally represented their parish, but, more often, participated as private individuals in the work of the Federations of Russian Canadians.[33]

The second Convention of the Federation of Russian Canadians was held in November 1944. There were delegates from 58 branches of the FRC and from 12 youth sections. There were also 10 delegates who were Doukhobors (including I.I. Verigin himself) and 7 delegates from the Orthodox Churches. At that time, the FRC had 3,492 members,[34] the largest number ever attained. With the end of the war, however, the feeling of the usefulness of such activities began to fade. The representatives of the Orthodox church left the organization primarily because the end of the war meant the beginning of a new period of revival of activity in the Russian-Orthodox parishes in Canada.

Soon after the end of World War II a new wave of immigrants headed to Canada from Europe, among them a considerable number of Russians. Some of these were "white" immigrants, who had settled in various countries of Europe and in China since 1920, and who fled as far as possible from the new boundaries of the USSR and its satellites. But the majority of the new Russian immigrants was made up of Russian workers and intellectuals deported by the Germans from the occupied territories of the USSR, plus Soviet prisoners-of-war who refused to return home.[35]

All these new Russian immigrants were staunch anticommunists. For most of them, the Orthodox Church in Canada represented the only moral source of strength on which they could count in this new and strange country and they contributed significantly to the revival of activities in and around the Russian-Orthodox churches. The clergy and old parishioners went out of their way to assist the newcomers.

The revival of the activities in Russian-Orthodox parishes was mostly manifested in the development of cultural programs: schools for children, courses of English and Russian languages, musical, singing and dancing groups, theatrical activities and sports teams.

This peaceful and constructive time seems to have ended for the Russian-Orthodox Church in Canada and all of America as we observe new changes in the form and content of the church and of its parish activities. These changes seem to involve new, mutually opposing tendencies described below.

Russian or American Orthodoxy?

Following the formal establishment of an autocephalous Orthodox Church in America, the problem of the authenticity of Orthodoxy as a religious doctrine and as the organization called on to preserve and protect the spiritual and cultural traditions of Eastern Christianity, finally surfaced and came to the fore. As long as the older generations of immigrants still prevailed in the Russian-Orthodox parishes, the church kept all the traditions, continued to use the "Old (Julian) calendar" and retained the traditional languages of ritual (Old Slavonic or Russian and Ukrainian dialects). New waves of Russian immigrants, and especially those who came after World War II, usually joined the parishes of the Russian-Orthodox Church Abroad, which tended to remain conservative. At the same time, the children of earlier immigrants born in North America, began to prevail on many parishes of the Orthodox Church in America to push for the introduction of English in church rites, the adoption of the "New" (Gregorian) calendar and for adaptation to the American way of life and local traditions.

Hence, with the establishment of the autocephalous Orthodox Church in America in 1970, and especially after the election in 1978 of Metropolitan Theodossius, himself a representative of that younger generation born in America,[35] the process of "Americanization" of the Orthodox Church in America was intensified substantially, provoking friction and conflicts in parishes where the more conservative members were still active.[36]

At the present time, the Orthodox Church in America and the Russian-Orthodox Church Abroad do not show any significant divergence on canonical questions and both churches consider themselves branches of the Eastern (Greek) Orthodox Church, the true and direct heir of the original Church of Christ founded by the Holy Apostles. They both believe in the ecumenical unity of Orthodoxy under the rule of four Eastern Patriarchs (Jerusalem, Antioch, Alexandria and Constantinople) and one Western Patriarch (the Pope of Rome), with the Patriarch of Constantinople being regarded as the supreme "Ecumenical Patriarch". Both the OCA and the ROCA condemn the Roman-Catholic Church for its "non-apostolic" innovations (the question of "filioque", the belief in Purgatory, the dogma of the Ascension of the Holy Virgin, the dogma of the infallibility of the Pope, etc.). Both Churches maintain traditional attitudes to life and morals. They both recognize the human and civil rights of women and Orthodox women participate actively in the life of the church: they look after the internal workings of the parish, manage economic and household problems of the parish, organize and work in parish schools, sit on the Parish Councils and chair them, act as Parish Elders, conduct and sing in choirs and serve as Readers. Women, however, may not enter the Clergy or approach the Altar. They can become nuns, however, and there are many Orthodox women's convents.

Both Churches are unanimous in categorically condemning homosexuality, lesbianism, bestiality and other sexual perversion, considering them sins to be overcome by the faithful through personal effort. Abortions and all kinds of racial, sexual or age discrimination are condemned as well. "Abortion is the most cruel act of age discrimination", said one of the Russian priests.[37]

Neither church makes any specific statement on the question of birth control and the attitude to this problem varies from one place to another; the general tendency in the Russian-Orthodox Church Abroad seems to be its condemnation whereas the Orthodox Church in America seems to accept it.

The major rift between the two churches seems to stem from their respective relations with the Ecumenical Movement, with other Christian churches, and especially with the Moscow Patriarchate. The Russian-Orthodox Church Abroad keeps cultivating among its members a sense of responsibility for the preservation of the purity of the teachings of Christ, as expressed in the Holy Scriptures, in the Holy traditions, in the writings of the Fathers of the Church and in the decisions of the first four Ecumenical Councils. A re-unification of Christians, therefore, is considered to be possible only on the basis of the complete restoration and acceptance of the teachings of Christ. The Russian Orthodox Church Abroad refuses to participate in the modern Ecomenical Movement, accusing it of trying to achieve unity by means of pragmatic compromises and of partial and tactical concessions to the detriment of the true teachings of Christ.[38]

The Orthodox Church in America, on the other hand, manifested a long standing interest in cooperation with other Christian Churches. In 1950, it joined the National Council of Churches in the USA and, in 1954, it was admitted as a full member in the World Council of Churches; since that time, it has played an active role in WCC activites.[39] The clergy of the Orthodox Church in America also attend conferences of Christian clergymen across the country and eagerly participate in religous, social and even political events in North American life. For example, young OCA priests frequently serve as Chaplains in the American Army; in Canada, Rev. Oleg Boldireff, one of the priests of the Orthodox Church in America, took an official part in the opening of the Provincial Parliament in Victoria, B.C., reading an Orthodox prayer.

Both Churches officially refrain from participation in the activities of any political party or group but their members have complete freedom of action in the political parties of their choice.

However, both churches condemn Communism and Communist regimes, especially in Russia, for their dogmatic atheism and especially for their open or covert persecution and repression of the Church and of faithful Christians. The Russian-Orthodox Church Abroad allows no compromise in its condemnation of the leadership of the Moscow Patriarchate, believing it to be the instrument of the Soviet government, that is, the instrument of a godless and atheistic power. Thus, the ROCA refuses to maintain any contact with representatives of the Patriarch of Moscow and forbids its members to attend joint church services with them.[40]

The Orthodox Church in America, having received the Thomos for its autocephaly from the Patriarch of Moscow, abstains from sharp attacks on him and permits the joint celebration of church rites with clergy from Moscow, although it condemns the persecution of Christians in the Soviet Union.[41] It should be noted, however, that there are still priests in the OCA, mainly of the older generation, who refuse to celebrate rites with clergymen from Moscow, but they represent a dwindling minority.

In conclusion, it would be useful to glance into the future. The two Churches, the OCA and the ROCA, having chosen different approaches to life's problems in their modern environment, likewise have a different perspective of their own future role.

The aspirations of the Russian-Orthodox Church Abroad are inseparably bound to the fate of Russia, which it envisages as becoming free from Communist oppression. That is why the ROCA is occupied primarily with taking care of the spiritual needs of Orthodox Russians, observing the traditions of Russian Orthodoxy and transmitting these to new generations who might, some day, be called upon to bring back these traditions in their purest form to a reformed Motherland. This is the way of idealistic conservatism, which might be successful if the anticipated renaissance of Russia were to happen soon enough. This hope is closer to the hearts of the Russian exiles, but in the long run, it alienates the younger people who were born and educated in a Canadian environment. For them, today's Canada is the reality of life whereas a free Russia in the future remains an ephemeral dream. The statistical data at the beginning of this chapter confirms this process of estrangement.

The Orthodox Church in America, on the other hand, sees its future in the strengthening and spreading of Orthodoxy on the North American continent and in the development of an American brand of Orthodoxy which would be better understood and, therefore, easily adopted by a larger proportion of the population on this Continent.

The Orthodox Church in America has its own way of "transplanting" traditional Russian Orthodoxy onto North American soil. As any kind of transplant includes a complex process of adaptation to the new environment the questions always arise: "How successful will the transplant be? What will be the price?"[42]

Tormenting questions inevitably stir the religious consciousness of Russian Canadians. What is more important — the preservation of the purity of the teachings of Christ or the survival of some kind or Orthodoxy on this Continent? What is more meritorious — the moral right to consider oneself a true Russian-Orthodox Christian or the right of conscience to regard oneself simply as a good Christian?

Everyone endeavours to answer these questions for himself, not only with the voice of one's conscience, but, very frequently in close relation with surrounding conditions, family circumstances career and other considerations. Many stop searching for an answer. They probably make up a large part of those 13 percent of Russian-Canadians who claim to have "no religion". And this process seems to be expanding.

Post Scriptum

While this book was being prepared for publication, a shift took place within the hierarchy of the Orthodox Church in America. I feel that the changes are of special significance for the further development of the OCA. My attention was first drawn to the premature retirement, in September 1981, of Sylvester Garuns, Archbishop of Montreal and Canada. In March of the same year, the Head of the Orthodox Church in America, Metropolitan Theodossius, moved his Chair from New York to Washington. The vacant New York Chair was given to a newcomer from Europe, Bishop Pierre L'Huillier. Born in France and a convert to Orthodoxy, L'Huillier graduated from the Academy of Theology in Moscow in 1962. In 1968, he was ordained by Metropolitan Nikodim in Leningrad's Alexander Nevsky Lavra (Monastery) as Bishop of Khersones. In 1979 Bishop L'Huillier was transferred from France to New York where he became Vicar Bishop, a position which places him on a high level in the policy-making hierarchy of the Orthodox Church in America.

In view of the close ties which L'Huillier has maintained with the Moscow Church, there will undoubtedly be some uneasy speculation as to how these changes may affect the further relationship between the OCA and the so-called Edmonton Patriarchate, as well as the Moscow Patriarchate in the USSR.

Notes

1. Kilbourn, William (ed.), *Religion in Canada. The Spiritual Development of a Nation.* The Canadian Illustrated Library, McClelland & Stewart Ltd., Toronto, 1968, p. 7.
2. Catalogue 92-735, Statistics Canada, (Bulletin 1.4-7) vol. 1, part 4, February 1974.
3. Catalogue 92-821, Statistics Canada, (Bulletin 2.2), 1976 Census of Canada.
4. Catalogue 92-735, Statistics Canada, (Bulletin 1.4-7) vol. 1, part 4, February 1974.
5. Catalogue 92-821, Statistics Canada, (Bulletin 2.2), 1976 Census of Canada.
6. *Kanadskii Pravoslavnyi Kalendar na 1971* g. (Canadian Orthodox Calender for 1971), Published by the Diocesan Council of the Canadian Diocese, Montreal-Toronto, pp. 40-48.

   Spisok arkhiereev, sviaschennosluzhitelei i prihodov Russkoi Zarubezhnoi Tserkvi s ikh adresami (List of Bishops, priests and parishes of the Russian Orthodox Church Abroad, and their addresses), 1979.
7. Okulevich, G., "*Russkie v Kanade*" (Russians in Canada), published by the Federation of Russian Canadians, Toronto, 1952, p. 307.
8. Forrest, A.C., in W. Kilbourn (Ed.) *op. cit.*, p. 66
9. Poniatowski, Michel, *Histoire de la Russie d'Amérique et de l'Alaska.* Librairie Académique Perrin, Paris 1978, p. 117.

   Ware, Timothy, *The Orthodox Church*, Penguin Books, A-592, Baltimore, MD, 1963, 1967, p. 187.
10. Handy, Robert T., *A History of the Churches in the United States and Canada.* Oxford University Press, 1979, p. 334.
11. *ibid*, p. 335
12. Okulevich, G., *op. cit.*, p. 15.
13. *Orthodox America 1794-1976. Development of the Orthodox Church in America.* Constance J. Tarasar (Ed.), published by the Department of History and Archives, the Orthodox Church in America, Syosset, NY, 1975, pp. 68-72, 74-75. The first such missionaries in Manitoba, Saskatchewan and Alberta were apparently Rev. Dimitri Kamnev from Seattle, and Rev. M. Maliarevsky from Minneapolis, as well as Rev. V. Alexandrov, Rev. Const. Popov. The first permanent Pastor appointed in Edmonton was Rev. Iakov Korchinsky, who founded the church of St. Barbara there.
14. *Ibid.*, pp. 69,74.
15. *Ibid.*, pp. 69-71, 302.
16. Okulevich, G., *op. cit.*, p. 307.
17. *Orthodox America 1794-1976. Ibid*, pp. 70-71.

18. Handy, Robert, T., *op. cit.*, pp. 345-350.

    Grant, John Webster, *The Church in the Canadian Era*. pp. 95-96; vol. 3 of the *History of the Christian Churches in Canada*. McGraw-Hill Ryerson Press, Toronto, 1972.

19. *Ibid*, p. 96.
20. *Ibid*, p. 98.
21. *Ibid*, p. 96, 139.

    Handy, Robert T., *op. cit.*, pp. 358-362.

22. Okulevich, G., *ibid*, p. 307.
23. Sollogub, A.A. (Ed.), *Russkaya Pravoslavnya Tserkov za granitsey, 1918-1968*. (The Russian Orthodox Church Abroad). Published by the Russian Mission in Jerusalem, and the Russian Orthodox Church Abroad, 1968, pp. 22-45.

    Archbishop John of Brussels and Western Europe, "*Russkaya Zarubezhnaya Tserkov*" (The Russian Church Abroad), Published by the Fraternity of St. Job of Pochaev, Montreal, 1979.

24. Grant, John Webster, *op. cit.*, p. 119. See also: *Orthodox America 1974-1976* pp. 188-194.
25. Okulevich, G., *op. cit.*, pp. 16-41.
26. *Ibid* p. 164.
27. *Ibid*
28. *Kanadskii Pravoslavnyi Kalendar na 1971* (Canadian Orthodox Calendar for 1971), *ibid*, pp. 59-65.
29. Okulevich, G., *op. cit.*, p. 187.
30. *Ibid*, pp. 194-196. The successor of the "Kanadskii Gudok" was "Vestnik" (Messenger), published in Toronto since November 1941.
31. *Ibid* pp. 198-204, 215, 217, 218, 222, 225, 229, 231, 235, 238, 244, 245.
32. *Ibid* pp. 216-217. Also "Vestnik" article "*The History of the First Years and the Fiftieth Anniversary*", April 5, 1980.
33. Thus, for instance, the Second All-Canadian Convention of the Federation of Russian-Canadians held in Toronto, November 1944, was attended by seven representatives of the Orthodox churches, among whom the following clergymen were mentioned: Metropolitan Veniamin, Archbishop Adam, Bishop Antony and the priests Ioann Diachina from Toronto and G. Marinets from Star, Alberta, the latter representing seven parishes. There were also the church activist Gregori Dutchak from Winnipeg and the priest Korablinov, also from Alberta. (See in G. Okulevich, *op. cit.*, pp. 233, 270)
34. *Ibid*, p. 233. This number should be increased by 400 young members of the Youth Clubs.
35. *Orthodox America 1794-1976*, *op. cit.*, p. 285
36. A very typical example of such internal conflicts happened at the St.

Peter and Paul parish in Montreal, where the Parish Council resisted pressure from its anglophone members; the latter, demanded that the Church services be celebrated in English. Finally, the anglophone members and the Parish priest, Rev. John Tkachuk, left the parish and founded their own parish elsewhere. In 1978, when the Head of the Church, Metropolitan Theodossius visited Montreal, he attended services in the new anglophone parish but did not communicate with the Russian Church. (Author).

37. Rosten, Leo (Ed.) *Religions of America, Ferment and Faith in an Age of Crisis.* Simon and Shuster, NY, 1975, pp. 112-121. In working on this part of my research, I was partly inspired by some selective topics touched upon in Rosten's reference book. I have also conducted a series of interviews on these topics with some Russian Orthodox priests belonging to both the Russian Church Abroad and the Orthodox Church in America. In my opinion the most representative among the Russian-Orthodox parish priests were: the Very Rev. Oleg Boldireff, Dean of St. Nicholas parish of the OCA, and Very Rev. Dimitri Sever, Dean of Holy Virgin's Intercession parish of the ROCA. I have had lasting and sincerely friendly relations with both for many years. In this article, I have tried to generalize as faithfully as possible the many conversations I had with all the priests, as related to the topics selected. (Author).

38. Panteleimon, Metropolitan, *"Pravoslavie i Inoslavnye khristianskie ispovedania"* (Orthodoxy and other Christian Faiths), Jordanville, 1950.

    Pomazansky, V. Rev. M., "Tserkov Khristova i sovremennoie obiedinitelnoe dvizhenie v Khristianstve" (The Church of Christ and contemporary movements for the Unification of Christianity); a Report to the XV Diocesan Conference, Jordanville, 1962.

    Grabbe, Archpriest Georghii, *"Sovremennoe Ekumenicheskoe Obnovlenchestvo i nashe otnoshenie k nemu"* (The Contemporary Ecumenical Revival and our attitude towards it). A Report to the Pastoral Conference, 1971.

    Grabbe, Archpriest G.,*"Kanonicheskoe polozhenie Russkoi Pravoslavnoi Tserkvi za granitsei"* (The Canonical Status of the Russian Orthodox Church Abroad). A Report to the AllChurch Council, 1974.

39. Orthodox America 1794-1976, *op. cit.*, pp. 246-248.

40. Sollogub, A.A., *op. cit.*, pp. 132, 137, 146 and, in particular, the "Message of Metropolitan Philaret" on this topic, Nov. 1-14, 1965, on pp. 346-353 in the same publication.

41. *"Ezhegodnik Pravoslavnoi Tserkvi v Amerike 1978"* (The Year Book of the Orthodox Church in America for 1978), New York, pp. 22-23, 59-60, 61-65.

42. Some of the problems of such a "transplant" are discussed in the opening article by Right Rev. A. Shmeman in the *Year Book of the Orthodox Church in America for 1978*, pp. 3-10.

Russian Baptists in Canada

(Compiled From Notes Provided by P.E. Kolibaiev)

The first Russian Baptists came to Canada at the beginning of this century. They settled in Winnipeg between 1901 and 1905 and twenty of the families organized a Russian-Ukrainian Baptist Church in that city with Ivan Shakotko as their preacher. Local Canadian Baptists gave strong support to the new community. Soon afterwards, Russian and Ukrainian Baptists of Saskatchewan and Alberta began to build small churches in various centres. Thus, a cohesive western community took root.

In Eastern Canada, their story began a little later and developed somewhat differently. The first church was organized in Toronto in 1908; the second in Montreal in 1910. An important event of the time was the publication of three hymnals, in Russian and Ukrainian, by I. Kolesnikov who also issued the bulletin *Dobry Drug* (Good Friend). In Ottawa, a Baptist Church came into being in 1916, folded five years later, and was revived in 1951 by new immigrants who had come from Europe following World War II. As the number of Baptists increased, new churches were founded in Hamilton, Niagara Falls, Toronto*, Windsor, Oshawa and Ottawa.

In the 1950s there were three unions of Slavic evangelical believers. In 1957, two Russian-Ukrainian unions amalgamated into one under the name of Union of Slavic Churches of Evangelical Christians and Slavic Baptists of Canada. Today, the executive committee of the Slavic Union of Churches comprises 13 members under the presidency of P.E. Kolibaiev. The Union maintains contact with the Russian Baptist Church in the United States, cooperates with them in missionary work, in publishing books and other literature in Russian and Ukrainian and broadcasts Baptist sermons to the USSR.

The so-called "third wave" of immigrants from the Soviet Union included a number of people who became interested in the Baptist faith. Some of them joined the Slavic Baptist Church in Calgary, under the ministry of I.E. Dovgalev, which organized a special school for children in the fall of 1981 with a membership of approximately 15 pupils, mostly from the families of third-wave immigrants.

In total, the brotherhood membership of Russian-Ukrainian Baptists churches in Canada represents approximately 1,500 individual members.

---

* At present, there are five churches in Toronto with a total membership of about 400. This is a count of individual members and does not include other family members.

Doctrinally close to the Baptists is a sect known as the *Pyatidesyatniks* (Pentacostals). In accordance with their religious beliefs, they deprecated higher education and had no lawyers or physicians in their ranks. They were, therefore, not in a position to help their own people and, consequently, very vulnerable. Searching for religious freedom, many eventually migrated to North America via Siberia, China and Australia. Approximately 1,500 of them live in Canada at present, 400 in Vernon, B.C., 200 in southern Ontario and others scattered in several parts of the country. (See also Chapter 7.)

Eleven

POLITICAL ORGANIZATIONS

As mentioned earlier, the Russian ethnic community is not a homogeneous unit, because it consists of people whose reasons for leaving Russia, the time and condition of departure, the experiences encountered in various countries during the transitional periods, not to mention the differences in class or national (ethnic) origin, were so diverse that one can say with confidence that there is not a single stratum of society from their former homeland that is not represented in Canada.

It is, therefore, not surprising that the political views of Canadians of Russian origin should be distinguished by their diversity. This phenomenon may not be very noticeable, partly because the Russian community is relatively small and partly because the individual immigrants are rarely vociferous.

We have no data on the distribution of the Russian minority among the various political parties in Canada. It is, however, clear that Russian Canadians do not participate in the political life of the country ***as a group***. This may be because it was not so long ago that they were "new Canadians" and, as people who had recently arrived, they were too occupied with thoughts of the past and with adapting to their new surroundings to become involved in the political life of their new homeland.

There is, however, a politically-active subgroup, the Federation of Russian Canadians (FRC), an organization that stands to the left of the political spectrum. It consists largely of people who left Russia at the end of the nineteenth and beginning of the twentieth centuries in search of a place to earn a living or to own a piece of land — the so-called economic emigrants. The organization has close ties with the Communist Party of Canada.

Other political parties and organizations have a completely different ideology, and their aims are diametrically opposed to those of the FRC. Refugees and people who left Russia after the 1914 war and October revolution were mostly enemies of Soviet authority, and many actually fought against it in the ranks of the White Army. In addition, soon after the end of the Civil War, some socialist-revolutionaries and a group of Mensheviks were expelled from the USSR. Abroad, they formed a moderate left-wing group among émigré organizations opposing Soviet politics.

All subgroups of the post-World War II immigrants, including those primarily from the USSR and secondarily from various countries outside the territories of Russia, generally had an anti-communist orientation. However, even among those immigrants, political views were not uniform.

Of the post-World War II political groupings of Russians in Canada, we will look at the following organizations: The National Labour Alliance of Russian Solidarists (NTS), The Union for the Struggle for the Liberation of the Peoples of Russia (SBONR) and the Kronstadt Group.

Common to these three organizations is their programme which, although differing in its aims, is directed towards consolidating their forces in the struggle for a democratic Russia. They are not strictly speaking Canadian organizations but affiliates of organizations scattered throughout the world where Russian emigrants have settled.

The Federation of Russian Canadians (FRC) is briefly outlined on page 166. Because its multi-faceted activities span several historical periods, the role of the FRC is described in various chapters throughout this book.

Other organizations, such as the Union of Monarchists, the Cadets' Union and Former Seamen, are steadily dying out. The activities of their small number of members consist mainly of social gatherings. Their retention of a national spirit, unbroken by many years outside Russia, is manifested by the periodic meetings of "Irreconcilability"* and occasional articles published in the Russian press outside the USSR.

* * *

Apart from the articles by V.I. Grebenschikov (NTS) and A. Klimoff (SBONR), the sections on Vlasov, the FRC and the Kronstadt Group were compiled as follows:

---

* Memorial meetings dedicated to honouring the victims of Bolshevik Terror during the Civil War in Russia and those oppressed by the Communist regime during subsequent years to the present.

Vlasov — the biographical sketch was prepared in consultation with the only surviving member of the Presidium of KONR, Dr. F.P. Bohatirchuk;

FRC — based solely on *"Russians in Canada"* by G. Okulevich and on articles from *Vestnik*, the official newspaper of the FRC; *Kronstadt Group* — based on the Group's own publications, as per references on page 166.

* * *

National Labour Alliance of Russian Solidarists (NTS)

The NTS, a Russian political organization, was born in Europe during the early thirties, and has been active ever since. Originally a youth organization, it was associated with the Russian All-Military Union (ROVS), a union of veterans of the Russian Civil War and those of the White Armies. The National Labour Alliance of the New Generation, as the movement was called at that time, sought a new ideological premise on which to fight communism. It soon became an independent political organization known as the National Labour Alliance of Russian Solidarists since the 1940s.

The marxist and communist doctrines of class struggle and *dictatorship of the proletariat* were countered with *solidarity of all members of society*. In its activities, the NTS strove to promulgate its ideological views and to propagate them within the USSR.

When the German-Soviet war began in 1941, many members of the NTS "infiltrated" Russian territory occupied by German troops. The members soon realized that the German government was not interested so much in combatting communism as in replacing Soviet authority with their own brand of authoritarianism. Together with new converted Russian anti-communists, they founded a "third force" under the slogan "neither Stalin, nor Hitler, but a Free Russia". In this respect, NTS members collaborated closely with the Russian Liberation Army (ROA) and with General A.A. Vlasov and later joined the "Committee for the Liberation of the Peoples of Russia" (KONR). Towards the end of the war, the German government arrested all the NTS leaders known to them. They were subsequently released by the Allied armies after the defeat of Germany and immediately resumed their political activities. Establishing their own printing house in West Germany, they started to publish anti-communist papers and pamphlets, distributing them among soldiers and officers of the Soviet occupation army in East Germany, and later even in the Soviet Union.

Russian Canadians

When the Allied authorities, the UNRRA, and later the IRO, started to vacate the refugee camps in Germany and to resettle the refugees in various countries of the world, many NTS members moved to Morocco, Australia and the Americas. Approximately 200 of them moved to Canada in 1948, others arriving between 1950 and 1952. The majority settled in Montreal and Toronto, smaller groups going to industrial and mining centres such as Hamilton, Sudbury and Rouyn-Noranda. They quickly re-established contact among themselves and with the centre of the organization in Frankfurt, West Germany. An NTS branch, headed by Valerian Lukyanovich Savin and comprising about thirty members, was established in Montreal in 1952. The following year, a "Canadian Division" of NTS was founded which eventually brought together the 120 or so members scattered throughout Canada, mainly in Quebec, Ontario and Manitoba. The objectives of this organization were as follows:

1. To make the Canadian public aware of the aims and essence of communism and Soviet power;
2. To make informative literature available to visiting Soviet citizens;
3. To collect money to aid the central NTS organization in Europe.

During the fifties and sixties NTS members were very active in Canada. Among the most successful initiatives were:

— The establishment of a "United Committee of Russian Social Organizations" in Montreal consisting of representatives of twelve Russian societies and three Orthodox churches with the purpose of organizing "Days of Irreconcilability". (Fig.34)
A particularly successful "Day of Irreconcilability" was held on November 9, 1952, marking the thirty-fifth anniversary of the Bolshevik Revolution in Russia. The Montreal press covered this meeting extensively and Radio Canada broadcast a number of speeches to the USSR.
— A number of meetings with members of Soviet groups visiting Montreal and Toronto.
— The development of close co-operation with the Veritas Institute* of Montreal, which was engaged in disseminating information on the activities of communist organizations in Canada.
— Several anti-Soviet demonstrations held in Montreal and Ottawa.
— To counteract communist propaganda, a rally in the very centre of the Ukrainian camp of Soviet patriots at Palermo near Toronto, where a "Day of Slavic Brotherhood" was being held and to which a delegation from the USSR had been invited.

---

* Presented by Rev. Rene Charbonneau.

— An anti-communist campaign during the Olympic Games in Montreal held jointly with NTS members from the USA.

By 1967, the Canadian branch of the NTS had lost much of its strength and dynamism. Some of the older members of the organization had moved, others left because of personal or family considerations. Moreover, there was no input from the younger members who were attracted instead by the Canadian way of life which led them in other directions. Some young people who shared the ideals of the NTS moved back to Europe for a more active political life.

References

Poremskii, V.D., "*The Political Mission of Russian Emigration*" . Report at the expanded editorial "Possev" Conference, September 12, 1954.

Leaflet — Invitation to the meeting devoted to "Irreconcilability with Communism and Soviet Authority" that took place on November 7, 1952, in Montreal in remembrance of the Bolshevik takeover of Russia.

Lettre apostolique "Sacro Vergente Anno", Aux peuples de la Russie, *L'Osservatore Romano*, 29 juillet 1959.

Communiqué pour la presse "Les Russes du Canada s'opposent au Communisme" that was registered for the International Service of Radio Canada for transmission by Voice of Canada.

Reports at the Meeting of Irreconcilability in Montreal, November 7, 1952 by A. Alpatov, V.I. Grebenschikov and K. Nikolaev.

A.D. Klimoff

The Union for the Struggle for the Liberation of the Peoples of Russia (SBONR)

SBONR is an organization whose role is a direct continuation of the activities of KONR (Committee for the Liberation of Peoples of Russia), sometimes called Vlasov's Committee.

The mass liberation movement started during the Second World War in German-occupied territories of the USSR. A group of civilians and former prisoners-of-war chose to take up arms and fight against the Soviet system even at the risk of being affiliated with another totalitarian regime, an affiliation they regarded as temporary. This group founded what was later to become KONR, under the leadership of former Soviet General Andrei Andreyevich Vlasov.

For many, this remarkable man's very name symbolizes the struggle for a free democratic Russia; for others, he is what Benedict Arnold is to Americans. His tragic story is on page 163.

SBONR — A Brief History and its Present Status in Canada

Brief Historical Review

Soon after the end of the Second World War, vigorous efforts were made to organize and unite Russian youth in German and Austrian refugee and displaced persons' camps. This was undertaken by an activist group of the Union of Youth of the Peoples of Russia (SMNR)* and it received wide response among Russian emigrants and particularly among the young. A result of this activity was the establishment, in August 1947, of BSMNR** whose members undertook to continue to struggle against the communist dictatorship in Russia on the basis of the democratic ideas of the Prague Manifesto of 1944.[2]

---

* SMNR was founded in 1944 by a decision of the Committee of Liberation of the Peoples of Russia.

** Militant Union of the Youth of Peoples of Russia.

By the end of 1947, Union membership had exceeded 4,000 in spite of the fact that former Soviet citizens were still terrified by memories of enforced repatriations that had occurred not long before.[3]

The appeals, pamphlets and proclamations of the BSMNR were widely distributed in the camps of refugees and displaced persons, and were avidly read. The ideological journal "Bor'ba" (Struggle), published since 1947, was the first, and for many years the only, loud voice that explained and supported the Liberation Movement of the Peoples of Russia against the slanderous Soviet counter-propaganda.[4] In its articles, "Bor'ba" analyzed the essence and ideology of the Liberation Movement of the Peoples of Russia, the true conditions existing in the USSR and described the attitude of the peoples of Russia towards communist tyranny.

BSMNR started to play an active role in German and international youth congresses; students took every opportunity and used every resource to explain the "Russian question" to foreigners, to distribute thousands of pamphlets and brochures in English, French and German, and to send ideological literature to the USSR.

In May 1948, it was decided to change the name of the organization to SBONR (Union of the Struggle for the Liberation of the Peoples of Russia), and it has continued to exist under this name to the present time. The change in name was prompted by the fact that, during the course of its political activities, the BSMNR outgrew its original "youth" orientation, becoming an organization of which 90% of the members were adults. They were ideologically mature and totally anti-communist. SBONR adopted the democratic basis of Vlasov's liberation movement.

During the first few years of its activity, SBONR began to devote more attention to the practical aspects of combatting communist influence and flagrant subversive communist activities in the West as well as in Eastern Europe.

By 1950, SBONR had become a truly popular, mass organization and, because of its consistent democratic policy, it has been able to attract many emigrants from the USSR who were non-Party people active in science and culture.

In 1951, SBONR initiated and was the main participant in the "Democratic Conference" in Munich which attracted significant numbers of the democratic intelligentsia, as well as the most recent emigrants from the USSR.

To present a unified, anti-Bolshevik front, SBONR has participated actively in the organization and operation of anti-Bolshevik centres abroad such as the Anti-Bolshevik Centre for the Liberation of People of Russia and the Coordination Centre of Anti-Bolshevik Movement (KTsAB) which consisted of four democratic organizations of Russian emigrants and five organizations of ethnic minorities.[5]

By July 1953, however, the diversity of views and arguments among individual organizations delayed the operation of the Coordination Centre, making further joint activity impossible and leading to an end of the Centre's existence.

Some organizations left the political area completely; others had to drastically reduce the scope of their activities. SBONR, likewise, had its share of troubles. The collapse of KTsAB served as a cause of a serious split in the ranks of the leaders and members of SBONR, the reasons for which were not ideological but tactical: the formation of blocks with other organizations; support for one of the diverse groups of KTsAB or another; and the difference in the interpretation of its Constitution. In spite of the fact that many well-meaning members exerted a great deal of effort to conserve the unity and strength of the Union, and even the fact that the 4th and 5th congresses of SBONR were directed towards the conservation and strengthening of the Union, the poison of indifference and absence of co-operation continued to spread. By 1963, the central leadership of the Union, concentrated in Munich, Germany terminated its activities.

Status in Canada

The advent of SBONR in Canada goes back to 1949 when the first chapter was organized in Toronto and the leaflet "Information Bulletin of SBONR in Canada" was issued on a regular basis.

In 1950, chapters were organized in Winnipeg and London (Ontario). The organizational work of SBONR proceeded successfully in Canada, and, at the second Conference of Canadian Chapters, called in September 1951 in Toronto, there were representatives from Toronto, Windsor, London, Hamilton, Sudbury, Montreal, Rouyn-Noranda, Winnipeg and Lethbridge. The publication of "Fakel" (The Torch), an ideological monthly journal of the Canadian Chapter of SBONR, began in 1952.

The crisis that beset the governing organs in the German branch of SBONR during the fifties after the collapse of the Coordination Centre had its effect on the operation of chapters in other countries, although to a much lesser extent.

Of all the SBONR chapters, those in the USA and Canada proved to be the most stable and viable. A possible explanation is that there were more young and dedicated members than in Europe. In addition, these countries had a relatively high standard of living which made these two chapters the most financially secure.

During the early sixties, both chapters started negotiations aimed at activating the operations of the entire Union and formulated plans that were crowned with success after a few years. The first step was the fusion, in 1964, of these two chapters into a new, expanded, North American Chapter of SBONR. At a subsequent conference of the two chapters, a new executive of the combined chapter was elected whose goal was to establish contacts with other chapters and to call the sixth convention of SBONR.

In November 1967, after a few years of preparation, the Sixth Convention of SBONR met in New York. In attendance were delegates from the Australian, Argentinian, Belgian, Venezuelan and North American Chapters. The convention confirmed the revised constitution of the Union, elected new executives of the governing bodies, and, most importantly, adopted a new ideological document - the Declaration of the Liberation Movement for the Peoples of Russia. The election of the new executives to the governing bodies meant that the Sixth Convention transferred the entire executive from Germany to North America.

One of the most important undertakings of the North American division of SBONR while organizing the Sixth Convention was the establishment of a SBONR publishing house. Having its own publishing facilities made it possible for the Union to publish the material they required for their operations, independent of any extraneous factors.

Another, no less important measure, adopted by the Sixth Convention, was the establishment of a Campaign Fund which was to support publications, give financial assistance to specific SBONR groups to facilitate carrying our specific projects and to give as much aid as possible to those who escaped from, or refused to return to, the USSR. In addition to income from special events, the Campaign Fund is maintained by contributions from Union members, friends and supporters of the organization.

The fruitful operation of the Union during the seventies confirmed the correctness of the resolutions and recommendations of the Sixth Convention. The successful Seventh Convention in Detroit in 1972, and the Eighth in Boston in 1977, reinforced the movement.

Conventions of the Union, called every five years, serve not only as the planning forum of the organization, but as the means for evaluating the strength of the anti-communist forces among the Russian immigrants in this country.

Notes

1. Dudin, Leo (N. Gradoboyev), "The Great Mirage", *Annals of the Russian Liberation Movement* (1941-1945), Vol. II, SBONR, London, Ontario, Library of Congress Catalogue Card no. 70-114953.

2. *Manifesto of the Committee for the Liberation of the Peoples of Russia*, Prague, 14 November 1944. Published by SBONR, Munich, 1960.

Also: Steenberg, Sven, *Vlasov*, Alfred A. Knopf, New York, 1970, p. 157.

3. Epstein, Julius, *Operation Keelhaul*, The Devin-Adair Company, Old Greenwich, Conn., 1973, 255 pages.

4. Klimoff, A., History of the Liberation Movement of the Peoples of Russia, Paper presented at the Ninth Congress of SBONR, 7 May 1982, Windsor, Canada, *Bor'ba*, NN 83-86, pp. 65-105.

General Andrei Andreyevich Vlasov

Of peasant stock, Vlasov was born in 1900 new Nizhniy Novgorod. His father worked as a part-time tailor to help educate him. In 1919, he was drafted into the Red Army where he found his metier, rising quickly through the ranks and gaining the respect of his superiors and subordinates alike as a soldier and a talented and patriotic military organizer. He joined the Communist Party in 1930. His subsequent career was brilliant, one of the highlights being his appointment as military advisor to Chiang Kai-shek, a post in which he revealed his diplomatic abilities. A few months before his fortieth birthday, Vlasov was promoted to Major General and, in February 1941, he received the Order of Lenin for his work in military organization.[1]

In the first year of the war, during the winter of 1941, Vlasov became the first Soviet general to defeat a German army: he saved Moscow and was proclaimed a hero, awarded the Order of the Red Banner and promoted to Lieutenant General.[2]

For his next posting, Vlasov was appointed Acting Commander of the Northwest Front. In an operation that was part of the effort to break the siege of Leningrad, he was flown in to join the army, which was surrounded near Volkhov, in an attempt to alleviate the desperate situation. However, being cut off from the main army, he was abandoned along with a few of his faithful aides. After wandering through swamps and forests for several weeks, he was finally captured by the Germans.

With plenty of time to think things over and to draw his own conclusions, Vlasov had, by that time, become disillusioned by the failure of the system he had formerly believed in. He realized that a country that was required to make endless sacrifices for more than 20 years in anticipation of the war was in a state of chaos; there was no party leadership when it was needed most. He witnessed the disintegration of the front, the misery of the people and the decimation of the army which was left without competent leaders as a result of the army purges of 1936 to 1939 when experienced senior officials were repressed or shot.

At that hour of truth in his soul-searching, Vlasov must have come to a decision; to fight against the system he no longer believed in . . . to fight for a free Russia.

His imprisonment and subsequent talks with other prisoners-of-war, including high-ranking Red Army officers and Colonel Vladimir Boyarsky in particular, showed him that he was not alone in his decision.

Encouraged by certain elements of the German command, some of whom opposed Hitler's ideas and especially his "Ostpolitik"*, Vlasov joined a group, composed mainly of former Red Army officers and civilians, which formed an organization that later became known as KONR and whose leader he became. His political programme was worked out and presented as the *Manifesto of KONR*, which called for:

> the overthrow of Stalin's tyranny, liberation of the peoples of Russia from the Bolshevik system and the restoration of the rights won by the peoples of Russia in the popular revolution of February, 1917, the acceptance of German military aid under honourable conditions, and the recognition of national states and their rights.

The Manifesto was reluctantly accepted by the Germans despite its frankly independent tone and the absence of any sign of subordination or references to the racist policies of the Nazis.

But Vlasov's dreams and efforts did not materialize. Afraid of his tremendous popularity, the Nazis kept him under tight surveillance. Vlasov had no control over any strategic decisions and the Nazis used his name without scruple to serve their own ends.

At the end of the war, Vlasov was offered a plane in which to escape to Spain but he refused, preferring to stay and die with his soldiers.

On June 24, 1946, he was turned over to the Soviets by the Allies and hanged as a traitor.

References

1. Izvestiya, February 23, 1941.
2. Izvestiya, January 24, 1942.

---

* Some of them were executed by the Nazis for having taken part in the unsuccessful attempt on Hitler's life and the coup d'état of August, 1944.

The Kronstadt Group

Between the fifties and sixties, a chapter of the Kronstadt Group was operating in Canada. It was so named in memory of the victims of the Kronstadt Rebellion of 1921. The rebellion was initiated by sailors of the Red Fleet, who were considered to be the pride of the Revolution, being the first and most active supporters of the Bolshevik coup of October 1917*. The founder of the Kronstadt group, S.G. Petrov-Skitalets, based the ideas and political progamme of the Group on a slogan put forth during the rebellion: "All power to the Soviets and not to the Communist Party"! In other words, "Let's have Soviets without Communists".

He explained the group's aims as follows:

> It (the Group) is a small circle of like-minded people, scattered throughout various continents, who consider it their moral duty, with respect to those who remain in their native land, to formulate and transmit through the "iron curtain" the idea of a new liberation program.[1]

The program of the Kronstadt Group was formulated in the *Thesis of the Paris Manifesto of November 14, 1944.*[2]

The basic slogan, however, did not meet with much enthusiasm among the Russian political emigrants and, after much discussion in "Novoye Russkoye Slovo" (a Russian daily newspaper printed in New York and one of the most popular émigré publications), it became evident that the majority did not support the group.[3]

Subsequently, the Kronstadt Group chose as its forum the "Seyatel" ("The Sower"), a journal published in South America by N. Cholovskii and an organ of the Federation of Russian Workers in South America.[4]

After the death of Petrov-Skitalets and other active members of

---

* The rebellion started among the sailors of the Soviet battleship *Petropavlovsk* and was supported by the soldiers and workers of the naval base at Kronstadt, 17 miles from Petrograd on the Gulf of Finland. The rebels called a meeting that adopted a resolution demanding the abolition of the Communist one-party domination of the Soviets. The resolution proposed free democratic elections to assert that the power would be returned to the people, i.e., to the free Councils of Workers', Soldiers' and Peasants' Deputies (Soveti rabochikh, soldatskikh i krestianskikh deputatov). The communists were quick to see the danger in the revolt spreading and reacted by calling the Kronstadt rebels "counter-revolutionaries". Reluctant Red Army soldiers were mobilized and 18 days later the rebellion was crushed, leaving 18,000 dead and many more deported to concentration camps.

the organization, the Group gradually curtailed its activities and, as far as is known, ended its existence by the close of the sixties.

In Canada, the Kronstadt Group consisted of several dozen members, mainly in Ontario and Quebec.

References

1. *Seyatel*, Buenos Aires, 1962, No. 105, p. 8.
2. Petrov-Skitalets, E., *The Kronstadt Thesis*, Robert Speller and Sons Publishers, New York, 1964, 134 pp.
3. *Information Bulletin of the SBONR*, North American Branch, London, Ontario, September 1964, No. 60, p. 11
4. *Seyatel*, "The Fate of the Kronstadt Group", July 1974, No. 146, p.4.

The Federation of Russian Canadians

The Federation of Russian Canadians (FRC) was officially born in 1942 out of the Russian Workers' and Farmers' Clubs and the Russian Committees to Help the Motherland.

The Russian Workers' Clubs, named after Maxim Gorky, were founded in Canada in 1930 by immigrants who had come to Canada from Poland, Western Byelorussia and Volynia in the 1920s and who hoped to return home after saving some money.[1]

Aiming to organize Russian and East European workers in Canadian cities, the clubs were active in the labour movement. In the first issue of the Club's newspaper, "The Canadian (Factory) Whistle" which appeared on April 8, 1931, the editorial article "Our Tasks" read as follows:

> Our first task is to bring together and organize the Russian proletarians in Canada who are under the influence of anarchic and White Guard elements. The Canadian (Factory) Whistle has to show the achievements of the workers in the country that is building socialism — the USSR.[2]

Accused of subversive propaganda by the Canadian Government, many members of the Clubs were deported between 1930 and 1934. In April 1940, publication of the newspaper was forbidden and, two months later, Russian Workers' and Farmers' Clubs were outlawed together with other communist and fascist organizations.[3]

During the war and the period of rapprochement between the Allies and the USSR, the climate for renewed activity became more favourable and the old members started to bring together activist groups who subsequently founded the "Russian Committee to Help the Motherland" (RCHM).[4] Several such committees were formed whose activities consisted of collecting funds and sending them to the USSR, as well as attempting to unite Russians and other Slavs to support the Motherland. (Fig. 35)

The Federation of Russian Canadians was founded in 1942, at the General Congress of the RCHM when the organizations and groups that took part in the fund-raising campaigns were in attendance.[5]

At a time when patriotic feelings ran high, "Vestnik" (The Messenger), the official newspaper of the FRC, which was founded on November 6, 1941, published patriotic articles and slogans, such as: "For the Motherland! For the Soviets!"

Recently, the Federation and its official newspaper, "Vestnik", celebrated their 50th anniversary. In the article "History of the First Years and the 50th Anniversary",[6] one reads that the organization considers its founding date to be not 1942 but March 5, 1930, the date on which the clubs named after Gorky were founded.*

The Federation maintains close ties with the Communist Party of Canada and "Vestnik" publishes articles taken from "Pravda" and "Izvestiya" verbatim, giving its readers the Soviet interpretation of international events.

The FRC also draws its inspiration from the USSR, as the following congratulatory telegram will attest. It was printed by "Vestnik" on the occasion of its 50th anniversary.

> All of us — honest Russo-Ukrainian Canadians — are proud of our Motherland and of the majestic achievements of the Russian people. They are a source of strength and inspiration for working people all over the world, wherever there is a fight for social and national freedom. In this way, the USSR helps many countries to get rid of hated reactionary régimes, to throw off the hated yoke of slavery and to take power in their own hands, becoming masters of their own destiny. All these historic changes are closely tied to the name of the Great Lenin and the Great October.[7]

According to date published in the May 1979 issue of *The Canadian Family Tree*, there were 15 FRC branches in Canada at that time. The FRC conducts active educational work among its members with extensive programs for children and youth, including music and dance groups, a chorus, etc. The newspaper "Vestnik" occasionally organizes competitions for the best essay on a given topic to attract the interest of young people.

---

* If the FRC considers its founding date to be 1930, given the fact that Russian Workers' and Farmers' Clubs were outlawed in 1940, it had simply emerged under another name in 1942. (Ed.)

By adopting a pro-Soviet stand, the Federation sets itself apart from other Russian organizations, founded by "white" and post-war immigrants.

References

1. Okulevich, G. *Russians in Canada*, Toronto, Canada, 1952, p. 69, (in Russian).
2. *Ibid.*, pp. 84-85.
3. *Ibid.*, p.195.
4. *Ibid.*, p.198.
5. *Ibid.*, pp. 209-212.
6. *Vestnik*, Toronto, April 5, 1980.
7. *Ibid.*, April 26, 1980.

Twelve

COMMUNITY LIFE AND CULTURAL-EDUCATIONAL ACTIVITIES OF RUSSIANS IN CANADA

Introduction

The small number of Russian Canadians and the fact that there was no mass settlement of Russian immigrants, with the exception of the Doukhobors, explain the absence of Russian organizations of national stature in Canada.

In general, early efforts to organize community life and cultural activity were concentrated around the churches. The church was a bulwark uniting people of different backgrounds who wished to retain their ethnic traditions and Russian language.

However, one look at the table of *Religious Affiliations of Russians in Canada** is enough for one to realize how divided Russian Canadians really are. It is not surprising that, because of the internal contradictions and frictions between people belonging to different faiths or jurisdictions within the Eastern-Orthodox Church and those who do not belong to any church at all but are nevertheless interested in "Russianness", there was a desire to hold cultural and social activities outside of the framework of the church.

Since the churches have their own activities which aim to keep the parish, and particularly the younger members, under its influ-

---

* See Chapter 10.

ence, there are sometimes feelings of rivalry directed against organizations that do not belong to its circle. This leads to the further fragmentation of the Russian Canadian society, which was not united to begin with.

Organized community activities take place under church auspices, in big community groups, and in independent cultural educational societies.

The need to retain one's ethnic identity and to belong to one's own group is strongest among first-generation Canadians. Exposed to an unfamiliar and often hostile environment, they cling to their past and their traditions to feel secure and fight the feeling of being third-class citizens.

Why would Russians continue to escape reality in this way? In answer to this question, one young woman whom we interviewed stated:

> Having arrived in Canada at the age of seven, having travelled the length and breadth of this country and loving it as I do, I have no hesitation in saying that I am a Canadian. But Canadians, unlike Americans, as we all know, do not easily accept others as being Canadians except in the legal sense of the word. One's origin is always probed, usually with the question of one's place of birth. For those of us born during or right after the Second World War, the answer is much more misleading that would be the one to the question "What language did you speak at home?"
> My peers were born anywhere west of the Soviet Union . . . in South America, China, Australia and even Africa. As my mother always said when officials insisted that I must be Polish, "A dove that is born in a stable is not a horse".

The second, third and subsequent generations become attached to the Canadian way of life and tend to lose interest in the Russian language and even in family history. Unhappy at being "different", some young people break with the past and try to become "one of the gang".

Interest in Russian heritage is usually reawakened with the arrival of each new wave of immigrants as, for example, was the case after World War II when new societies and active cultural groups flourished in major cities where New Canadians settled.

The organizations founded at that time consisted mainly of refugees from the Soviet regime who were apprehensive of infiltration by communists into their societies. For this reason, the charters of these organizations deny membership to persons belonging to a communist party. This clause determines their ideological "face" and sets them apart from those groups, founded by previous waves of immigrants, that had leftist leanings.

As the Doukhobor and FRC organizations are described in other chapters of this book, reference is made only to the most viable independent organizations in the larger Canadian cities such as Montreal, Vancouver, Toronto and Ottawa.

Although the aims of these organizations and the pattern of their activity are basically very similar, we considered it worthwhile to include, for the record, some details of their background and activities.

Montreal

One of the oldest Russian communities is in Montreal, where the first steps at organization were taken in 1923. At that time, a Cultural-Educational Society affiliated with the Church of the Holy Apostles Peter and Paul was formed.

One of its founders and long-time president was B.V. Orlov. To further the preservation of the Russian heritage and language, the Society put on concerts, social evenings and staged performances of Russian classics. Lectures were organized with speakers frequently hailing from other Canadian and American cities. In 1923, A.B. Zharkovskii organized the "Pushkin" library, which is still in operation.

The arrival of the first immigrants after the Second World War breathed new life into the Russian community. In 1949, the Society for Aid to New Canadians was formed, which provided some financial assistance to new arrivals. In many cases, the Society assisted in bringing over immigrants' relatives who were still overseas.

Acquiring some confidence in their new environment, the "New Canadians" began to take part in the actitivies of the Society. Among the organizers were Father O. Boldireff, N.S. Grebenshchikova, L. Guryanova and A.F. Romar. A theatrical group was formed with M.S. Petrov, Mr. and Mrs. Lashkhabanov, Mr. Shelekhov and Mrs. N. Grebenshchikova among the most active members. Named "Vozrozhdenie (Renaissance), it achieved great success, staging plays in other cities including New York, under the direction of Boris and Wanda Arleninov.

There was also an extensive programme for children and the younger generation which included Russian-language schools and courses, sports teams, childrens' summer camps and scouts, and dancing and singing groups.

The musical groups were the most active. A string ensemble grew into the Andreev Orchestra which, at the beginning of the fifties consisted of 25 people. The "Gusli" folk-music youth group also achieved considerable success under the direction of Mr. and Mrs. Andrianov, giving professional concerts in several cities.

In the field of immigrant aid, the Canadian Division of the

Tolstoy Foundation Fund, which existed in Montreal from 1953 to 1964, organized mutual aid and financial assistance to immigrants and worked to get visas for relatives. The financial base of this activity was a grant of $25,000 from the Federal Government of Canada. Operations were expanded to the point where the annual financial turnover reached $100,000.

In 1954, a Russian Branch of the Canadian Legion was founded under the direction of Captain B.V. Orlov. Membership included veterans of the First and Second World Wars as well as those who had served in the Serbian Royal Army. The Russian Branch continues to help veterans to establish their status as legionnaires and to obtain veterans' pensions.

In the town of Rawdon (Quebec), where there were so many Russians that it seemed almost a Russian town, a monument to Russian soldiers was erected in the cemetery of the Holy Seraphim Chapel. An annual requiem is held in honour of Tsar Nicholas II and his family, King Alexander of Yugoslavia and all the victims of communism. The ceremony is usually followed by a military parade which includes local branches of the Royal Canadian Legion from neighbouring towns.

The Cadet Union was founded in Montreal in 1952. To this day, its aims are to provide mutual aid, uphold the honour of the name "Russian" and disseminate information about Russian history, which is frequently presented in a biased way, either through ignorance or by intent. Founded by A. Perekrestov, E. Rubanistyi, Y. Mazaraki, N. Vydykhan, E. Lyashenko, Rev. O. Boldireff and M. Kazanovitch, the Cadet Union is active today under the leadership of G.P. Levchuk. Under its aegis, congresses of Russian Imperial Cadets are held from time to time since the first one took place in Montreal in 1968. Congresses are now held every two years around the world, the last being in Paris in 1980. The Cadet Union also publishes a journal called "Cadet Roll Call".

The Monarchist Union, presided by A. Apraksin meets periodically. Among the members are representatives of Russian nobility, the core of high society in Imperial Russia. The village of Labelle in the Laurentians, not far from Montreal, provided a summer retreat for these families. Upon entering the small village church, one forgets the years spent in exile, overtaken by the feeling of being back in "old" Russia, which ceased to exist a long time ago.

As mentioned before, in the fifties, there were, summer camps for Russian scouts near Montreal and Toronto. As participation in scout camps left a long-lasting impression in the minds of the young generation, a brief description of the Russian Scouts Organization is in order.

R.N. Polchaninoff

*Russian Boy Scouts**

Only a year after Robert Baden-Powell's movement to organize English boys "for training in character, citizenship and leadership" officially became the Boy Scouts, an affiliated movement began in Imperial Russia, culminating in the foundation by Oleg Pantuhoff of the Russian Boy Scouts on April 30, 1909. The aims of the movement were similar to English scoutism, the difference being emphasis on the Russian nation and religion.

In Russia, the movement did not survive the Revolution, which occurred eight years later. The new rulers proclaimed the Scouts as a symbol of a rich and decadent society. In the Soviet Union, the education of children was taken over by the Party, whose aim was to prepare young children (Organization of "Pioneers") for the "Komsomol" (Young Communists) and eventually for Communist Party membership.

Many Russian scouts emigrated with their parents and it says much for the strength of the Russian Boy Scouts and the enthusiasm of their members that, before long, a rebirth took place. An important fact was that Pantuhoff himself became an emigrant and it was he who founded and headed the Organization of Russian Scouts Abroad until his death in October 1973. His career as Chief Scout spanned 64 years which, of course, is unique in the movement, worldwide.

As the Russian Scouts found themselves scattered in various countries of the world after the Revolution, the aim of the movement was strengthened by the wish to preserve the "Russianness" of the children, organizing them not by place of residence but by principle of ethnicity. Due to the relatively small number of members which resulted from this principle, the Organization of Russian Scouts includes girl scouts as well.

In the 1920s and 1930s attempts were made to keep the organization bipartite: The Boy Scouts' insignia was a lily and the Girl Scouts', three snowbells. However, after World War II, the two branches were formally united under a common insignia: a lily.

As the number of "white" immigrants in Canada was small between the two World Wars, it is not surprising that there were no attempts to organize Russian Scout troops. This changed at the end of

---

* Registered under the name of The Organization of Russians Scouts Abroad (Organizatsiya Russkikh Skautov za granitsei) on August 30, 1922 at the International Boy Scouts Bureau.

the 1940s, when World War II immigrants started to arrive in Canada. The newcomers began organizing the first scout troops: in Toronto[12], the Scout Instructors were Sabrodsky and V. Martysevich; in Montreal,[3,4,5] A. Kaminsky, E. Kruchinsky, V. Bykadorov and S. Medvedev. In 1952, a special Lone Scouts detachment for people living far away was organized under Instructor L. Semeniuk.[6] Administratively, all these units were part of New York ORYuR*, represented by Sci. Andrei Illinsky.

In 1951, following the arrival from Europe of the Scm. R. Polchaninoff and the organization of the North American Region, the Canadian troops came under the management of its own leader, Scm. G.P. Joukoff, who was appointed as representative of ORYuR.[7] He served in that capacity from 1956 until his death in April 1957.[8] The Russian Scouts were then taken over by the North American Region. After it was divided into Eastern and Western American Regions in 1980, the Canadian territory was incorporated in the Eastern American Region of ORYuR-NORS*.[9] The Canadian summer camps[10,11] which operated from 1952 to 1956 were no longer organized and the Russian children from Canada joined the summer camp in the Adirondack Mountains of New York State.

Memories of those happy days live on forever, as the following description by the young woman quoted earlier attests:

> There were two summer camps near Montreal. A family owned a piece of property just outside of Rawdon, Quebec, a village about 40 miles from Montreal. They made their property available to the scouts and suddenly it became a Russian enclave and Rawdon a place to go to. The scouts were divided into male and female camps and activities were divided into schedules according to age groups, the younger ones belonging to the "belki" (squirrels, equivalent to Brownies) and the "volchata" (wolfcubs). We lived in tents, built gates and fences around the perimeter, raised the mast, built latrines and set up the kitchen area, which was placed halfway between the boys' and girls' camps. We built our own beds from small tree trunks, filled our mattresses with straw and washed our dishes in the stream.
>
> Every morning we were awakened to the sound of a trumpet, raised the flag, performed gymnastics, washed, then had breakfast. There were games, chores, "pokhody" (long marches), tests, lessons in Russian history, the hated afternoon naps, beloved campfires. We laughed and we sang and the songs learned around the

---

* ORYuR — Organizatsiya Rossiĭskikh Yunykh Razvedchikov (Organization of Russian Boy Scouts).

** NORS — National Organization of Boy Scouts. The American District was referred to by the double name, ORYuR-NORS, following the reorganization in 1979.

fire became one of our strongest bonds and was one of the pleasures we passed on to our parents.
The scouts "died" in Montreal as did several other attempts at "maintaining our heritage".
However, I will never forget Rawdon, the tiny church built outside the priest's house where we sang Sunday mass under the towering pine trees or that feeling of knowing that there is a spot that you can say you belong to."

In 1965, scout work in Canada was revived under the direction of Sci. N. Smirnoff[12,13] and Tatiana Novotny[14]. In the 1970s, due to increasing interest from parents and children, a camp was established on the picturesque banks of the Muskoka River.

By 1970, all three Canadian troops had disintegrated.[15] As recently as 1979-1981, Scm. P. Naumov organized a troop in Montreal.[16] Although the activities of ORYuR-NORS in Canada have been substantially reduced due to the universal process affecting Russian youth growing up outside Russia, i.e. the loss of interest in their heritage, the excellent ideas of Russian-scoutism have not totally disappeared. Interest in it may yet be renewed when the older scouts start bringing up families of their own.

References

1. *Vestnik Razvedchika*, No. 34, March 1954.
2. *North American Region Orders*, No. 12 #8, October 1, 1954.
3. *Vestnik Razvedchika*, No. 17, December 1950.
4. *Vestnik Severo-Amerikanskogo Otdela*, No. 12, November 1952.
5. *Byulleten' Monrealskoy Druzhiny ORYuR*, No. 3, May 1953; *North American Region Orders*, No. 3 #6, April 20, 1956.
6. *Ibid.*, No. 6 #2, October 15, 1952.
7. *Chief Scoutmaster's Orders*, No. 57 #5, April 17, 1956.
8. *Vestnik Ruká*, No. 56, May 1957.
9. *Chief Scoutmaster's Orders*, No. 57 #5, April 17, 1956.
10. *Vestnik Razvèdchika*, No. 24, June-July, 1952.
11. *Vestnik Ruka*, No. 44, March 1956.
12. *North American Region Orders*, No. 61 #2, January 29, 1966.
13. *Ibid.*, No. 65 #2, December 24, 1966.
14. *Ibid.*, No. 67 #4, June 7, 1967.
15. *Ibid.*, No. 81 #8, December 10, 1970; ibid., No. 83 #5, January 1, 1971
16. *Eastern American Region Orders*, No. 7 #2, May 21, 1981.

Vancouver

At the beginning of the twentieth century there was only a small number of Russian immigrants in British Columbia. These were mostly peasants, as well as people belonging to various religious sects. In the cities, there were a few revolutionaries who had fled tsarist Russia after the 1905 revolution. After the Civil War in Russia as the number of immigrants increased owing to the "whites" who established themselves primarily in Vancouver. In 1928, Russians built the first Orthodox Church (the Church of the Holy Resurrection) as well as to a hall for meetings and performances. Formed in 1935, the Russian-Orthodox Society took upon itself the financial and legal responsibilities of the Church.

At the same, time the activities of other Russian groups in Vancouver were developing along quite different lines. In 1931, a Russian Workers' Club was organized — one of the Maxim Gorky Clubs which were in operation in Eastern and Central Canada. This club was the predecessor of the Federation of Russian Canadians and, from 1941 on, all its activities were held in the building called the Russian Peoples' House.

With the substantial increase in the number of Russians in Vancouver after the Second World War, the notion arose of creating a single Russian cultural centre which would be independent of various church jurisdictions. So it came about that, in 1955, the Society of Friends of the Performing Arts was organized, headed by R. Makovkin. Its location was in East Hastings in a building provided by Mr. Ivankhnyuk; it was modified by the Society members and used for artistic performances and evenings.

In March 1956, a commission headed by M. Boriskovich, formulated a constitution for a Russian Centre, which was adopted at a meeting of 130 people and legally registered in Victoria. Initially named the "Russian Centre of British Columbia", it was later changed to the "Russian Social Centre" in Vancouver. The first president was Mr. Andreyev, who retained this post for many years. He was succeeded by Mr. Stromilov, Mr. Kholodilin and Mr. Buyan who has been president from 1973 to date.

The following groups function within the framework of the Society: theatre, choir, balalaika orchestra, library and a youth circle. At one time, there was also a committee dealing with aid to invalids, and a news bulletin.

In November 1957, the Russian Social Centre acquired the former movie house "Kitsilano Theatre".

Due to the death or departure of a number of the organizers and insufficient interest on the part of the younger members, there has been a drastic decline in the vitality of the Society in recent years.

In an attempt to avoid the liquidation of the Centre, it was suggested that the building be converted into a senior citizens' home. Because of the differing views on the matter, this was not approved. Then, at an extraordinary meeting in 1969, it was decided to create an *ad hoc* committee to try to rejuvenate the Centre. The committee called for action and the people responded. A new administration was elected which undertook the task of renovating the neglected building and reorganizing the activities of the Society. The balalaika orchestra was re-established under the leadership of M. Luzgin, who made special trips from Seattle; and a children's school and dance studio was organized under the direction of Mrs. Lozovskaya and Mrs. Maurer. Augmented by a choir and a balalaika ensemble, the dance group participated in ethnic performances and festivals and groups representing the Society appeared on radio and television.

As is provided for in the constitution, all those who speak Russian and are interested in the activities of the Centre are invited to functions held by the Society. Thus, representatives of all immigration waves participate in its various programmes.

It is encouraging to note that the activities of the Centre are supported by the young generation, which gives assurance that it will not wither but, indeed, grow and develop in the future.

Toronto

In 1950, a group of Russian immigrants arriving from Europe after the Second World War founded a Russian Club in Toronto, which they named the "Russian Cultural-Educational Society". Among its founders were D. Vendeli, E. Svetlichnaya, V. Petrov, N. Blagoveshchenskiĭ, A. Klimoff, M. Manuilov, M. Lyalin and E. Ermolayev. The aim of the society was to unite Russians in Toronto and the surrounding areas, regardless of their church affiliation.

Initially, the Society held its social and cultural activities in rented quarters. By 1950, the Society was in a favourable position financially to be able to purchase a building and, henceforth, all activities took place under one roof. The new premises also housed a library consisting of 2,500 volumes. In 1973, the Society purchased a larger building and registered under a new name, the "Russian Cultural Aid Society".

From the very beginning, the Society published a journal called *Edinenie* (Unity), which was subsequently renamed *Russkoe Slovo v Kanade* (Russian Word in Canada). Its editor, up to the temporary cessation of publication in 1981, was K.I. Matiash.

Cultural activities are no different from other organizations. Of the more popular are the artistic programmes and traditional Russian fair presented by the Society's *Novgorod Pavilion* during "Caravan" week.

An optimistic sign of the Society's viability is the fact that 1981 was the first time in its history that the younger generation had taken an active part in the operation and management of the Society.

Ottawa

The social life of Russians before the Second World War centred exclusively around the Bukovinian Church that was the only Eastern-Orthodox Church in Ottawa at the time. Among the parishioners was a small number of White Russians who emigrated to Canada from Southern Russia, Turkey and the Balkans. The families of V. Berdnikov and N. Statkevich were members of the church committee and were the first old-timers to welcome the representatives of the new wave of immigrants who came to Canada in the late forties.

For a long time, however, the number of ethnic Russians was so small that the question of organizing cultural-educational activities did not even arise. With the increase in the Russian population in the early fifties, two Orthodox Churches were organized. As a result, most of the Russians left the Bukovinian Church; but, because of the different Church jurisdictions, i.e., the Russian-Orthodox Church Abroad and the Orthodox Church in America, close relations between parishioners were not encouraged.

Staying aloof from the mainstream of cultural activities were small numbers of Doukhobors and those who, although Russian speaking, did not participate in church activities or married non-Russians, gradually losing their mother tongue, as well as the tradition of their fore-fathers.

Late in 1973, the idea occurred to establish a society in which all people of Russian background, regardless of church jurisdiction, would meet on neutral ground. By that time, the number of Russians in Ottawa had reached several hundred. The group of twelve who shared this idea and took the initiative consisted of people who represented different waves of immigration, social backgrounds and church affiliations.

It was decided to call the Society the A.P. Chekhov Society, after the Russian writer, doctor and humanist. A committee was established to draw up a constitution and elected its first president, O. Mokievsky-Zubok. Today, that position is held by T.F. Jeletzky.

In addition to the Society's aims of preserving the cultural heritage and of bringing together Russian-Canadians and, indeed, all people interested in Russian culture, other objectives outlined in its Constitution were:

> — to raise the image and prestige of the Russian-Canadian, a loyal Canadian citizen, whose reputation in the past had frequently been tarnished by the activities of small but vociferous groups of extremists of Russian descent;
> — to take every opportunity to explain the difference between the concepts "Russian" and "Soviet", and "Russian" and "communist", which are frequently confused by the media and, consequently, in the mind of the Canadian public.

The Society was officially inaugurated at the beginning of 1974. In addition to ethnic Russians who naturally formed the majority and represented various streams of immigration, but primarily the waves which followed the First and Second World Wars, there were members of different nationalities inhabiting the Soviet Union, as well as others interested in Russian culture.

The activities of the Society are partially supported by a grant from the Directorate of Multiculturalism, Department of the Secretary of State, and include lectures, concerts, special activity groups, language courses and a library. Other programmes include arts and crafts exhibits, an annual ball, social evenings, and the latest project — the present book of collected essays.

Concluding Remarks

In addition to the Russian ethnic groups and organizations mentioned here, there were a number of other, smaller groups dispersed all over Canada. Some did not leave any records; others were short-lived. In particular, this applies to independent organizations whose existence was restricted by meager financial means, small membership and, last but not least, the absence of permanent quarters.

Those organizations whose activity was part of church life fared better. All churches, rich or poor, had a parish hall where any group could hold its functions without having to look for premises of its own.

After a certain period of adaptation to Canadian life, interest in keeping one's memories decreased and, without additional motivation, seemed to dissolve in everyday life. There were, however, instances when the desire to preserve the Russian heritage proved strong enough to resist the general apathy common to the generations born outside the homeland. Such motivation persists in the Russian-Orthodox Church Abroad (ROCA) because of its belief in its missionary role, bound to the fate of Russia. Russian Orthodoxy in its purest form, as well as language and tradition, are to be preserved for the day when they can be brought back to a reformed Motherland freed from communism. The tendency to organize activities to preserve the Russian heritage is also observed among the Doukhobors and in the clubs affiliated with the Federation of Russian Canadians, which keep close ties with the USSR by sending groups of young people to the "Motherland". These visits and exchanges continue to motivate people to preserve their Russian culture.

On the other hand, Russians who have no ties with organized Russian communities or groups are the first to become assimilated by Canadian society and are no longer sufficiently motivated to keep the ways of their ancestors.

* * *

Several individuals contributed to the foregoing chapter on the cultural-educational activities of Russians in Canada. The breakdown of the various sections is as follows:

Montreal — compiled from notes provided by Rev. O. Boldireff and T. Galko;
Russian Boy Scouts — Scm. R.N. Polchaninoff
Vancouver — extracts from a report by Nina Krink on the occasion of the 20th anniversary of the Russian Centre, August 20, 1980;
Toronto — compiled from notes provided by R.F. Piotrovsky and N.G. Kosachova;
Ottawa — T.F. Jeletzky.

M.I. Mogljansky

Thirteen

RADIO BROADCASTING IN RUSSIAN

In addition to Canadians of Russian origin, there are more than a million Canadians of Polish, Ukrainian and Byelorussian descent, many of whom have a good understanding of the Russian language. To these one can add Canadians of non-Slavic origin who were born and brought up on the territory of the Russian Empire or, latterly, the Soviet Union. Moreover, during the last two decades, some anglophone and francophone Canadians began to study Russian. Several universities established Russian departments offering courses in Russian language, history and literature.

Before 1950, however, one rarely heard Russian radio broadcasts in Canada intended for Canadian listeners, although in the large cities small, private radio stations were regularly or intermittently broadcasting programs in Polish, Ukrainian, Italian, Greek and other languages. In the early seventies, television stations in the large cities started to broadcast programs in a number of languages other than English and French, and the Government encouraged ethnic groups to develop their own programmes.

We know of only a few, not very successful, attempts to carry out regular broadcasting in Russian. For example, in the mid-1950s, several local residents in Montreal, headed by Andrei Kodzhak (now head of the Russian department at New York University) started half-hour broadcasts in Russian on one of the local, private radio stations. These programmes were financed by commercial advertising, as is the custom in Canada. Although these broadcasts were well structured and conducted on a highly professional level, they remained on the air for only a few months as they did not attract sufficient attention neither from Montrealers who understood Russian nor from the business community.

Another attempt was made at the end of the sixties in British Columbia by a musical group of the Russian Cultural-Educational Society. Even before that, an attempt at broadcasting in Russian was initiated by a group of local Doukhobors. In both cases, almost exclusive use was made of taped programmes from the Russian Section of Radio Canada International.The broadcasts included parts of the programme cycle devoted to the history of Canada in celebration of the centennial of the Confederation of Canada. These attempts, however, were even less successful.

Recently, a private radio station in Toronto started to broadcast some short programmes in Russian on a show called "Neva". These, however, appear to have pro-Soviet leanings.

How could it be that, in a country where hundreds of thousands of people understand Russian from childhood and where there are people who make a special effort to study this language, there are no regular broadcasts in Russian?

The author considers the main reason to be the absence of a unified organization, similar to the Polish and Ukrainian ones across the country, one that could unite Russian Canadians, represent their interests and concern itself with the conservation of the Russian language, culture and traditions. The Federation of Russian Canadians, which grew out of Workers' and Farmers' clubs before and during the Second World War, had a certain influence, primarily among representatives of the labour movement. However, soon after the war, many former citizens of the USSR who did not want to be repatriated came to Canada from West European DP camps. Meeting members of the Federation, they began to tell them about the forced collectivization of peasants, the liquidation of millions of people in Gulag camps, and Stalin's terror. In addition, an eyeopener was the disclosures of Igor Gouzenko who had defected from the Soviet Embassy in Ottawa. The influence of FRC diminished.

Unlike the FRC, Russian cultural and educational societies and church parishes in large Canadian cities did not have a financial base and, therefore, could not embark on any complex and expensive enterprise as radio broadcasting.*

Another reason for the lack of regular Russian-language programmes is that Russian Canadians can listen to broadcasts of the International Service of Radio Canada and the Voice of America, not to mention other overseas stations that can be heard in Canada.

---

* An exception is the large and active group of Russians in Vancouver which, for many years, has regularly broadcast musical programmes.

Finally, for those who know Russian, or for non-Russians studying the language, there is a large selection of tapes, cassettes and records in Russian to suit all tastes.

Radio Broadcasts in Russian for Overseas Listeners

The Russian Section of the CBC International Service was established in October 1950, and since 1951 has transmitted a daily short-wave broadcast in the Russian language. A few words are in order regarding the International Service of the CBC in general, as many native Canadians do not know that it even exists.

The International Service was founded in 1944, during the Second World War, to give accurate information concerning events at the front and in the world in general to people living in countries that were occupied by German troops and who had no access to such information. This is why the International Service primarily broadcast to Norway, Denmark, The Netherlands, Austria, Czechoslovakia, Italy, Belgium and France. After the war, when the Soviet Union converted the East European countries into its satellites, established the "Iron Curtain" and initiated the so-called "Cold War" against the West, it was decided to start broadcasts in Russian, Ukrainian, Polish and, after the uprising in Hungary in 1956, in Hungarian. In view of the expanded trade and cultural relations between Canada and South America, the International Service started to broadcast programmes to that continent as well.

The International Section of Radio Canada (before the early seventies this was the "CBC International Service" and, more recently, "Radio Canada International") is not large, either in terms of the number of workers or languages in which broadcasts are made (only eleven are used, including English and French), in the size of its budget, or the time it has on the air.

An important supplementary function is performed by the Transcription Service which annually sends thousands of records and tapes throughout the world at the request of radio stations of various countries.

The policy of the International Service was not to be involved in propaganda or interfere in the internal affairs of other countries. Its terms of reference have always been restricted to the transmission of accurate information regarding the situation in our country and in the rest of the world, devoting particular attention to life in Canada in all its aspects. It is possibly for this reason that the International Service of Radio Canada has acquired a significant number of regular listeners during the years it has been in operation. This is supported by the number of letters (more than 30,000 per year) from various countries. The above figure would probably be substantially greater if listeners in countries of the Soviet bloc did not fear repression on the part of the authorities for writing to Radio Canada.

Let us, however, return to broadcasts in Russian. The tone of the broadcasts of the Russian Section was established from the very beginning by the late Dana Wilgress, a Canadian diplomat who had been the head of Mission in the USSR during the Second World War. In the first broadcast of the Russian Section, he mentioned that Canadians continued to hold friendly feelings towards the peoples of the Soviet Union who, as comrades-in-arms during the Second World War, had fought against a common enemy. He also mentioned how willingly and generously Canada gave assistance to the Soviet Union during the war. Speaking of the aims of the broadcasts, Wilgress emphasized that they would exclusively send accurate, objective information about all aspects of life in Canada, current news gathered from all over the world and a cross-section of commentaries by Canadian journalists.

As regards the internal situation in the Soviet Union, listeners frequently wrote how much they appreciated the fact that Radio Canada abstained from comments on Soviet life, saying that, living on the other side of the ocean, a person can never understand the way of life in another country as well as the citizens of that country can.

Although the Russian Section was always one of the largest, there were never more than eight or nine staff members, including the head of the section.

The requirement to prepare and broadcast two to four broadcasts daily for a total of 45 minutes to one hour did not permit any division of labour. Each producer had to be ready at any time to put together programmes and reports, to record interviews on any subject, prepare news bulletins and work in the studio on live programmes. Whenever possible, consideration was given to each producer's expertise as well as his ability as a broadcaster.

Until recently, each Section had a lot of freedom in selecting material for broadcast and the management rarely interfered with the work of individual sections. This independence existed to an even greater extent in the area of relations with the Federal Government in spite of the fact that, up to the end of the sixties, the International Service was not simply a division of Radio Canada, as it is today, but was under the direction of the Ministry of External Affairs with an independent budget approved by Parliament.

The daily programmes of the Russian Section usually consisted of three parts: news bulletins and commentary on the news highlights of the day; a review of the Canadian press (compiled in such a manner as to acquaint listeners with the various points of view of our newspapers regarding any given question); and a Feature Programme. Some of the most popular features among listeners were: "Answers to listeners' letters", "Thoughts and affairs", "Canadian encyclopedia", "History of Canada", "Religious life in Canada", "Musical journal", "Jazz in Canada", "Science and Technology News", and "Notebook of a philatelist".

The broadcasts gave extensive coverage to major events in Canada such as parliamentary elections, major religious holidays, anniversaries of Canada's confederation (particularly the hundredth anniversary in 1967), the Montreal Exhibition in 1967 and the Olympic Games in Montreal in 1976.

The Russian Section also transmitted interviews with many prominent Canadians or visiting foreigners. Among them were such people as: George Ignatieff, a Canadian diplomat; Boris Volkov, the pioneer of Canadian Ballet; Aleksandra Lvovna Tolstaya, the head of the Tolstoy Foundation and daughter of Leo Tolstoy; Aleksandr Kerensky, the head of the Provisional Government in Russia after the February revolution in 1917; Pitirim Sorokin, sociologist; Lyudmila Chiryaeff, the founder and director of Les Grands Ballets Canadiens*; Sergei Rostropovich, cellist; and other Russian writers, poets, painters, sculptors, scientists and engineers living in Canada. There were also interviews with visitors from the USSR who were involved in the arts and science exchange program, as well as some members of the Politburo of the CPSU** and of the Soviet government.

At the beginning of the sixties, during the so-called "thaw" in the Soviet Union, an agreement was concluded between Radio Moscow and the International Service of Radio Canada to exchange programmes on various subjects. In this connection, L.C. Chipman, director of the Russian Section at the time, visited Moscow, as did three producers of this Section later on. This agreement, however, amounted only to an exchange of musical and sports recordings in English. As far as is known, of all the recordings (other than music) that the Russian Section sent to Radio Moscow, the only one used was that of an interview with Igor Stravinsky, recorded in Toronto before he made his first visit to the Soviet Union after half a century abroad. Another rare occasion was the performance by a local Moscow symphony orchestra of a work by Yuri Fiala.***

For understandable reasons, the most interesting responses from listeners were those that were sent while the listeners were

---

* Montreal-based ballet company of national renown.

** Communist Party of the Soviet Union.

*** Fiala is a member of the Canadian Association of Composers.

visiting the West, or after they had emigrated to Israel, the United States, Canada or any other free country. The overwhelming majority of these letters was not only laudatory but contained suggestions on how to make the broadcasts even more interesting. Some letters mentioned that not only the person writing but many of his friends regularly listened to the Radio Canada broadcasts. They said that they had not written for fear of political reprisals in spite of the fact that after the "thaw" that took place under Khrushchev in the mid-1950s, Soviet authorities stopped jamming Russian and Ukrainian broadcasts by Radio Canada International.

In the mid-1970s, the management of the International Service was replaced by a new team whose members adopted a fully supportive attitude towards "détente". This lead to a general restructuring of the Service, followed by a subsequent curtailment in the freedom of selection of broadcast material by the staff, who were no longer permitted to write or transmit political commentaries of any kind.

These changes in management, staff and policies of the International Section (and, in particular, the Russian Section) attracted the attention of some members of the Federal Parliament, who frequently asked for an explanation from the Government.*

---

* See the late Mr. Cossitt's remarks in Hansard, October 26, 1976, p. 455 and December 21, 1978, p. 2, 338.

Appendix I

Newspapers and Magazines in the Russian Language in Canada from 1915 to 1981

The following are contained in the list provided by R. Bogusis from the publication *Checklist of Canadian Ethnic Serials*, National Library of Canada, Ottawa. It is published by permission of the Newspaper Division, National Library of Canada. Canada, par B.L. Burrell. For abbreviations used see pp. 188-89.

CHECKLIST OF CANADIAN ETHNIC SERIALS

Compiled by	Ruth Bogusis
Edited by	Liba Blazek
Editorial direction	Sabine Sonnemann

Newspaper Division
Public Services Branch

Ottawa
1981

Canadian Cataloguing in Publication Data

Bogusis, Ruth
Checklist of Canadian ethnic serials

Text in English and French.
Includes publications in various languages.
Bibilography: p.
Includes index.
ISBN O-660-50732-3
DSS cat. no. SN3-148/1981

1. Serial publications — Canada — Bibliography. 2. Ethnic press — Canada. I. Blazek, Liba. II. Sonnemann, Sabine. III. National Library of Canada. Newspaper Division. IV. Title. V. Title: Liste des publications en série ethniques du Canada.

Z6954.C2B63 O15.71'034 C81-090052-lE

Minister of Supply and Services Canada 1981
Available in Canada through authorized bookstore agents and other bookstores or by mail from
Canadian Government Publishing Centre
Supply and Services Canada
Hull, Quebec, Canada
KIA OS9
Catalogue Number SN3-148/1981 Canada:$50
ISBN 0-660-50732-3 Other Countries: $60
Price subject to change without notice

Abbreviations used in the list compiled by Ruth Bogusis

Libraries

ACAI	Arctic Institute of North America, University of Calgary	Calgary
ACUCES	Canadian Ethnic Studies, University of Calgary	Calgary
ACU	University of Calgary	Calgary
AEP	Alberta Legislature Library	Edmonton
BVIV	University of Victoria	Victoria
BVAU	University of British Columbia	Vancouver
BVA	Vancouver Public Library	Vancouver
DLC	?	
DOBIS	Dortmunder Bibliothekssystem/National Library automated data base/	
OLU	University of Western Ontario	London, Ont.
OTMCL	Metropolitan Toronto Library	Toronto
OTU	University of Toronto	Toronto

References

Ayers	N.W. Ayer & Son's Directory, Newspapers and Periodicals. Philadelphia. N.W. Ayer & Son, 1880-
C.E.S.	Canadian Ethnic Studies
Gregory	Gregory, Winifred, ed. American Newspapers 1821-1936: A Union List of Files Available in the United States and Canada. New York: The H.W. Wilson Co., 1937.
McKim's	McKim's Directory of Canadian Publications, Montreal, Toronto, Winnipeg, Vancouver and London /England/: A McKim Ltd., 1892-1942.
McLaren	McLaren, Duncan. Ontario Ethno-Cultural Newspapers 1835-1972: annotated checklist. Toronto: University of Toronto Press, 1973.
OONL	Items seen but not held in National Library of Canada. Bibliographical information retained in base *Canadian Ethnic Serials Checklist* file.
ULCN	Union List of Canadian Newspapers held by Canadian Libraries. Ottawa, National Library of Canada, 1977.

Abbreviations Indicating Periodicity:

b̸	irregular	m	monthly
d	daily	b	bi-monthly
c	semi-weekly	q	quarterly
i	three times a week	t	three times a year
w	weekly	f	semi-annually
e	bi-weekly	a	annually
s	semi-monthly		

Other Abbreviations

u	unknown
uu	unknown, no reference
mn	microfilm, negative
mp	microfilm, positive
nhg	no holdings given
?	information incomplete or questionable
[ ]	incomplete holdings

Sample Entry

Kanadai Magyar munkas[1] July 16, 1929 - Dec. 28, 1967[2]
Hamilton, Ont.; Toronto, Ont.[3]
w,c,i,w,:[4] Hungarian[5] (In Hungarian)[6]
Eng. title: Canadian Hungarian worker[7]
Cont'd by: Uj szo[8]
Desc:[9] Title varies; Canadai magyar munkas July 16, 1929 - May 20, 1931 published in Hamilton, Ont.; June? 1931 - Dec. 28, 1967 in Toronto, Ont.
Frequency varies: w to July 26, 1934; c Aug. 2, 1934 - Aug. 24, 1935; i Aug. 27, 1935 - Dec. 30, 1935 - Dec. 30, 1939; w Jan. 1940 - Dec. 28, 1967
Has supplements: Farmmelleklet and Az Uttoro.
HUBN[10] or Jan. 13, 1968-
OONL[11] or July 1929 - Dec. 1967; mp nhg[12]
Ref:[13] C.E.S.: June 1970, p. 79
McLaren: p. 88
ULCN: p. 243

1. Title
2. Publication dates
3. Place of publication
4. Frequency
5. Ethnic Group
6. language of Publication
7. Title in other language(s)
8. Publishing history
9. Description (notes)
10. Foreign location
11. Canadian location
12. Holdings
13. Reference Source(s)

RUSSIAN

Bor'ba Jan. 1968-
Munich, Germany]; London, Ont.
b̸; Russian (In Russian)
Ref: C.E.S.: Apr. 1970, p. 62

Canadian Russian 1909?-1910?
Toronto, Ont.
w; Russian (In Russian)
Ref: C.E.S.:Apr. 1976, p. 253
McLaren: p.136

The Doukhobor inquirer Feb.1954-1955
Saskatoon, Sask.
m; Russian (In English)
Sponsor: Union of Young Doukhobors
Cont'd by: The Inquirer
ACUCES nhg
Ref: C.E.S.: Apr. 1976, p. 254

Dukhoborcheskiĭ rassvet u
u; Russian (In Russian)
Ref: C.E.S.: Apr. 1976, p. 253

Evangel'skai͡a vera Sept./Oct. 1954?-
Toronto, Ont.
b,f,q; Russian and Ukrainian (In Russian and Ukrainian)
Eng. title: The Faith of the gospel
Ukrainian title: Ievanhel'ska vira
Ref: C.E.S.: Apr. 1970, p. 87

Fakel 1949-u
London, Ont.?
b̸; Russian (In Russian)
ACUCES nhg
Ref: C.E.S.: Apr. 1970, p. 62

Golos istiny 1959-
Winnipeg, Man.
m; Russian (In Russian)
Ref: C.E.S.: Apr. 1970, p.62

Gudok Oct.1940-June 1941
Toronto, Ont.
m?; Russian (In Russian)
Ref: C.E.S.:Apr. 1970, p.62

Ievanhel's'kyĭ visnyk May 1929-1930?
Winnipeg, Man.
m, b; Russian and Ukrainian
Eng. title: Evangelical herald
Desc: Title in Ukrainian
ACUCES nhg
Ref C.E.S.: Apr. 1976, p. 254

Informatsionnyĭ listok 1965?-u
London, Ont
b; Russian (In Russian)
Sponsor: Russian Liberation Movement, Canada
Continues: Informatsionnyĭ listok Soiuza bor'by za osvobozhdenie marodov Rossii, (SBONR) otd. Kanada
Cont'd by: Informatsionnyĭ listok SBONR
ACUCES nhg
Ref: C.E.S.: Apr. 1970, p. 62

Informatsionnyĭ listok Chekhovskogo kluba 1974-
Ottawa, Ont.
b; Russian (In Russian)
Sponsor: Chekhov Club
Ref: C.E.S.: Apr. 1976, p. 254

Informatsionnyĭ listok SBONR u-u
London, Ont.
b; Russian (In Russian)
Sponsor: Russian Liberation Movement. North American Branch
Eng. Title: Information bulletin
Continues: Informatsionnyĭ listok
ACUCES nhg
Ref: C.E.S.: Apr. 1970, p. 62

Informatsionnyĭ listok soĭuza bor'by za osvobozhdenie narodov Rossii; (SBONR), otd. Kanada 1949-u
London, Ont.
b; Russian (In Russian)
Sponsor: Russian Liberation Movement, Canada
Cont'd by: Informatsionnyĭ listok
Desc: Corporate body varies: SBONR, otd. Kanaĭda, or: SBONR, Kanada
ACUCES nhg
Ref: C.E.S.: Apr. 1976, p. 62

The Inquirer 1955-Sept. 1958
Saskatoon, Sask.
m, q; Russian (In English)
Sponsor: Union of Young Doukhobors
Continues: The Doukhobor inquirer
ACUCES nhg
Ref: C.E.S.: Apr. 1976, p. 254

Iskra 1945-
Grand Forks, B.C.
w, s; Russian (In English and Russian)
Sponsor: Union of spiritual Communities of Christ
Desc: Frequency varies: w to 1969; s 1969 -
OONL or [1946-1947] - [1950-1956] - [1959-1960]-[1962]
Ref: DOBIS

Iskra Soi͡uza dukhovnykh obshchin Khrista u
Grand Forks, B.C.
w; Russian (In Russian and English)
Sponsor: Federation of Spiritual Communities of Christ
Continues: Sten-gazeta
Ref: C.E.S.: Apr. 1970, p. 62
C.E.S.: Apr. 1976, p. 255

Kanadiĭskai͡a Pravoslavnai͡a Rus' Sept. 28, 1916-1917
Winnipeg, Man.
s; Russian (In Russian and Ukrainian)
Ref: C.E.S.:Apr. 1970, p. 63 and 98

Kanadskiĭ gudok Apr. 1931-Apr. 4, 1940
Toronto, Ont.; Winnipeg, Man.
m,s,w,c: Russian (In Russian)
Cont't by: Vestnik
Desc: x Title varies: Kanadsky gudok
Subtitle: Organ russkikh rabochikh Kanady.
Some early issues have articles in Byelorussian
Apr. 1931-Dec. 1, 1931 published in Toronto, Ont.; 1932-1940 in Winnipeg, Man.
Frequency varies: m Apr. - Aug. 1931; s Sept. 1, 1931 - Apr. 23, 1932; w May 7, 1932 - Oct. 26, 1933; c Nov. 1, 1933-1940?
OONL mp Apr. 1931-Apr. 4, 1940; or May 1, 1931; Mar. 22, 1932; July 4, 23, 1935; Feb. 13, 1936; [July 29, 1937-Dec. 16, 1939]
Ref: Ayer's: 1937-1942
C.E.S.: Apr. 1970, p. 62
McKim's: 1936-1940
McLaren: p. 137
ULCN: p. 77

Kanadskiĭ pravoslavnyĭ kalendar' 1952-1972
Toronto, Ont.
a; Russian (In Russian and some English)
Sponsor: Russkai͡a pravoslavnai͡a tserkov'. Kanadskai͡a eparkhii͡a. Eparkhial'nyĭ sovet. Kafedral'nyĭ sobor Khrista Spasiteli͡a.
Eng. Title: Canadian Greek-Orthodox calendar
Cont'd by: Pravoslavnyĭ tserkovnyi kalendar'
Desc: English title varies: Canadian Orthodox calendar. Church bulletin.
OONL or 1952, 1957, 1959-1961
Ref: C.E.S.:Apr. 1970, p. 63
DOBIS

Khristianin Jan. 19, 1968-
Toronto, Ont.
m; Russian (In Russian)
Sponsor: Torontovskai͡a khristianskai͡a missii͡a
Eng. Title: The Christian
Desc: Monthly (except August)
ACUCES nhg
Ref: C.E.S.: Apr. 1976, p. 254

Kuban' skyĭ kraĭ 1951-u
Toronto, Ont.
q; Russian (In Russian and English)
Eng. Title: Kuban Cossack bulletin
Ref: C.E.S.: Apr. 1970, p. 63

Mir Jan. 1973 -
Grand Forks, B.C.
m,ɓ; Russian (In English and some Russian)
Continues: Union of Young Doukhobors. Newsletter
Desc: A Doukhobor youth publication
ACU nhg
BVA 1973-
BVAU 1974-
BVIV 1973-
OONL 1973-
OTU 1973-
Ref: DOBIS

Pravoslavnoe obozrīenie 1946-
Montreal, Que.
b; Russian (In Russian)
Eng. title: Orthodox observer
ACUCES nhg
OONL or 1977-
Ref: C.E.S.: Apr. 1970, p.63
DOBIS

Pravoslavnyĭ tserkovnyĭ kalendar' 1973-
Toronto, Ont.
u; Russian (In Russian and some English)
Sponsor: Russkaia͡ pravoslavnaia͡ tserkov. Kanadskaia͡ eparkhiia͡
Eng. title: The Orthodox Church calendar
Continues: Kanadskiĭ pravoslavnyĭ kalendar'
Desc: Title varies: Pravoslavnyj cerkovnyj kalendar'
OONL or 1973-
Ref: DOBIS

Pravoslavnyĭ vĭestnik v Kanadīe Oct.? 1961-
Montreal, Que.
m; Russian (In Russian)
Eng. title: Church messenger
ACUCES nhg
Ref: C.E.S.: Apr. 1970, p. 63

Prikhodskie vedomosti 1972-1975
London, Ont.
ɓ; Russian (In Russian)
Sponsor: Prikhod Nerukotvornogo Obraza Khrista Spasitelia͡
Russian Orthodox Church of Holy Sudary of Christ the Saviour
Desc: Church bulletin
Ref: C.E.S.:Apr. 1976, p. 254

Prikhodskoĭ listok u
Montreal, Que.
ƀ; Russian (In Russian and English)
Eng. title: Parish news
ACUCES nhg
Ref: C.E.S.: Apr. 1970, p. 63

Primiritel’ u
Windsor, Ont.
b; Russian (In Russian)
Eng. title: Reconciliation
ACUCES nhg
Ref: C.E.S.: Apr. 1976, p. 254

Rabochiĭ narod 1918
Winnipeg, Man.
m; Russian (In Russian)
Desc: Only several iss. published
Ref: C.E.S.: Apr. 1970, p. 63

Russian life 1915-u
Edmonton, Alta.
s; Russian (In Russian?)
Ref: McKim’s: 1917

Russian monthly instructive political journal
Jan. 1935-May 12, 1936
m; Russian (In Russian?)
Ref: MacDonald: p. 83

Russkai͡a gazeta 1925-1926
Montreal, Que.
u; Russian (In Russian and English)
Eng. title: Russian gazette
OONL or Aug. 23, 1925
Ref: ULCN: p. 311

Russkiĭ golos Apr. 4, 1913-June 20, 1916
Edmonton, Alta., Winnipeg, Man.
w; Russian and Ukrainian (In Russian and Ukrainian)
Eng. title: Russian voice
AEP or 1915-1916
Ref: C.E.S.: Apr. 1970, p. 63 and p. 113
ULCN: p. 13

Russkiĭ narod Nov. 1914-May 1, 1919
Winnipeg, Man.
w,s?, ƀ; Russian and Ukrainian (In Russian and Ukrainian)
Eng. title: Russian people
Desc: Transliteration varies: Russky narod
DLC or May 6, - Nov. 12, 1915; Jan. 10 - Oct. 3, 1918
Ref: Ayers: 1918-1919
C.E.S.: Apr. 1970, p. 63 and p. 113
Gregory: p. 768
McKim’s: 1917-1921

Russkiĭ narodnyĭ kalendar' 1914-u
Edmonton, Alta.
a; Russian (In Russian and Ukrainian)
Desc: Calendar-almanac of Russkiĭ golos. Title varies : Russkiĭ narodnyĭ kalendar' na . . . god
Ref: C.E.S.: Apr. 1976, p. 254
C.E.S.: June 1970, p. 199

Russkoe slovo 1910-1924?
[New York, N. Y.]; Montreal, Que.
d; Russian (In Russian)
Desc: Newspaper
Ref: Beaulieu: 1965, p. 151
C.E.S.: Apr. 1976, p. 254
McKim's: 1918-1921

Russkoe slovo v Kanade 1951-
Toronto, Ont.
m; Russian (In Russian)
Sponsor: Russkoe kul'turno-prosvetitel'noe obshchestvo
Eng. title: Russian word in Canada
ACUCES nhg
OONL or [1951-1955]-[1961] - [1970] -
OTMCL 1972-
OTU 1954-
Ref: C.E.S.: Apr. 1970, p. 63
DOBIS
McLaren: p. 137

Slyshym 1968-1969
London, Ont.
ɓ; Russian (In Russian)
Sponsor: Soi͡uz bor'by za osvobozhdenie narodov Rossii [Russian Liberation Movement]
Desc: Only 3 iss. published
ACUCES nhg
Ref: C.E.S.: Apr. 1976, p. 255

Solidarnost' May 1930-1931
Toronto, Ont.
m; Russian (In Russian)
Desc: Only 8 iss. published
Ref: C.E.S.: Apr. 1970, p. 63

Sovremennik Mar. 1960-
Toronto, Ont.
a?, ɓ?; Russian (In Russian)
OONL or 1960-
Ref: C.E.S.: Apr. 1970, p. 63
DOBIS

Sten-gazeta Feb. 28, 1943-Mar. 1945
Grand Forks, B.C.
w; Russian (In Russian)

Cont'd by: Iskra Soi͡uza dukhovnykh obshchin Khrista
Ref: C.E.S.: Apr. 1976, p. 255

The True vine Jan. 1972-1974?
Montreal, Que.
Russian (In English)
Sponsor: Russkaia pravoslavnai͡a tserkov' zagranitseĭ v Kanade [Russian Orthodox Church outside Russia, in Canada]
Desc: Official English language publication of the Dept. of External Mission of the Synod of Bishops of the Russian Orthodox Church outside of Russia
ACUCES nhg
OONL or [1972-1974]
Ref: C.E.S.: Apr. 1976, p. 255
DOBIS

Union of young Doukhobors. Newsletter 1969?
Vancouver, B.C.?
m; Russian (In English and Russian)
Cont'd by: Mir
Desc: A Doukhobor youth publication
Ref: C.E.S.: Apr. 1976, p. 255
DOBIS

Vestnik Nov. 6, 1941-
Toronto, Ont.
w,c,w; Russian (In Russian)
Continues: Kanadskiĭ gudok
Desc: Frequency varies: w to Jan. 15, 1942; c Jan. 21, 1942 - Dec. 13, 1967; w Dec. 1967:
MWU or 1953-1958
OONL mp Nov. 6, 1941 - ; or [Nov. 6 1941 - Dec. 28, 1960]; Jan. 4, 1967-
OTMCL mp 1941
Ref: C.E.S.: Apr. 1970, p. 63
McLaren: p. 137-138
ULCN: p. 244

Vol'nai͡a Kuban' Nov. 1949-1950?
Toronto, Ont.
m; Russian and Ukrainian (In Russian, Ukrainian and English)
Eng. title: Bulletin of the World Alliance of Kuban Cossacks
Ukrainian title: Vil'na Kuban'
Desc: x Russian title added in 1950.
English language added in 1950.
English title varies: Nov.-Dec. 1949:
Kuban Cossack Monthly
ACUCES nhg
Ref: C.E.S.: Apr. 1976, p. 255 and 286

Voskresnyĭ listok 1959?-
London, Ont.
w; Russian (In Russian)

Sponsor: Prikhod Nerukotvornogo Obraza Khrista Spasitel͡ia
[Russian Orthodox Church of Holy Sudary of Christ the Saviour]
Desc:Church bulletin
Ref: C.E.S.: Apr. 1976, p. 255

Vremia 1940-June 17, 1941
Kamsack, Sask.
ƀ; Russian (In Russian)
OONL or [1941]
Ref: C.E.S.: Apr. 1970, p. 63
OONL

Zaria July 1972- *
London, Ont.
ƀ; Russian (In Russian)
ACUCES nhg
Ref: C.E.S. Apr. 1976, p. 255

Zhizn' prikhoda Dec. 1975-
London, Ont.
ƀ; Russian (In Russian and English)
Sponsor: Prikhod Nerukotvornogo Obraza Khrista Spasitel͡ia
[Russian Orthodox Church of Holy Sudary of Christ the Saviour]
Eng. title: The Parish life
Desc: Church bulletin
ACUCES nhg
Ref: C.E.S.: Apr.1976, p.255-256

Zhizn' very 1948-u
Winnipeg, Man.
u; Russian, Ukrainian (In Russian and Ukrainian)
Ref: C.E.S.: Apr. 1970, p. 63 and p. 126

Zhyve slovo 1957-u
Swan River, Man.
b; Russian and Ukrainian (In Russian and Ukrainian)
Eng. title: The Living Word
Ref: C.E.S.: Apr. 1970, p. 63 and 126

---

* Note: *Zaria* is a publishing house.

Appendix II

A Supplement to the List of Russian Serials Published by R. Bogusis

Compiled by R.N. Polchaninoff from materials published by Michail Schatoff in *Half a Century of Russian Serials, 1917-1968*, Cumulative Index of Serials, published outside of the USSR. Edited by N.A. Hale, Russian Book Chamber Abroad, New York, 1970-72. For explanation see p. 201.

*Argus;*Baltiĭskiĭ almanakh-literaturno-khudozhestvennyĭ sbornik
Publ. Shkliar Riga-Kaunas-Toronto (Monthly)
1923-24 no. 1-4
1928 no. 2
1934 no. 1-2

Drug
Montreal, Quebec
1952

Edinenie
Zhurnal svobodnoĭ demokraticheskoĭ mysli
Ed. Manuilov
Toronto/1950/
1950 no. 1-3 mimeo

Edinstvo
Toronto/1950
1950 no. 1

Kanadskiĭ farmer
Canada
1921

Krug
Pub. 6-ǵo Kruga - "Kniaz' Igor" Organizatsii͡a Rossiĭskikh Yunykh Razvedchikov
Ed. V. Bykadorov
Montreal /1954/
1952 no. 1-3

Miloserdnyĭ samarianin
Russkiĭ zhurnal v Kanade
Ottawa (Monthly)/Irreg/1954
no.1 - newspaper; no.2 - magazine
1954-56 no. 1-14

Monarkhicheskiĭ vestnik
Pub. Montreal'skii otdel Rossiĭskogo narodno - monarkhicheskogo dvizheniia 1955
1955 no. 1-5

Novyĭ put'
Print. by the Christian Press Ltd.
Winnipeg, Manitoba
1955 no. 1

Obozrenie
Molokanskoe obozrenie
1945-49

Biulleten'
Montreal'skoĭ Druzhiny ORYuR
1953 no. 3-5
(? no. 1-2)

Russkiĭ narod
Organ Soiuza Osvobozhdeni͡ia Prikarpatskoĭ Rusi v Kanade
Winnipeg, Manitoba
1919-21

Biulleten'
Russkoe Kul'turno-prosvetitel'noe obshchestvo
Toronto, Ontario
1950 no. 1-2

Samoderzhavnik
Zov russkikh gosudarstvennykh liudei
Organ priverzhenstev podlinno russkoi pravoslavnoĭ samoderzhavnoĭ narodnoĭ monarkhii
Pub. Ed. Ī͡u. Penionzhkevich (Iurpe)
Quebec (Irreg) /1954/
1954 (July) no. 1
1955 no. 2
1958 no. 4

Svobodnoe obshchestvo
Organ Federatsii anarkhistov. Later united with newspaper Volna
Ed. V. Dodkin
Magazine /1920/
1920-21 no. 1-4

Vesti antikommunisticheskoĭ bor'by
Pub. Russka͡ia sektsi͡ia Kanadskogo instituta Veritas
Montreal
1953 (Nov.) mimeo

Zelényĭ vestnik
Informatsionnyĭ listok NTS
Montreal
1955(November) no. 1 mimeo

Zemli͡a i voli͡a
Organ Partii sotsialistov - revoli͡utsionerov
Toronto /1918/
1918-1924

Zov
Pub. Berlinskiĭ komitet pomoshchi pravoslavnym bezhentsam imeni Doktora A. Trushnovicha (Predstavitel'stvo v Monreale)
1955 no. 3 mimeo

Gvozd'
Stengazeta druzhiny "Moskva" (ORYuR)
Montreal, Quebec
195- no. 1-2 handwritten

Dukhovnyĭ sputnik
(Dukhoborcheskiĭ organ)
1959 (April)

Pis'mo Rodine
Pub. SBONR
/Leaflets for distribution in the USSR/
London, Ontario
1963-66 no. 1-21

Troĭka; Katalog
Toronto, Ontario
1966

"/" - information of the compiler
"()" - in M. Schatoff's original
ORYuR - Organization of Russian Young Scouts
Organizatsii͡a Rossiĭskikh Yunykh Razvedchikov, Svodnyĭ Otri͡ad Gen P.N. Vrangeli͡a v Monreale 1980: March, May (no numbers)

Appendix III

Some Statistics on Canadians of Russian Descent

Early statistical data on Canadians of Russian descent are scarce. Since there is no universally-accepted definition of the term *Russian*, and the term *nationality* may be interpreted in many ways, there are frequent discrepancies in the figures, particularly in the early records.

The first census in Canada that mentions the name *Russian* among other ethnic groups is the census of 1851-1861. However, no registration figures are entered.

In 1871-1881 the Russians were grouped together with the Poles with no indication as to the actual numbers of each group. After 1881 the paragraph *Russian* appears in every subsequent census but there is no certainty that other nationalities were not included in the group of "Russians". It is equally possible that a number of Russians were registered along with the Poles, Finns and later, Ukrainians, Byelorussians and others for reasons outlined in the Introduction and elsewhere.

TABLE 1

Total Population of Canada and Number of Russian Canadians

Census Year	General Population (Totals)	Number of Russian Canadians
1851	2,436,297	None registered
1861	3,229,633	None registered
1871	3,689,257	607
1881	4,324,810	1,227
1891*		
1901	5,371,315	20,014
1911	7,206,643	43,142
1921	8,787,949	100,064
1931	10,376,786	88,148
1941	11,506,655	83,709
1951	14,009,429	91,279
1961	18,238,247	119,168
1971	21,568,310	64,475

* Data on ethnic origin were not recorded in this particular year.

Source: *Census of Canada*, 1971, Vol. 1, Part 3, Catalogue 92-723, (Bulletin 1.3-2), p. 1-1, Table 1: "Population by Ethnic Group for Canada".

Russian Canadians

Early data on immigrants to Canada classified by *nationality* are contained in the annual books of records, *Immigration, Facts and Figures*, issued by the directions of J.A. Calder, Minister of Immigration and Colonization, 1920.

Table 2 is excerpted from the above publications and covers the period between 1900 and 1920. The Ukrainians, Byelorussians and other settlers coming from the provinces which were under the rule of the Russian Empire are not mentioned because they have probably been included in the group of Russians.* Doukhobors, however, are listed separately although ethnically, as well as by place of birth, they are Russian.

TABLE 2

Total Immigration to Canada by Nationalities
From July 1, 1900 to March 31, 1920

Year	Polish	Russian NES**	Russian Doukhobor	Finnish	Mennonite
1900-01	163	1,044	—	682	—
1901-02	230	2,467	12	1,292	52
1902-03	274	5,505	—	1,734	38
1903-04	669	1,955	—	845	11
1904-05	745	1,887	24	1,323	—
1905-06	725	3,152	204	1,103	—
1906-07	1,033	1,927	—	1,049	—
1907-08	1,593	6,281	—	1,212	—
1908-09	376	3,547	—	669	—
1909-10	1,407	4,564	—	1,457	—
1910-11	2,177	6,621	41	2,132	—
1911-12	5,060	9,805	24	1,646	—
1912-13	9,945	18,623	108	2,391	—
1913-14	9,793	24,485	4	3,183	—
1914-15	1,976	5,201	—	459	—
1915-16	8	40	—	139	—
1916-17	12	25	—	249	—
1917-18	—	42	—	113	—
1918-19	4	42	—	2	—
1919-20	76	51	—	44	—

* *Immigration, Facts and Figures* list Ukrainians who came to Canada from Galicia, Bukovina and the Carpatho-Ukraine as Austro-Hungarians. After the Treaty of Riga in 1921, the provinces populated by the Ukrainians were divided among the newly-proclaimed states of the USSR — Poland, Romania and Czechoslovakia. Ukrainians who came from these provinces after 1921 were sometimes registered by nationality, meaning citizenship, i.e., as Poles, Romanians, Czechs.

** NES — Not Elsewhere Specified.

Another source of information on immigrants at the beginning of the twentieth century is the handbook, *Historical Statistics of Canada*, M.C. Urquhart, editor.*

The scarcity of data on East Europeans is reflected in the following table from Urquhart's work. (Note that the table should be read from the bottom up).

TABLE 3

Series A316-366. Ethnic Origin of All Immigrants to Canada, ifrom overseas and the United States, 1901-1960.

Year	USSR	Eastern Europe Polish	Baltic States	Year	USSR	Eastern Europe Polish	Baltic States
1960	581	3,401	1,455	1929	11,867	6,424	5,852
1959	548	3,960	1,297	1928	17,325	8,583	5,743
1958	657	3,171	1,809	1927	12,179	8,481	6,252
1957	972	3,096	3,734	1926	10,795	5,552	5,738
1956	866	2,438	1,852	1925	3,077	1,952	1,698
1955	857	2,073	1,393	1924	5,594	2,908	6,363
1954	1,129	2,461	1,760	1923	3,668	4,157	255
1953	1,484	3,308	2,605	1922	206	2,758	785
1952	3,968	5,638	5,504	1921	513	2,853	460
1951	9,254	13,078	12,954	1920	1,441	3,554	1,198
1950	4,468	6,732	5,236	1919	44	24	25
1949	7,539	12,359	8,334	1918	45	2	15
1948	11,482	13,915	9,531	1917	32	—	129
1947	2,374	2,735	2,113				
1946	384	730	98	1916	27	15	276
1945	119	332	47	1915	43	7	91
1944	75	106	17	1914	13,110	2,373	637
1943	56	72	28	1913	47,665	13,339	3,508
1942	47	77	29	1912	35,065	10,077	2,135
1941	62	117	29	1911	18,661	6,028	1,637
1940	67	112	58	1910	9,610	5,454	2,262
1939	1,936	439	147	1909	4,405	4,092	1,348
1938	2,070	633	143	1908	3,649	7,346	453
1937	1,359	675	151	1908[1]	7,193	15,861	1,212
1936	909	414	122	1907[1]	2,230	2,685	1,049
1935	582	447	94	1906[1]	3,418	6,381	1,103
1934	648	436	127	1905	1,914	7,671	1,323
1933	472	410	117	1904	1,955	8,398	845
1932	586	474	120	1903	5,505	8,656	1,734
1931	652	680	212	1902	2,479	6,550	1,292
1930	9,256	5,207	3,558	1901	1,044	4,702	682

1 For 1901 to 1906, fiscal year ending 30 June of the year given. Nine months for 1907 ending 31 March. Fiscal year ending 31 March 1908. Calendar year 1908 to 1906.

* The University Press, Cambridge; MacMillan Co. of Canada, 1965, p. 28.

Despite its title, *Ethnic Origin of all Immigrants to Canada*, the table leaves it up to the reader to decide who are the people arriving from Eastern Europe. In the table all arrivals are divided into three groups: USSR, Polish and Baltic States.

Needless to say, this classification does not show the ethnic origin of the people but the country they came from. The confusion is compounded by the erroneous interpretation of historical dates — one has only to realize that there was no such country as the USSR between 1901 and 1917. Only when the Russian Empire, which included the Baltic States and part of Poland, disappeared from the map of Europe after the revolution and civil war in Russia, did the USSR emerge as a state.

Registration by ethnic origin became more precise in immigration statistics after World War II. Until 1967, a separate column was used for this category (See Table 4). In October of that year, however, new immigration regulations came into effect, viz:

> These Regulations are universally applicable and completely nondiscriminatory. Since a prospective immigrant's racial origin has no bearing in determining his admissibility to Canada, all references to this subject have been removed from all immigration documents. There is, therefore, now no way available to the Immigration Division to compile data on the ethnic origin of immigrants.*

A researcher trying to gather data on Russians coming to Canada has to rely on such circumstantial evidence as former citizenship, place of birth, former permanent residence, religion and mother tongue.

---

* *1967 Immigration Statistics*, Introduction, "Origin of Immigrants", Canada Immigration Division, Department of Manpower and Immigration, Cat. No. MP22-1/1967, Ottawa, 1968, p. 2.

TABLE 4*

Russian Immigration to Canada 1946-1981

Year	"Russians" by Ethnic Origin	"Russians" by Citizenship (Soviet Citizens)	"Russians" by Place of Birth (in Russia or USSR)	"Russians" by Last Permanent Residence
1946	154			
1947	234			
1948	1,405			
1949	885			
1950	604			
1951	2,273			
1952	1,072		*Totals for 1946-1961:*	
1953	485	18,075	28,992	12,299
1954	355		(See Note 2)	
1955	241			
1956	234			
1957	375			
1958	252			
1959	202			
1960	158			
1961	209	105	570	79
1962	198	81	494	56
1963	177	75	416	61
1964	201	80	413	77
1965	260	159	543	157
1966	281	265	635	268
1967	Iden-	301	698	294
1968	tifi-	221	490	183
1969	cation	145	394	112
1970	of	136	406	131
1971	immi-	159	349	155
1972	grants	319	498	315
1973	by	293	696	427
1974	ethnic	252	899	602
1975	origin	230	1,437	278
1976	was	319	1,305	315
1977	dis-	279	998	299
1978	con-	236	990	379
1979	tinued	183	1,650	1,332
1980	in	167	2,438	147
1981	1967	120	1,307	868

* Statistical data used in compiling the above table provided by courtesy of the Program Data Directorate, Immigration and Demographic Policy, Employment and Immigration Commission, Ottawa, 1982.

Note 1: Between 1946 and 1955, the number of immigrants registered by *ethnic origin* as Ukrainians and Poles was 34,339 and 61,578, respectively. The number of immigrants registered as Russians during this period was 8,180.

Note 2: Between 1946 and 1961, immigration statistics taking into account *citizenship, place of birth* and *last permanent residence* do not appear to have been compiled uniformly. For example, these indicators were not used sequentially in every table; rather, either one or another indicator was used, or a combination of two. Therefore, we have given only the totals for the above years, as presented in annual immigration statistics. These are 18,075, 28,992 and 12,299 respectively.

One would think that one of the most dependable factors in detecting the number of Canadians of Russian ethnic origin would be their mother tongue. As Tables 5 and 6 show, however, the number of people who remember being of Russian extraction is nearly three times higher than the number of those who consider Russian language their mother tongue. The latter are on the decline as the younger generations become assimiliated and Russian is no longer spoken at home.

TABLE 5

Population by Mother Tongue for Canada
1941-1971
(Russian Canadians)

	1941	1951	1961	1971	1976
Total population	11,506,655	14,009,429	18,238,247	21,568,310	22,992,605
Russian Canadians	83,708	91,279	119,168	64,475	—
Number of Russian Canadians who consider Russian their mother tongue	52,431	39,223	42,903	31,745	23,485
Number of Russian Canadians who speak Russian at home	—	—	—	12,585*	—

*Urban population: 7,895; provincial, 4,690.

Source: *Census of Canada*, 1971, Vol. 1, Part 3, Catalogue 92,725, (Bulletin 1.3-4), April 1973; *Census of Canada*, 1976 Vol. 2, Catalogue 92,821, (Bulletin 2.2), February 1978.

TABLE 6

Distribution of Russian Canadians who speak Russian at home, by Province, in 1971

	Total Population	Russian Canadians	Number of Russian Canadians who Speak Russian at Home
Canada	21,568,310	64,475	12,585
Newfoundland	522,100	40	—
Nova Scotia	788,960	245	5
Quebec	6,027,765	4,060	1,440
Ontario	7,703,105	12,580	3,075
Manitoba	988,250	4,040	360
Saskatchewan	926,245	10,030	1,435
Alberta	1,627,875	10,235	650
British Columbia	2,184,620	22,995	5,615
Prince Edward Island	11,640	10	5
New Brunswick	634,555	105	—
Yukon	8,945	70	—
North-West Territories	8,785	65	—

Source: *Census of Canada*, 1971, Catalogue 92,774, (SP-4) May 1974.

The following four tables contain information onthe occupational composition and distribution of Russian Canadians, as well as some population statistics on the USSR.

TABLE 7

Occupational Composition of Russian Immigrants Arriving in Canada from Overseas after World War II

Occupational Group	Year 1946	1947	1948	1949	1950	1951	1952	1953	1954	1955	Total for the Decade
Managerial	—	—	—	—	—	—	—	2	2	—	4
Professional	1	8	20	11	10	58	76	43	21	23	271
Clerical	4	6	10	11	5	46	52	21	12	6	173
Transportation	—	—	—	—	—	—	—	5	2	2	9
Communication	1	—	24	6	—	26	9	—	—	—	66
Commercial	—	—	—	—	—	—	—	9	4	5	18
Financial	1	5	7	6	1	12	12	1	—	—	44
Service (Including Domestics)	—	18	180	118	55	122	49	39	16	19	617
Agriculture	1	30	364	205	142	206	51	36	14	5	1,054
Fishing, Trapping,											
Logging	—	59	2	2	10	47	7	—	1	—	128
Mining	—	9	19	10	10	44	8	—	1	—	101
Manufacturing, Mechanical	3	15	125	75	57	306	136	41	34	31	823
Construction	1	4	79	25	12	89	28	17	11	10	276
Labourers	—	—	30	7	6	220	72	34	38	19	426
Not Stated	1	3	13	9	6	13	19	3	2	1	70
All Workers	13	157	873	485	314	1,189	519	251	158	121	4,080
All Dependents	141	77	553	400	290	1,084	553	234	197	120	3,629
Total Immigration	154	234	1,406	885	604	2,273	1,072	485	355	241	7,709

Source: *1956 Immigration Statistics*, Department of Citizenship and Immigration, Statistics Section, Ottawa, 1957 (Reprinted 1976).

TABLE 8

Distribution of Russian Canadians, by Major City in 1971

City	Russian Canadians
Vancouver	7,310
Toronto	5,270
Montreal	3,605
Calgary	3,010
Edmonton	2,295
Winnipeg	2,100
Saskatoon	1,935
Hamilton	
Kitchener	
London	
Ottawa	Between 500
Regina	and 1,000
St. Catharines	
Victoria	
Windsor	

Source: *Census of Canada*, 1971, Vol. 1, Part 3, Catalogue 92-723, (Bulletin 1.3-2), October 1973

TABLE 9

Population of the USSR. 15 January 1970
(Data on the largest ethnic groups in USSR)

Ethnic group	Total
Russian	129,015,140
Ukrainian	40,753,246
Uzbek	9,195,193
Byelorussian	9,051,755
Tatar	5,930,670
Kazakh	5,298,818
Azerbaijani	4,379,937
Armenian	3,559,151
Georgian	3,245,300
Moldavian	2,697,994

Source: Bureau of Statistics of the USSR.

NOTE: Canadian immigration statistics register all representatives of different republics under one code number as "arrivals from the USSR."

Table 10

Distribution of Russian* Population in the Republics of the USSR**

Republic	Total Population (in thousands)	Russian Population (%)
Russian SFSR	97,864	83,3
Ukrainian SSR	7,091	16,9
Moldavian SSR	293	10,2
Byelorussian SSR	659	8,2
Lithuanian SSR	231	8,5
Latvian SSR	559	26,6
Estonian SSR	240	20,1
Georgian SSR	408	10,1
Azerbaijan SSR	501	13,6
Armenian SSR	56	3,2
Turkmen SSR	263	17,3
Uzbek SSR	1,091	13,5
Kazakh SSR	3,974	42,7
Kirghiz SSR	624	30,2
Tadzhik SSR	253	13,3

*Russian, meaning ethnic Russian.

**Source: S.I. Bruk, ed., *Numbers and Distribution of the Peoples of the World*, Academy of Sciences of the USSR, Moscow, 1962, p. 71.

Explanation of Illustrations

Fig. 1. Early Russian map, prepared by Ivan Lvov, a nobleman from Yakutsk, showing the Chukchi Peninsula, Diomede Islands and Alaska which was believed to be an island at that time; circa 1710.

Note the unusual map projection where North and South are reversed. Hence, the lettering is upside down while the topography is depicted in the normal fashion.

Source: *Atlas geograficheskikh otrkytii v Sibiri i severo-zapadnoi Ameriki 17 i 18 vekov,* (Atlas of Geographic Discoveries in Siberia and Northwestern America in the 17th and 18th centuries), edited by Academician A.V. Efimov, USSR Academy of Sciences, Moscow, 1964. Map No. 55.

Fig. 2. Russian Imperial Coat of Arms on totem pole: double-headed, crowned eagle with a shield depicting St. George fighting the dragon. Tlinget tribe of Indians, south-east Alaska, circa 1860.

Source: National Museum of Man, Marius Barbeau Collection.

Fig. 3. Totem pole at old Kasa-an, showing figures of two Russian-Orthodox priests; copied from an old Russian church in Sitka, Alaska. Kasa-an, Kaigani Haida.

NMC 74-2561
S.I. 45,123C—Smithsonian Institute, Washington, D.C.

Fig. 4. Interior view of a stationman's shack, showing four Russians employed in railway construction.

C-56822—Public Archives of Canada.

Fig. 5. Russian Immigrants arrive at Quebec, circa 1911. Most of them went to farm virgin lands in western Canada.

PA 10158—Public Archives of Canada.

Fig. 6. Jaroslaw School, one of the first Russian rural schools, Skaro, Alberta, circa teens.

Russian settlement located 45 miles northeast of Edmonton and 12 miles from Lamont.

NA-2664-2—Provincial Archives of Alberta.

Fig. 7. Typical Russian-Ukrainian Settlement of the early 1920s.

C-17574—Public Archives of Canada.

Fig. 8. Meal-time aboard the *Lake Huron* for Doukhobors en route to Canada, 1899.

C-5628—Public Archives of Canada.

Fig. 9. Posters advertising Emigration to Canada.

C-63084 and C-6196—Public Archives of Canada.

Russian or Ukrainian families on board ship on their way to Canada, circa 1910-1914.

C-38706—Public Archives of Canada.

Fig. 10. Among the immigrants who came after the Revolution and the Russian Civil War was the Grand Duchess Olga, sister of the last Tsar, Nicholas I. She is shown in her Toronto home with her two sons.

Source: Private collection.

Fig. 11. Four post-World War I Russian immigrants. From left to right:
O. Rodomar, prominent social worker and director of Phillips Industries; Rev. and Mrs. O. Boldireff; Professor P. Babkin, internationally-known physiologist. Circa 1950s.

Source: Private collection.

Fig. 12. Four brothers of the Ignatieff family who made significant contributions in the field of science and humanities. Circa 1950s. From left to right: Alexei—mining engineer; George—diplomat and Chancellor of a major Canadian University; Leonid—professor of Russian; Vladimir—biochemist in agriculture.

Source: Private collection.

Fig. 13. The Harbin Volunteer Fire Department, showing fire lookout tower "Magirus", Harbin, China; circa 1930.

Source: Zhiganov, *Polytekhnik,* Anniversary Issue, 1969-1979, No. 10, Sydney, Australia.

Fig. 14. Street in Harbin, China, circa 1930-31. All store signs are in Russian. One could imagine that the photograph could have been taken in pre-revolutionary Russia, except for the few inscriptions in Chinese characters.

Source: Zhiganov, *Polytekhnik,* Anniversary Issue, 1969-1979, No. 10, Sydney, Australia.

Fig. 15. Russian refugees from Shanghai approaching Vancouver, B.C. on board the *S/S Empress of Russia,* 1924.

Courtesy A. Malysheff.

Fig. 16. Two members of the Russian colony established by Col. O. Dournovo. Mr. and Mrs. Borovikov in the clearing where construction of one of the houses is in progress; August 5, 1924.

PA 124422—Public Archives of Canada.

Fig. 17. General Burghardt, descendant of Prince Bagration-Mukhtarsky, on the farm which he built in Brightview, 50 miles southwest of Edmonton, Alberta. Circa 1928.

Courtesy Mrs. I. Nelischer.

Fig. 18. United Nations Relief and Rehabilitation Administration (UNRRA) DP camp in a former women's prison which at one time was the palace of Bavarian princes. Bayreuth, 1946.

Source: Private collection.

Fig. 19. International Refugee Organization (IRO) Hospital, Bayreuth, Bavaria, Germany, 1946. Physicians and administrative staff. In the centre, wearing a beret is Ms. Mary Taylor, Canadian director of the hospital.

Source: Private collection.

Fig. 20. Immigrants crowd the deck of the *S/S Beaverbrae* before disembarking at the Port of Quebec. Circa 1951.

PA 124423—Public Archives of Canada.

Fig. 21. Port of Halifax, examining new arrivals in Immigration Examination Hall, Halifax, N.S., March 1952.

PA 111579—Public Archives of Canada.

Fig. 22. Group of students from the New Canadians English-language course, Ottawa, 1951. Standing at the left in a white blouse is Mrs. Whittle, the instructor.

Source: *Argosy of Commerce*, 25th Anniversary Issue, 1954. Marvin Flatt Photography; photo ref. 10,872,630.

Fig. 23. The price of freedom. A certificate given to the bearer proving that he paid $500.00 to be liberated from Soviet citizenship.

Source: Private collection.

Fig. 24. St. Nicholas Russian-Orthodox Church (OCA), Ottawa, Ontario, 1982.

Source: Private collection.

Fig. 25. St. Vladimir Russian-Orthodox Church (ROCA), Edmonton, Alberta, showing the Hieromonk Grigori Moiseyevsky.

Source: Private collection.

Fig. 26. St. Barbara's Russian-Orthodox Church (MP), Edmonton, Alberta.

Source: Private collection.

Fig. 27. Russian block house serving as a fort for protection against attack, Sitka, Alaska, 1880s.

NA 1807-50—Glenbow Alberta Institute, Calgary, Alberta.

Fig. 28. Indian burial huts with Orthodox crosses, Sitka, Alaska. 1880s.

Courtesy Glenbow Alberta Institute, Calgary, Alberta.

Fig. 29. Russian contingent at Greek-Orthodox Church, Edmonton, Alberta. A Russian priest is blessing the soldiers prior to their departure to the front; World War I.

B 7229—Provincial Archives of Alberta, E. Brown Collection.

Fig. 30. Blessing of the water at the Russo-Greek-Orthodox Church, Eastgate area, Alberta. The original church shown in the rear was completed in 1912. It was replaced by a new building in 1946. Circa 1930.

NA 2497-3—Provincial Archives of Alberta.

Fig. 31. Russian wedding, Calgary, Alberta. Rev. Vassilii Olshansky is performing the ceremony.

Courtesy Mrs. Vera van Veen.

Fig. 32. Russian-Orthodox church choir, Calgary, Alberta, mid-1930s.

Source: Private collection

Fig. 33. "Three Wise Men"—Soviet missionaries on assignment to serve parishes in Alberta and Saskatchewan.

Source: Edmonton Journal, January 8, 1979.

Fig. 34. Invitation Card to the Annual Assembly of Opposition to Communism, Montreal, November 1952.

Source: Private collection.

Fig. 35. "Aid to Russia" Fund during the Second World War. Calgary Stampede Parade with float sponsored by the Russian-Canadian Club, affiliated with the Federation of Russian Canadians, Calgary, 1946.

NA 1241-1097, Glenbow Museum, Provincial Archives of Alberta.

Fig. 36. Presentation of "Russian and Ludmilla" by Toronto youth group, directed by N. Suchachova. Ottawa, 1974.

Source: Private collection.

Fig. 37. National tricolour flag of old Russia, Canada Day celebrations, Ottawa, 1977.

Source: Private collection.

Fig. 38. Doukhobor group at annual ball of Chekhov Society, Ottawa, 1977.

Source: Private collection.

Fig. 39. Scene from "The Bear" by Chekhov Society drama group, Ottawa, 1975.

Source: Private collection.

Fig. 40. Members of the Royal Canadian Legion, Russian Branch 226, Montreal, 1955.

Courtesy Rev. O. Boldireff.

Fig. 41. Canadian Centennial celebrations at the Russian Centre in Vancouver, 1967. Unveiling a portrait of Sir John A. MacDonald.

Source: Private collection.

Fig. 42. Arts and Crafts Show, Chekhov Society, Ottawa, March 1977.

Source: Private collection.

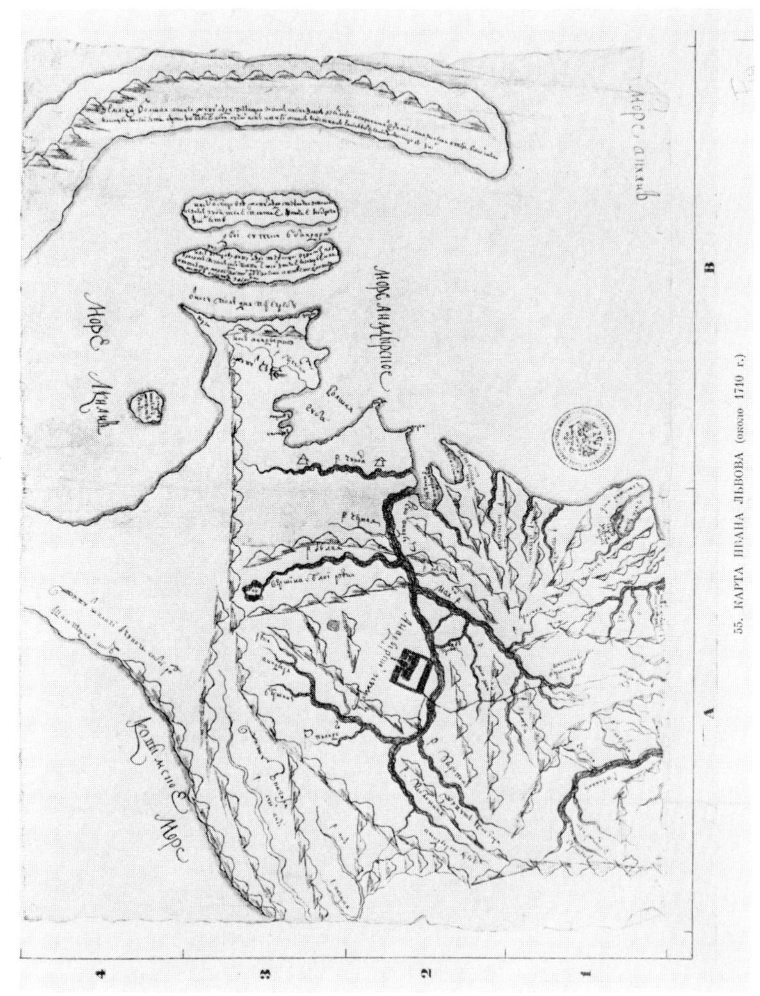

Fig. 1

Fig. 2

Fig. 3

Fig. 4

Fig. 5

Fig. 6

Fig. 7

Fig. 8

EMIGRATION TO CANADA.
THE ATTENTION OF
SHOEMAKERS & TAILORS
who desire to Emigrate is called to the advices received from the Government Agent at Toronto, who writes, there is a great want of Tailors in the Province, and I could distribute upwards of 500 in a week from this Station. They command very high wages. The demand for
SHOEMAKERS
also is almost unlimited. The rates of wages given to competent, industrious workmen is from about $8 to $10 or $12 a week, to men of special aptitude and intelligence from $12 to $14 or $15 a week is frequently given.
BUILDING MECHANICS, CABINET MAKERS, COUNTRY BLACKSMIT
LABOURERS, & FARM LABOUR
CAN FIND IMMEDIATE EMPLOYMENT AT HIGH WAGES.
FREE GRANT OF LAND TO ACTUAL SET
Free Passages are not grante
For further particulars and information concerning Canada, apply to
WILLIAM DIXON, Esq., Canadian Govern
11, Adam Street,
For rates of passage money, and to book to Cana
Ocean Mail Steam Company, apply to ALLAN BROTHE
James Street, Liverpool; or to
EDWARD REED,
36, Finsbury Circus, LON
Public Archive
Canada
160 акрів = 130 моргів австр.
вільної
землі
200 мільонів акрів під управу
в західній
КАНАДІ
для
кождого
оселенця
6196

Fig. 9

Fig. 10

Fig. 11

Fig. 12

Городская Добровольная Команда.
«Каланча». «Магирус».
Новый Город.

Fig. 13

Fig. 14

Fig. 15

Fig. 16

Fig. 17

Fig. 18

Fig. 19

Fig. 20

Fig. 21

Fig. 22

ГОСУДАРСТВЕННЫЙ БАНК СОЮЗА ССР

КВИТАНЦИЯ РЫ № 977042

18 июля 1973 г.

Принято от

адрес плательщика

согласно извещению №

Наименование получателя

Старший бухгалтер (бухгалтер)

М. П.

Fig. 23

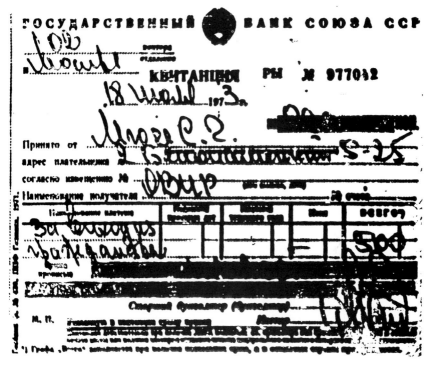

Fig. 24

Fig. 25-1

Fig. 25-2

Fig. 25-3

Fig. 26

Fig. 27

Fig. 28

Fig. 29

Fig. 30

Fig. 31-1

Fig. 31-2

Fig. 32

Russian missionaries, from left, Very Rev. Arseniy Melnik, Very Rev. Peter Vlodek, and Very Rev. Nikanos Shymko

'Three Wise Men' came from afar for Christmas

Everyone likes to be with friends at Christmas and the Most Rev. Ireney of St. Barbara's Russian Orthodox Cathedral is no exception.

He was all smiles when a trio of missionaries from the Soviet Union arrived Saturday in time for morning services at the church on 96th Street and Jasper Avenue.

As the Three Wise Men, they had come a long way to celebrate Christmas -- and it was a joyous reunion.

The Most Rev. Ireney, Vicar of the Patriarch of Moscow and all Russia and administrator of the Patriarchal parishes in Canada and the U.S., would now have help in running his parishes in Alberta and Saskatchewan.

He had waited since mid-summer for replacements for the two priests who had returned to the Soviet Union.

After Christmas, the three will be assigned to parishes outside Edmonton — the Very Rev. Peter Vlodek from Lutz to the Nisku-Calmar area; Very Rev. Arseniy Melnik, from Sumy, near Kiev, to Vegreville; and Very Rev. Nikanor Shymko, also from Lutz, to Chipman.

They do not speak English and have never been to Canada. But, they say, due to a shortage of priests to serve the 20 parishes in Alberta and two in Saskatchewan, they have come to fulfill their obligations as their predecessors have done for the last 81 years.

They were reluctant to talk on human rights issues facing dissidents in the Soviet Union or what effects arms talks between the Soviet Union and the U.S. will have.

Fig. 33

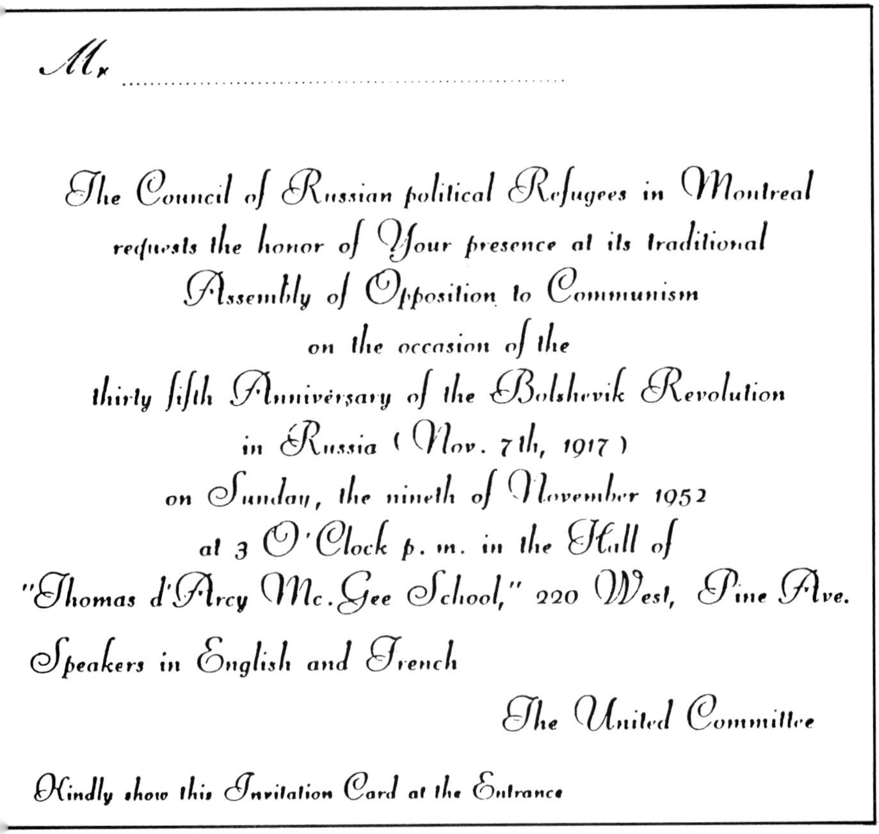

Mr ....

The Council of Russian political Refugees in Montreal
requests the honor of Your presence at its traditional
Assembly of Opposition to Communism
on the occasion of the
thirty fifth Anniversary of the Bolshevik Revolution
in Russia (Nov. 7th, 1917)
on Sunday, the nineth of November 1952
at 3 O'Clock p. m. in the Hall of
"Thomas d'Arcy Mc. Gee School," 220 West, Pine Ave.

Speakers in English and French

The United Committee

Kindly show this Invitation Card at the Entrance

Fig. 34

JAN 2 3 1942
RUSSIA
GIVE
TO THE
AID TO RUSSIA FUND
Support the
CANADIAN
AID TO RUSSIA
FUND
JAN - 1943
JAN 2 6 1943
They Need Our Help Now!
Let's Not Fail Them
Mail Your Contributions to:
Room 906, Royal Bank Building,
675 W. Hastings St.,
Vancouver, B.C.
Donated By
Ingledew's
623 Granville St.
RUSSIA

Fig. 35

Fig. 36

Fig. 37

Fig. 38

Fig. 39

Fig. 40

Fig. 41

Fig. 42

Index

Russian Canadians

Ziganov 119 White Horse, Yukon 3

* * *

The views expressed in this book do not necessarily reflect the position or policy of the Government of Canada.